CW01391835

What's Done
Cannot
Be Undone

What's Done Cannot Be Undone

Athena Stevens

ONE PLACE. MANY STORIES

HQ
An imprint of HarperCollins*Publishers* Ltd
1 London Bridge Street
London SE1 9GF

www.harpercollins.co.uk

HarperCollins*Publishers*
Macken House, 39/40 Mayor Street Upper,
Dublin 1, D01 C9W8, Ireland

This edition 2025

1
First published in Great Britain by HQ,
an imprint of HarperCollins*Publishers* Ltd 2025

Copyright © Athena Stevens 2025

Athena Stevens asserts the moral right to be identified as the author of this work.
A catalogue record for this book is available from the British Library.

ISBN: 978-0-00-855730-0

Set in
11.5/16.7 pt. Minion by Type-it AS, Norway

All rights reserved. No part of this publication may be reproduced, stored
in a retrieval system, or transmitted, in any form or by any means,
electronic, mechanical, photocopying, recording or otherwise,
without the prior permission of the publishers.

Without limiting the author's and publisher's exclusive rights, any unauthorized
use of this publication to train generative artificial intelligence (AI) technologies
is expressly prohibited. HarperCollins also exercise their rights under Article
4(3) of the Digital Single Market Directive 2019/790 and expressly reserve this
publication from the text and data mining exception.

Printed and bound in the [UK using 100% Renewable Electricity at
CPI Group (UK) Ltd, Croydon, CR0 4YY]

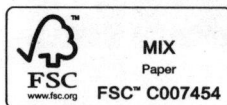

FSC
www.fsc.org

MIX
Paper
FSC™ C007454

For more information visit: www.harpercollins.co.uk/green

To Marmee and Daddy, equal and opposite
forces, ever dynamic, who have given me wings
to fly and a steadfast ground to land upon.

And to those who have been vectors of protection and stability
in my life, whether within my sight or beyond my knowing.

'I joke about it because it's the only way
I can open my mouth without screaming.'

– *HAWKEYE PIERCE*, M*A*S*H

Trigger warning: There is a lot of trauma in this book. From now on, assume there's a 'trigger warning' on every page. I don't want to write them out myself – my publishers are telling me to keep my word count down.

Chapter 1

What happens to me happens again and again. But those who it most commonly happens to have the least amount of energy to explain it, let alone a way to be heard.

In my life, I am always looking for a point of stability – something to lean up against that can bear my weight. Having cerebral palsy, my fight/flight/freeze/fawn sympathetic nervous system is on unnecessary high alert, constantly causing startles in my day-to-day life that knock me off balance. There is rarely an internal 'centre' to be found within a body that over-contracts, then over-loosens, its muscles in order to correct itself. This attempt at balance, to minimise the severity of my condition, remains still unmastered within my body after years of physical therapy and classes in movement for performance. There was even some ballet, when the community dance teachers didn't automatically turn me away due to my disability.

With the endless quest for a stabilising force, I find a centre within my Self. Even though I know I am enough, I actively look for ways to make sure I am bearing the weight of inconvenience that comes with my disability: I don't leave my things scattered throughout the green rooms; I come to the theatre with a single-dish meal ready to pop in the microwave as soon as the principals take their places; I go home without making a big deal of it.

Cerebral palsy puts me in a constant quest for balance, but it's never within my body. Even as I find myself lying flat on the floor, I push my limbs deeper against the ground, hoping that the ground, which pushes back up against me, will somehow cradle me with its forces against gravity. When I can't find myself supported enough physically, I look for the other forces, habits and occupations that I can hold on to.

I read philosophy and listen to podcasts. If bearing too much weight is going to cause my world to crumble, then I want to know how everything in it works. Because if I know how it all works, then I will be able to predict what I can count on, and what I need to avoid for my own safety. I try to learn constantly, so I can know, within reason, what to expect.

Habits are my other sources of stability; the daily atomic practices that build upon each other to form consistency. The writing of 750 words a day that equal the first draft of a new play after fifteen days. The daily physical therapy, brought from my childhood, to ensure that the slight scoliosis of my spine remains slight. Always taking the same route to work, interacting only with the people who have thus far proved themselves to be kind. Always playing the same sneak-out-and-avoid-goodbyes game every evening.

If we are not careful, life has a way of throwing us the unthinkable. So, I try to be full of care, full of thought, full of anchoring, in order to avoid falling.

*

This is a terrible idea.

I have flipped off the switch in my brain that automatically filters out unwise choices – just for the night. The mechanism is usually in hyperdrive, calculating possibilities and probabilities where harm might occur. Harm to my body, harm to another's body, harm to feelings, harm to reputation. *Will people assume that I don't know what I'm doing if they see me?* Possibly. Probably.

'Stop worrying about how you look. Other people aren't looking at you. They are too busy thinking about themselves,' people tell me. They make it sound as if I am vain. Or weak.

But I have seen what happens when I am not living up to other people's expectations, or when they want to believe that I am not coping. People want to be seen to care about me, they always have.

'Seen to care' is the key phrase here. It's not the same as 'care'.

'But you deserve to have fun,' The Dresser said when we came up with the idea last week. Working as a West End understudy midway through a run affords you the strangest ways to pass the time. You hear muffled words come over the stage relay for the hundredth time, the cues you already know by heart, and you're meant to be in a state of 'ready'.

If the unlikely event that you were hired for happens and a principal cannot go onstage, a show stop is called and the understudy has moments to get backstage, get the wig and costume on, and look as identical as possible to the performer you are replacing. Then the show goes on; the audience is none the wiser.

If you are not needed onstage, then once the performer you are covering makes their final entrance, you're released for the night, free to go home.

Although I'm understudying the title role, I am done a good thirty minutes before anyone else.

This is how I came up with my terrible idea. The game is simple: I walk through the inaccessible labyrinthine gut of the theatre building while The Dresser packs up all of our stuff and makes small talk with all the people who 'didn't notice I had slipped out'.

The fun is in seeing how far I get before The Dresser catches up to me. Shuffling with an uneven gait through a journey of nine fire doors, 113 stairs and overly long, plushly carpeted hallways that hold the locked offices of the theatre staff.

Walking with unsure footing past these doors is always the most tantalising bit of the night. *Who works behind these closed doors, and what opportunities could we create together?* is the question my mind always goes to, when really what I should be thinking is, *What would someone think if they opened the door and found me – unstable, out of breath, pale with effort and about to fall over?* I would excitedly start my elevator pitch to frantically try to justify why a wild, out-of-joint body like mine is walking unsupervised past their always-locked doors. Though let's be honest, I wouldn't get that far.

Yesterday, I passed through two-thirds of the door-lined hallway before The Dresser caught up with me from three storeys away. I know it is a dangerous game to be without The Dresser; to be without my able-bodied friend, both physically and emotionally. I could fall. Or someone could doubt that I belong backstage in the West End, and that would crush me. But everyone else is allowed to play these kinds of games. They were allowed to play these games growing up, even if they were going to fall at least once on the cement. I was expected to stay strapped into a wooden posture chair, learning how to hold myself up.

I know that playing this game The Dresser and I call 'chase' is more than silly – it is unwise. It's a terrible idea. What constructive purpose could it serve?

*

My mother was worried that when the time came, she would not be able to get me out fast enough. She swore to herself that she would keep trying, no matter what. It was to be our first mother-and-daughter joint effort; she was determined to put this first parcel of maternal worries to bed because everyone was telling her to do so. Surely her mother's instinct could not be so developed yet? After all, she was fresh out of nursing school, imagining the worst. And there was an epidemic that baffled everyone. But needles seemed to be a key factor in how it spread. That, and homosexuals, but she hadn't come into contact with the latter thus far.

Needles were a different matter. She and every other nurse in history were always accidentally jabbing themselves with used sharps. The head nurse told her she was young and that she would worry less about this in time. Her obstetrician used the same language.

My mother knew that if her dismissed fears were correct, every second too long would mean that my dendrites and neurons would be starving. The pressure was literally on her pelvis to minimise the damage for me. She was the only person who dared to glance at a long-term vision of what would happen if her labour and delivery progressed in this manner. She was the only one who seemed to admit that things could go wrong. She told every nurse and doctor that she was a registered nurse herself; she had the qualifications to know that something was not as it should be.

She also had the instinct of a mother.

It was more convenient for others to lean on toxic optimism. 'Worry less' and 'it'll all be fine' nearly killed me.

But things don't always work out for the best, no matter how much you might shut your eyes and wish otherwise.

*

I know very little about what happened. I don't know the name of the doctor who insisted my mother keep pushing. It was only after 2018 that I learned my life was saved by a doctor from Vietnam and one from Nigeria. They took control as soon as they saw that damage was being done. Learning this renewed my love for people who leave where they come from, set up lives where they will always be considered an 'outsider' and still manage to stick to their conscience.

Other than two admittedly generalised immigrant faces, I have no details about who else was involved. The documentation and court files are available. My father has always offered that I 'come to him if I ever have any questions'.

But I don't. In the age of Google, I know that the doctor's name would lead me down a path of cyberstalking. My quick, detail-oriented brain, which this doctor certainly had more than a hand in forming, would latch on to discovering everything it could possibly glean: is he retired? Dead? Did he move hospitals? Did he get a promotion? What are his children doing? Do they know about me? Does he think about me? Has he admitted to himself the impact he's had on my life or convinced himself otherwise? Can I find his address on Google Earth and see the colour of his front door?

This way madness lies, certainly.

I knew when my father offered to give me any details I wanted, it would be opening a Pandora's box that I had assumed was easy to keep locked. Up until that point in my life I had been told 'the doctors made a mistake' as an explanation for my disability. People make mistakes. Mistakes can often be fixed. I had long come to terms with this explanation and my life kept moving forward. It's all right. It was a mistake. Poor, mistaken doctor, wherever you are, know that I have forgiven you.

But forgiveness is not an action you need to do once and then it's over. I have realised that not only is contending with a birth-induced brain injury going to be a daily occurrence, but searching for forgiveness for the person who caused that brain injury will be ongoing as well. In fact, rather brilliantly, on the days when the first task is particularly difficult, the second feels practically impossible – a supreme case of mind-fuckery. Forgiveness is a daily choice. I have the choice to forgive moment by moment. I want to make the right choice, every time. Forgiveness, I think, is easier when you don't know someone's name.

So, here's what I do know: the events of my birth didn't start on that day. Discovering that I was headed into this world from the wrong direction was not some sort of plot twist that suddenly surprised everyone. It's not like my pre-natal self decided to do some sort of somersault with jazz hands and tap shoes because I couldn't wait for my big debut. They knew. Weeks or even months before my Birth Day, the doctor who would deliver me saw the scans, pointed out my position to his colleagues and even to my mother, but then decided to continue on with the traditional birth plan with no change.

'She'll probably straighten herself out again in a few weeks. Don't worry. It'll all work out in the end. You'll see, Mrs Stevens. Go home and try to relax. You've got a big day coming up.'

We think of 'not taking action' as a wise substitution for 'not making a decision'. This form of patience is lauded. Jumping to conclusions will get you into more trouble than simply waiting. We need to see the lie of the land, not act rashly, and take our time to make sure we are doing the right thing. Refusing to make a decision is, in itself, a decision. By waiting to take action in the weeks my mother packed and repacked her suitcase for the hospital, harm was done by not acting. By not calling my mother into a consultation, talking about worst-case scenarios, and 'what ifs', choices were being made on an hour-by-hour basis.

In the moments of chaos that are to come, remember that. There will be memories that I have to pull out and slow down, examine for dramatic effect. Know that my life didn't change in an instant on the First Day. Rather, the refusal to be decisive towards giving my mother a caesarean section was not admirable or wise. It was kicking the can further down the road, hoping the decision became so clear that it basically made itself. Like so many catastrophes, there were many warning signs, chosen to be ignored, which caused what happened. As much as I now have to find the effort to forgive on a daily basis, others took efforts then to convince themselves nothing had to be done.

Is it any wonder that I grew up with a sense of fate and the inevitable? When we studied bell curves in maths class, I looked at the smallest sliver of representation at the far ends and thought, 'That's me. That's where I landed on day one.' I am the case where things didn't work out, despite the odds being ever in my favour – to use a phrase that will later be synonymous with my generation.

I am fascinated by outliers: the marginal percentages of mistakes piling up on top of each other until their catastrophic ends meet and a radio announcer screams, 'Oh, the humanity!'

It shouldn't come as a surprise that I became obsessed with Apollo 1. The number of times the astronauts pleaded with the government, saying, 'Something is not right. These equations don't add up. You are putting us in danger.' It was a natural progression to go from Apollo 1 to the *Challenger* explosion. I was fascinated that a tiny little O-ring, cracked and frozen, could bring down a mechanical marvel, and all the hope encapsulated in that rising rocket was sent, ultimately, to 'touch the face of God'.

My dad drove me to school the morning of 9/11, and the last thing I heard before I got out of the car was that a small plane had flown into the World Trade Center in the slightly muffled and banal voice of Terry Gross on NPR. I turned to my father and said, 'How can that happen?'

'People make mistakes. It just happens,' he said, before taking my wheelchair out from the back of the car and rolling it closer to the passenger's side where I was standing.

How could so many 'mistakes' happen? I thought, watching one plane after another crashing throughout the morning as we shuffled, dazed, between our classrooms.

*

I make my move and slip away from The Understudy's dressing room while my colleagues seem absorbed in something else. My Understudy Mum reads her book and my Understudy Dad's attention has been overtaken by something on the BBC. In reality, we are all the same age, and the two of them cover every other role in the play except mine. The character I am covering has cerebral palsy and the director is insisting the production shell out for another actor to cover that part: one who, like the principal performer, has an authentic brain injury from birth. I suppose you could say that this was a role I was born to play, although given the physical condition of this theatre, I'm not convinced I was born to play this role here.

I signal with a nod to The Dresser on my way into the hallway. She knows what it means as I slowly close the dressing-room door behind me. The game is on.

Taking a left into the hallway, I pass by old production posters and a framed photograph of Timothy Spall from decades ago, taken on the stage downstairs. There's magic in these walls, I remind myself. And while understudying a West End title character has never been on my bucket list, with each passing week of the production I have felt a stabilising force growing within me from being in a long run of a production.

Let any of those shut office doors fling open upon me tonight. Let them question whether or not I belong in this theatre. I'll ask the stage manager to reveal my pay stubs. I'll call on my Understudy Parents to bear witness that I am one of them.

Then I'll turn the tables and ask why someone in this supposedly liberated and creative industry doubted my belonging.

These thoughts fortify me as I open the door into the stairwell, letting the door close slowly, so the shift in air stays imperceptible. Then I make the same movements I do every night to go down the first concrete flight of stairs.

My left hand holds on to the top of the stairs' banister.

I lower myself to the ground, keeping my weight well behind the precipice of the stairs.

With my right hand, I grab the lower stair rail, giving myself another fixed point of stability as I take the weight off my feet and prepare to scoot down the stairs on my bum.

This is how I've approached going down any flight of stairs ever since I was a child.

Only this time, something new happens.

There's no noise. No startle within my body. I'm not overexcited or getting ahead of myself. Indeed, everything has gone to plan.

But my left arm has pulled my weight over the base of my heels, and over the edge of the stairs.

The sound that comes out of my mouth is one that I have never made before.

And I am falling headfirst down a flight of concrete stairs.

Chapter 2

Every action has an equal, and opposite reaction.
Forces come in pairs.
An object at rest will stay at rest and an object in motion will
stay in motion unless acted upon by an external force.

As I am falling down the stairs, I hear these words repeated in the voice of my high-school physics teacher, Ms Up/Down. In my head I see her marking the forces involved in my fall, hand-drawn arrows that show vectors of both magnitude and direction. Nothing falling to Earth can accelerate at a rate faster than 9.8 metres per second, and that only happens in freefall. My limbs and torso are making contact with each step as I roll down, causing a force of friction that works against my acceleration. The vocalisations coming out of me are caused by my body making forceful contact with each individual step, causing air to accelerate through my windpipe. All these factors, input into the equation on Ms Up/Down's whiteboard, mean that the forces acting upon me will reach their greatest potential when I hit the floor. In other words, this is going to hurt like hell when it's over.

Then I remember the biological probability that adrenaline

is flooding my system. So, the pain from whatever injuries I am currently sustaining as I fall won't be truly felt until that hormone clears out. So, in reality, this is going to really hurt in about an hour or so, when I'm getting into bed.

Just as well. I've been suicidal all week. Maybe this will be what ends it all. I'm OK with that.

The bed I'm going 'home' to isn't mine. I haven't been able to go to the home I own for over two months, as the lift isn't working. Guinness Homes, the building's management company, and I are in a PR battle, and their latest move is telling the press that they have put me up in posh serviced housing, so why am I not thankful? Let's just say they make better beer than property managers.

My housing debacle isn't the only thing contributing to my recent thoughts of suicide. One of my good friends, who claims to be 'liberal' and an 'ally', has apparently hit his limit with me. He labels me 'aggressive'. I tell him he's misspelled 'assertive'. He didn't appreciate the correction. Add the fact that the days are getting shorter, and I am sliding quickly into depression. Earlier today, I spent hours staring out of the floor-to-ceiling window four storeys above the churning Thames, and wondered if the fall would be high enough to do the deed. I calculate the angles, the probability, the speed, graphing it all in my head. And now, here I am, tumbling down this concrete flight of stairs. If it was meant to happen, it will happen now. I just needed to lose my balance.

All of that mental maths was a waste.

This is all it took—

And—

Here we are—

This is it—

No.

I have a split second between my body ceasing its downward tumble, and The Dresser and The Understudy Parents bursting in at the top of the stairwell.

First: analyse and assess. I've not been knocked out. I'm alert and logical. What hurts most?

My knee. My left knee.

I see what looks like a moth-eaten hole torn in my jeans. Underneath, there is a tiny superficial graze where the first layer of my skin has rubbed off. The pink mark is the size of a shirt button. There is no blood. All four of us look at the tiny wound in disbelief. The wound that I see matches the amount of pain I feel, which is to say, practically none. I fell down an entire flight of stairs, and ended up with a scratch and a slight twinge.

'Where else hurts?' A mixture of urgency and protective compassion is in Understudy Mum's question. She brushes the hair out of my face.

But that's it. There is no other place that hurts or feels odd. I rub my tongue over my teeth to see if any of them are chipped, but my pearly whites are accounted for. I feel no bruises forming. My hearing and vision are fine.

All I can think is: *That was my chance at an exit, and it didn't happen. Great. I'm meant to stay on Planet Earth for longer.* While I am so thankful that I'm not in agony, trying to wrap my head around the meaning my brain is piecing together from what has just happened is really frustrating.

The others ask me what I need. Now every muscle in my body is back to facilitating between tension and stability. This is the very nature of my cerebral palsy: my body hurries itself between being so low in muscle tension that it could melt into a puddle on the floor and then jerking upright with a full-body spasm as if to say, 'No! I am here! I can hold myself upright just as well as those other bodies, so don't you dare underestimate me.'

'I need a hug,' is my response. The Dresser pulls me into herself tightly, which is the exact sort of hug I am always in need of. The kind of hug where another body lends me its stability, telling my muscles on an atomic level that they can slow down. This kind of hug mutes the electrical surges firing through my uneasy form.

Still holding on to The Dresser, I open my eyes and look over her shoulder. It's only then that I notice how narrow the concrete stairs are. How did I fall down without hitting either the brick wall or the railing on either side? I hug my friend more tightly.

Once back at (not my) home, I pull back the crisp white duvet of (not) my bed. My hands and psyche are still shaking as I look out the window over my slice of the Thames. Sometimes I can't help but think that the simplest explanation for surviving falls like these is a group of spirits who have been assigned the task of ensuring I survive as long as I am meant to. In my mind, they look like the Fab Five from *Queer Eye* and shout to each other, 'Protect the head!' and 'Watch that wall!' as the most unlikely alignments occur to keep me safe. The voice of Karamo rings out, Gandalf-like, 'Not today, Satan. It is not her day to die.'

How else can I explain surviving so many should-be-lethal falls in my life?

*

The people around my mother did not realise that they sealed my fate. Each second without oxygen sent me down a rung of the ladder of social standing. After all, this was before the first George Bush signed the Americans with Disabilities Act into law in 1990. A young, white, university-educated couple from rural Missouri, and the well-educated doctor who claimed that my mother didn't know her own body, are all included in 'all men are created equal'. But a disability, made worse with each passing second of labour, brought forward by the misjudgements and stubbornness of the doctor, is enough to remove me from that list. It is seen instead as a mere catastrophe to be overcome with character. In the event of disability, the formation of a good work ethic should overcome it.

All of this is to say: the factor observed first and foremost in my life will be the effects of what other people have done to me, rather than anything else that I myself may do. Fame cannot alter this; nor can fortune, talent, skill. Nobody can foresee that having a mouth move out of joint in a strained effort to sharpen my articulation will be interpreted by a percentage of the population as a lack of intellect. Not one person in the delivery room put together the realisation that the events of that day, my Birth Day, were sealing the reality that many who meet me will assume that my role is to be a second-class citizen: uneducated, disenfranchised and extremely 'thankful' for any 'help' I may receive.

In the chaos and power struggle between Older-Doctor and Panicked-Woman-in-Labour-Knowing-What-Was-Happening-Inside-Her-Body, no one understood that the outcome of these moments would result in certain taxi drivers being unwilling to take my direction when I try to explain the road closures around my flat. That it would mean shop and restaurant staff rolling their eyes when I tell them they need to clear the cleaning equipment out of their accessible loo because the overly large room doesn't exist to be their establishment's store cupboard.

With each moment, oxygen deprivation caused a smoothing of the wrinkles in my brain, which will one day make men sleeping rough on the street come up and offer to help me as I go by them. Some men do this because they genuinely want to – and can – aid someone who has seen as many levels of suffering as they have; because a voice in the back of their head reminds them they ought to do something whenever they see someone less fortunate than themselves. Still others will jump to help, and then demand a payment beyond that of a polite 'thank you'. They puncture the illusion of their 'good deeds' by using it as a balance book to gain the ego-stroke they are after.

Nobody in that labour and delivery room knew that it would be impossible for me to tell the difference between these agendas until the harm is already done. Nor did they know that such agendas would be seen not only in homeless men, but in people who purport to facilitate my education, my safety, my career.

When the neurons that send signals from my brain to my fingers were killed, there went not only my shot at being a classical pianist, but also the ability to feed myself. I will forever have the handwriting of a serial killer, something that makes writing in one of those much-coveted pink kawaii lockable diaries impossible. I will ask for a Casio My Magic Diary for Christmas, dreaming of the day that a real computer is small and cute enough to carry around in my bag. The lack of fine motor control in my hands gives me a profound disadvantage in using scissors or glue. These details, brought on by someone else's refusal to take action, were used to justify putting me into classes created for people with cognitive disabilities.

Without the gift of foresight, it would have been easy perhaps for a third party to justify why the professionals in the delivery room waited so long to change their course of action. How could any of those able bodies in the medical profession know that their lack of action was careening me towards this life? What happened to me was always described as a mistake: 'The doctors made a mistake.' Mistakes to me, therefore, meant life-long disability inflicted on the innocent. Mistakes were airplanes flying into buildings. Mistakes were life-ending, or, at the very least, life-altering.

Mistakes cannot happen.

*

The older I get, the more I realise I can't rehab my way out of cerebral palsy. It is clear to me that, as Shakespeare wrote, 'What's done cannot be undone.' Nor can I put definitive boundaries on what has been done to me. I understand that the damage created doesn't simply impact the way I move, nor does it merely affect the way the world moves around me. The way an assault of loud noises or emotions makes it impossible for me to keep my balance; how I can't stop the sadness, which seems unending, once grief begins. And yet, I feel that if I cannot stay upright, if I cannot keep in tune with the music onstage, I risk falling and smashing the pieces of my life that were already splintered on the First Day into a fine powder, unable to be re-joined and made whole again.

It is impossible for me to tell which bits of my mind and soul exist that are authentically me without a brain injury. I do not know if there is a corner of my life or my work that has not been touched by a doctor decades ago. Often, I feel as though I am not an actor, performing with autonomy to create my own fate. Rather, I wonder

19

if I am not a marionette: the inability to move my limbs the way I envision; a faceless doctor's arms enveloping the proscenium arch, pulling the strings that move me around the stage. At some point, I know his power ends and my power begins. But often when I try to demarcate whose is whose, the strings attached at my joints start to tangle, leaving me with even less control than I imagined myself to have.

*

I was 'born' dead.

As the minutes pass with my vital signs at zero, any attempt to untangle my Self from the brain injury is becoming increasingly difficult to decouple.

What my physical body will become is also changing. My feet will remain small from the reduced amount of walking they will undertake. A lack of running around to the point of being breathless as a child means that my lungs will never develop to their full capacity, an inconvenience I curse every time I have to sight-read Shakespeare for an audition. From the age of six, I will need an orthodontic palate expander to lessen the effects of an overly engaged tongue constantly pushing against my teeth, correcting their protrusion outwards and preventing every single shirt I wear from being soaked with saliva.

Fifteen years after women started chanting 'my body, my choice', my own body was formed as a result of my mother not having a choice. The medical profession of America in the 1980s decided that caesarean sections had become too frequent, as if mothers-to-be were asking for them like fizzy cola bottles. And so, despite my mother having her own medical degree and a job working with high-risk newborns, the events of my Birth Day were dictated by the whims and fashions of what was considered to be a 'safe and standard' medical agenda.

Newsflash: this story doesn't have a happy ending. I can't overcome cerebral palsy. I still have a brain injury. It will suck as much in the last chapter as it does in these frozen moments at the beginning of my story. The violence of a doctor's inaction took an able body away from me for life. My disability is not part of who I am; it is a product of trauma.

*

As I type this, I use one finger – the middle one on my left hand. It hovers over my yellow BT21 Chimmy keyboard and I move my entire arm from the shoulder in order to press each letter one by one to form the words on the screen in front of me. This is a chapter I am choosing to write by hand at my typing speed of six words per minute, rather than dictating into my iPhone for my fellow theatre director to type up. I want to see these words pop up on the screen at the rate I can physically type them. I want to chew over every turn of phrase as I labour to put this chapter down. I want to take the time to know that I've formed this chapter word by word, knitting it together as intricately as DNA knits together to form a baby.

Every few years a well-meaning person suggests voice-dictation software to aid getting my thoughts onto the screen more quickly. They have no idea to what extent my life is a graveyard of failed technology. From my teenage years I have worked for hours, sometimes daily, to refine and perfect my speech in the hopes that some technological engine might understand it. However, a few months ago a software developer told me that such programs were built for doctors and lawyers: professions with limited vocabulary and repetitive sentence structure. Thus, it is my talent and choice of occupation, and not my articulation, that has made what everyone claimed to be a simple solution virtually impossible.

Nevertheless, word by word, this chapter will be finished, just the same as every script I have written, every character I have performed or social inequality I've had to explain. Line by line, my mouth has wrapped itself around the soliloquies of Juliet. Minute by minute, my hands have typed at a keyboard, forcing my mind to slow down and refine the dialogue it hears before it gets on the page. Hour by hour, I have waited for gatekeepers to unlock their doors, ignorant to the fact that, while my body is slow because of someone else's decisions, my mind has become twice as fast.

In drama, we talk about every story having an inciting incident: the singular event that sets the main character on the path of both adventure and crisis. The inciting incident is where the story begins. It is the 'once' when we say, 'once upon a time'.

Forget that I have managed to spin life into verse, soliloquy and song. Put down the fact that my life has become a shield of achievement to hide behind.

Do not force-feed me my own fairy tale – I am already in possession of the autonomy required to shape its ending. I have managed to stitch together a ball gown from the shreds of fabric that were left for me. Bought a carriage with the gold coins tossed in my path as recompense. I will make good on the promise and power that is contained within the miracle that is being alive.

But first, sit still in this moment's violence of taking away my brain's connection with my body.

This should never happen.

My life was thrown off balance from the start by complacency and inaction.

Be still and know that something profoundly unfair and irreparable has occurred.

I wasn't 'made better' because I was broken.

I shouldn't have been broken at all.

Chapter 3

'This little girl won't stop smiling!' the nurses said when they passed me to my mother or walked by my bed in the neonatal intensive care unit.

'Isn't it amazing how she smiles despite the fact that we nearly killed her during her birth?' is what they were avoiding actually saying.

My mother knew that my smile was not a smile. It was a muscle contraction. My 'smile' was a sign that something was wrong. Without a hint that another world existed, my parents were taken from the expected world of high-pitched cooing over brightly coloured baby cradles and yanked into a vortex of despair. All the expectations of what their baby would be like shattered from moment one.

For the next few months, my mother took me to mummy and baby classes only to come home in tears when I was not keeping up with what other children were doing. She looked around, saw children developing, learning how to reach for toys.

She dangled a teddy bear above my head. Was I even seeing it?

My mother took me to every free physical therapy session she could find. Increasingly, therapists told her that I missed milestones

– something she already knew. If my young brain could get as much input as possible in the early years, some of the effects of missing these milestones might be mitigated.

We had no money. Mum continuously bought powdered milk with her government-subsidised coupons. She took me home, turned on *Mister Rogers, Sesame Street, Zoobilee Zoo*, and copied the same manipulations she saw the physical therapist do to me in the clinic. She waited for me to do something other than stare up at the ceiling; waited for a sign that, despite the correlation of being ignored in the hospital and the very clear physical clues that something wasn't right, there was a brain in there that was capable of something – capable of loving her.

At fourteen, I stumbled across an old photo book with a black-and-white cover, the sticky, magnetic pages only showing one or two pictures. They were odd pictures – not family celebrations or me as a baby. The pictures were of an apple; a puzzle; a glass of milk; a TV. Underneath was a label of what they were. 'Apple'. 'Puzzle'. 'Milk'. 'TV'. Common nouns that require no adjectives, because we all know the Platonic ideal of a thing when we say the words. This was a book my mother made for me to communicate with her in case I wasn't ever able to speak. She wanted to be prepared for that reality, if it were to come to pass.

I once asked my mother what I did when most children are described as toddlers, as I, of course, was not 'toddling'.

'Therapy,' she said. I knew she was right. Not only was she right – I had done therapy – but that one single word had taken up my full existence for the first years of my life while other children were 'toddling around'.

The hours of exercises given to her during free physical

therapy clinics included what we would come to call 'elevators': squats at varying heights, from sitting on a bench at 'ground' to fully standing at 'ten'. She would ask me to go to the second floor, then ten, then seven, then back down to the ground, and back up to five.

'Don't just slam your bottom down – sit down with control … No, that was too fast. You need to do it again.'

We didn't work only on standing. Learning how to hold my head straight was going to take several years.

As soon as we could afford it, my mother would put up a floor-to-ceiling mirror on the only blank wall of our living room. Family from out of town made comments about how she was trying to 'enlarge the room'. Then, when my parents could scrape together some money again, she bought PVC pipes and elbow connectors to form a barre that I could hold on to for support. That addition certainly did not enlarge the room. But it did make our priorities clear to any visitors thereafter.

During the holidays, my father would put Christmas cards around the perimeter of the mirror, different points of gold foiled doves and silver stars for me to focus on as I learned to activate the muscles in my neck required to hold up my head. The cards with long family updates of New Baby's first steps or Big Brother's first football games would go straight in the bin.

In January, the glittery cards would come down, leaving the images that were always taped on the mirror at my eyeline: a picture of Abraham Lincoln. Another of William Wilberforce. A Bible verse: 'I can do all things through Christ who strengthens me.' A photo of Nelson Mandela. And a quote from Winston Churchill: 'This is the lesson: never give in, never give in, never, never, never,

never – in nothing, great or small, large or petty – never give in except to convictions of honour and good sense. Never yield to force; never yield to the apparently overwhelming might of the enemy.' The last, I would be asked to memorise and recite when called upon from the age of four.

While my parents' world fell into exclusion and isolation, a world of expectation was nested in my mind. Staring at these images for hours, I was told that anything was possible; I could be like these people. No, I *would* be like them.

There is one memory that particularly stands out from that time in my life, other than sitting on a therapy ball, or being held up at the barre. It was a rare moment of on-the-couch-ness. I think my mum must've been doing laundry, as that is how I got out of the physical labour that was usually required even to watch television. We were watching *Rumpole of the Bailey*.

'If I did law, I wouldn't want to be a judge.'

My mother stopped folding the laundry and looked at me. 'A judge is the best that you can be in law – why wouldn't you want to do that?'

'Because they wear silly wigs and dresses all the time.'

I could tell by the look on my mother's face that I had said the wrong thing, although I wasn't sure which thing I had said that was wrong, so I quickly tried to recover. 'I know I could be a judge, I just don't want to.'

'Now listen to me: whatever you do, regardless of if it's being a janitor or going into law, whatever you do, always aim for the top of your field. Don't settle for anything less than you could be.'

Step one in how to make your child a cut-throat Anglophile before she can walk.

With placemats about George Washington as I was fed breakfast, my father reading the *Little House on the Prairie* series every night, and the added fairy tales about girls who worked hard, never complained and became princesses, the inner workings of the world made sense. If you do things right, if you follow the script, you will excel.

*

'I can't believe you are acting this way. After all we have done for you!'

I'm at JFK International Airport, ready to disembark for a week-long trip that involves two professional readings for off-Broadway theatres. Everyone else has cleared the airplane except for me and The Dresser. My wheelchair has yet to be delivered to the gate, so the Virgin Atlantic flight attendants are expecting me to get into a wheelchair that is not my own and that I am unable to move independently. They need to 'clear their plane'.

I know from experience that the second I step off the plane, I am no longer Virgin Atlantic's responsibility. My wheelchair, which could be anywhere in the airport or back at Heathrow, is no longer Virgin's problem. It's the typical diffusion of responsibility: the notion that somebody somewhere will do the right thing.

'I've always depended on the kindness of strangers,' as Tennessee Williams put it. That worked out well for Blanche.

The flight attendant is now trying to get me over the threshold of his airplane. So, I do the only thing I can think of: I take a seat in first class.

'I am not leaving until my wheelchair is delivered here.'

'I am just appalled! We were so nice to you, and this is how you treat us.'

I take out my phone and switch on the voice recorder, showing him that I am doing so.

'You're not allowed to record us. That's illegal. Put that phone away.'

'I work as an accessibility advisor to Heathrow Airport, which we have just left. I also work with the Virgin Atlantic accessibility manager. I am sure she will be interested in hearing our conversation, so please do keep going.'

'How dare you do this to us!' What follows implies that any concern over me recording our conversation is very short-lived.

*

The summer of 1989 was so hot, ugly orange cicadas with their bulging eyes came out of the earth en masse. For years afterwards, Sunday School teachers would use that summer and the constant screaming of enormous red bugs as an illustration of what the plague of locusts in Exodus must have been like.

We could not afford to turn on the air-conditioning. Instead, there were two box fans on either side of the living room, facing in opposite directions so that a breeze would come through when I was at the barre. I assumed that their main purpose was for me to stick my face up against them and sing songs through the small slits in the plastic against the spinning blades.

'No, now stop that, you're wasting time,' my mother said as she put the can of wasp spray down, and stepped away from the corner where she was spraying. A nest had been built outside our picture window and the soulless insects now came in through our empty air vents, looking for someone to blame for the Chicago heat.

'Why do I have to do therapy anyway? It's summer, nobody

works in summer.' The logic of childhood got the better of me in front of Nelson Mandela, Abraham Lincoln and Winston Churchill at that moment. Screw all these guys and all they accomplished for humanity. Maybe I could do all things through Christ who strengthens me, but I didn't want to. I wanted to go and play in the fire hydrant with the kids I saw outside. Or take a nap.

If this meant I wouldn't be a princess or a queen or the president of the United States, fine. Lots of people weren't any of those things, and they got a summer holiday without cicadas and wasps.

'When am I going to be done with this therapy and not have to do it ever again? Where's the end of it? Nobody else has to do this. Why me?'

My mother sat me down. I had been sloppy in my exercises. I wasn't trying hard enough. I was bored at the repetition. I was four years old.

*

The head of the Women's Equality Party, Sophie Walker, and I have finally stepped out after two days of meetings. We spent them analysing political opportunities, equal pay, paid social care, and the reality that the UK Government is spiralling out of control.

I just want to go home, but now I'm on a bus, being told by a bus driver how to operate my own chair.

'You are in a wheelchair, therefore you have to face backwards and put your brakes on, or I can't drive away.'

I tell him that I have no brakes because I have a 250kg electric chair, which I have more experience driving than I'm guessing he does. Granted, I might be wrong. I will concede he might have a PhD in physics and I don't see him complexly because I'm a judgemental snot. But I don't feel like being fucking Rosa Parks this evening.

'Please open the door and lower the ramp so I can get off this bus.'

'All you have to do is turn around and face backwards.'

'Please open the door so I can get off this bus.'

'Just do as I say, and we can get going.'

'Please open the door and lower the ramp – I would like to get off your bus.'

By now, other passengers are getting restless, and they are asking him to open the door. I don't think for a moment that they are taking my side. Everyone wants to get home.

It would be easier for all involved if I just left.

When I am finally released from the vehicle of patronising hell, the March wind is colder than I expect. It is dark, and I drive my chair the three miles home because the idea of risking the wrath of another bus driver is too much for that evening. I remind myself that this only happens about 1 per cent of the time. I also know, mathematically speaking, that simply because it happens on average once out of one hundred doesn't mean it can't happen twice in a row.

The next day I receive word that I have been nominated for an Olivier Award, both as an actor and as a playwright.

My first thought upon hearing the news: having an Olivier nomination won't stop people telling me I don't know how to ride a bus.

Chapter 4

I learned at a very young age that my fate depended on other people finding favour with me. This began with going to school at the age of three. The only special programme for disabled children in my area was outside my school district, and so I was bussed out to another school. This one had bathrooms kitted out with grab-bars, and long tables for individuals who still needed their diapers changed at the ages of five, seven, nine.

The large room in the centre of the building was covered in blue mats. We were made to get out of our chairs, which doubled as hardwood straitjackets, and lie down as the adults lifted our legs as high as they might reach. For some, it was a few inches off the mat; for others, their legs went all the way to a near-ninety-degree angle.

'This is where kids like you go to school. This is where you belong.'

In class, I sat next to a boy who constantly moaned and hit himself. We played football during lunch with a blow-up black-and-white ball. A potato sprouted in a clear jar suspended from the ceiling, so we could watch its roots grow.

There was the boy who spoke with no disarticulation, but he only talked about *The Wizard of Oz*. He repeated lines from the movie, talking as if he were the Tin Man whenever he took his turn in class. We rode the bus together, with me perched on an oversized seat. I loved the big yellow school bus that came to our apartment every morning. As my mum put me on it and waved goodbye, he sat next to me. Slowly, my pre-kindergarten self realised that he could mimic, and I thought it was learning. I taught him to say, 'One plus one equals two.' I knew that was a fact. I knew that was reality. I also taught him, 'Two plus two equals four.' And then I asked what two plus two equals, and he gave the right answer.

There was a girl who, when we sat together as a class, would bang her head on the table, and the adults never prevented her from doing it. I wanted to stop her. The fact that I couldn't scared me. Thankfully, she always wore a medical helmet.

Another boy was always getting into trouble – some sort of hyperactivity made him shout out, thus causing my entire body to spasm.

'This school was built for you.'

I couldn't escape the underlying feeling that something didn't fit. By the age of four, I put together that my Saturday-morning music class was full of learning-disabled students, with the exception of myself.

I was learning at a faster rate than any of the other children around me. The teachers praised me for it. They then spent hours trying to control or, maybe in their own way, teach the others.

There was one exception: Miss Goodman. During an Individualized Education Plan (IEP) meeting[1] the school's

---

1   Individualized Education Program/Plan: the yearly educational road map listing all the services, accommodations and overall needs for a child with disabilities, to be supplied by the school.

physiotherapist told my mother that walking wasn't an appropriate goal for me. 'No walking will happen during her therapy sessions at all.' My mother put up a fight, again wasn't believed and wasn't listened to – that is, until Miss Goodman volunteered.

'It is reasonable to expect this child to walk. And if no one else will work on it with her, I will give up my lunch hour, tape her hands to the walking frame and teach her how to walk.'

I first knew Miss Goodman liked me when she gave me three lemon icing sandwich cookies at lunch when everyone else got two. We were lucky that any of us got cookies that day. The boy who had a habit of shouting and refusing to stay in his seat kicked the blow-up football into the potato in the glass jar, shattering it.

Miss Goodman firmly reprimanded him: 'I told you to only kick the football on the floor so that something like this wouldn't happen.'

For most of us, this restriction matched up with our own physical limitations.

'When you don't listen to adults … when you don't listen to me … bad. Things. Can. Happen. We're not going to have any potatoes growing in jars any more. You won't get to see what its roots look like. You obviously can't listen enough to follow directions. And so, those are the consequences.'

The intensity with which Miss Goodman convicted the whole class, even though it was just one boy's fault, was striking. It was as if Gareth Southgate had lined us all up for some sort of penalty kick at the hanging jar and coached us until someone finally got a goal.

I didn't like the wild boy who couldn't stay in his seat and screamed at inopportune moments. He never did anything to me, though, and I knew as long as I didn't attract his attention, it would stay that way. I could just be in my chair, looking at the worksheet about shapes, pointing or telling my assistant the answer, thinking about what was written on the blackboard ... and he would leave me alone.

At the age of four, some boys you like, and some of them won't stop talking about *The Wizard of Oz*. An adult says something, or someone makes a comment about 'leaving her alone', and you think: 'Yeah, that's what I want. This boy is weird, and I don't know why.'

If you asked me who was most likely to kick the ball off the floor, I could've easily pointed to him and said, 'He doesn't behave right ever.'

It wouldn't be the kid who took his food by a tube and drooled on his stuffed animal friends, would it?

There was a sketch on *Sesame Street* about a puppet who broke something without meaning to. And that's how I knew the word for what had happened: an accident. I knew that an accident was less likely when you were being careful, and if there was anyone in our nine-student class who wasn't careful, it was the boy who the teacher yelled at day after day.

So, of course, I saw what was coming, and I didn't do anything to stop him.

Miss Goodman was right. I let the potato jar get broken, even though there were three other adults in that classroom. Aides, they were called, even at the height of the Aids epidemic. Not personal assistants, or carers, or teacher's assistants. Everyone told us that they were our 'aides'. This became even more confusing when you spoke to those who weren't part of this 'special' world – the looks you would get when you said you had 'aides' following you at school ...

At almost five years old, I wore my heart on my sleeve, and I had already learned to keep quiet and remain small when there was trouble. Miss Goodman must have seen this, must have somehow noticed me avoiding eye contact with her, looking at the chipboard tray table locked in place with black Velcro straps collecting pools of saliva in front of me.

When the other kids went out to recess, we began our walking lessons. She took me out of my chair and strapped my hands to the silver walking frame. She used soft, gentle words of encouragement, not at all the same as those she had sputtered in reaction earlier that day.

I was getting so strong and doing so well, becoming so grown up as I placed one foot in front of the other in what was most likely more of a modified, controlled fall than an actual stride. I remember my hands hurting more than my feet as they remained taped tightly to the frame – it was impossible for me to make the micro-adjustments everyone else inevitably does throughout their bodies when they grasp hold of an object.

'Won't you be impressive walking into kindergarten on your first day at a new school next August?' She meant the statement as a form of encouragement and admiration, but the news that I would be attending a different school than the one the rest of our class was headed for was a surprise.

My mother had said for months that I did not belong in a classroom with children like this. I didn't know enough to know if I would like a different kind of school, but I knew enough to know my parents wanted it, so it must be a good thing.

If I proved myself smart enough, blended in enough with the other children, maybe, just maybe, I could attend school with kids whose inner worlds were a little more like mine.

*

I wake up. My neck and upper back are stiff. I'm in a continuous debate with myself as to whether this is middle age or cerebral palsy. Or maybe it's just crappy sleeping habits that I inherited when I was at university and suddenly woke up one morning face down in a pillow like a dead fish.

I don't have bad posture. Seventeen years of physiotherapy, followed by another God-knows-how-many hours working in theatre and physical movement, means that my posture is like that of a ballerina.

'Give yourself some slack in your back,' my friend, The Movement Director, encourages me. 'I know you think you're being normal, but actually it's so perfect you look strange compared to everyone else.' In the Covid time in which the world has stopped, I'm back doing my therapy to keep my ability to walk.

Later that day, as I remind myself to sit up straight, I remember The Movement Director's words and try to find a softness in my back. I immediately go into a panic that I am slouching again. I gaze into the mirror and try to find balance. Shifting the curve of my lower spine forward and back. I don't know what straight feels like. I never have.

I am aware of the irony of choosing a career in the performing arts where 'your body is your instrument'. This is my instrument, and I barely know how to keep it in balance.

I watch the daily Covid-19 briefings obsessively, scanning for details as to what's going on and what could happen. My director at Shakespeare's Globe Theatre reckons that we will be back to normal in July. When I tell her she is nuts, she changes the subject, continuing on with her plans.

Staying inside by government order is not strange to the friends who are living with me during the lockdown. They came from Lithuania with their two-year-old and are stuck on what was meant to be a fun getaway. They have been within the walls of my flat for three months.

I love playing with their little girl every day, teaching her to count to three in English, and then five, and then ten.

Peppa Pig grates on my nerves, and when I hear the music playing as I sit down to try to write something, I grit my teeth a little harder. I also want a bacon sandwich.

Bing is OK. *Bing* is about a little-boy bunny who has an adult friend named Flop, who is surprisingly smaller than Bing and looks like he's knitted out of an old orange sock. Flop acts as the sort of inner emotional stability that any toddler needs.

Arguably, most adults need a Flop to tell them that it's OK to be sad. Or that sometimes, despite your best efforts, things don't work out right. Flop is voiced by Mark Rylance, who I am currently working with on a focused government effort to recreate America's New Deal for Covid Britain. So, I listen to his voice tell Bing that sometimes things don't work out, and then I hear him through our emails talking about how desperately we need change in our government.

Behind The Little Girl watching anthropomorphic animals, I sit at my kitchen table with the Lithuanians and The Roommate. She is in shock at the news of George Floyd.

She has been in a fragile state for weeks as we have been confronted with the restrictions. Now she watches protests on her laptop screen. We don't show it on the big television in case little eyes see something no one should have to see. The Roommate is shaken – you can see it in her movements and motions as she goes about the kitchen, trying to make a cup of coffee. She burns the frozen croissants that we now make during what is called 'croissant o'clock' – sometime between 10 and 11 a.m. on the days that pass otherwise timelessly during the pandemic. There is an unsettlement I can feel about her when she comes out from her room. There is a determination not to bring up what she has seen as the rest of us continue with our day, sipping coffee and arguing about if the outside or the inside of a croissant is the better bit.

Finally, she breaks.

'Doesn't it keep you up knowing people are like this? I had no idea. It seems like Black people get shot down all the time in America. Is that how it is?'

The Lithuanians spent considerable time in the States. For them, growing up in the Soviet Union, those with the supposed power to protect you were not necessarily out for justice. They weren't always your friend, despite what it said on their uniform or how the media framed it.

But I know the question is aimed at me.

'The people who are meant to protect you very often choose not to.'

The Roommate retreats back into her room. I sit at the table, watching The Little Girl play with Lego. On television there is a new talking animal trying to come to grips with another problem in life.

*

I looked down at a slip underneath the pink dress. It had lacy frills that I so loved to see, but I knew I was meant to keep the slip hidden underneath.

In my IEP meeting at my new 'normal' school, my mum was going on and on about how intelligent I was and how I should be put into mainstream education classes on a permanent basis. Now five years old, I had proved that I could do it over the past year, and there was no reason not to continue. I excelled in every subject – what was the problem?

In the middle of this impassioned plea, she sees the pink dress hiked up to my waist and yanks it back down over the lace and tulle of my underskirt.

And then she starts in with another point.

The year with mainstream students had made me soar from height to height. Two boys had a crush on me in class. I had friends. With the exception of the one time I had forgotten to ask my mother to sign a permission slip for a field trip, I couldn't think of anything I had not done perfectly.

At one point, I insisted to my father that I wasn't improving enough. He pulled out a self-portrait I had made at the beginning of the school year, and the one I had brought home in March. My parents had attached the masterpieces with plastic alphabet magnets on our almond-coloured fridge that groaned in the middle of the night against the shattered tiles of our kitchen.

'Look at this. See how much more detail, how many more colours you used in this one than you did before? You improve every day – that's what growing up is.'

On the weekends, my father and I were left home alone while Mum earned nearly a week's worth of wages in forty-eight hours as an overnight nurse. It was there I learned to mix Lego and Barbies, to look for Narnia in the closet where we kept our vacuum cleaner and coats for the winter. Mega Bloks and Duplo were easier to manipulate in my less-than-nimble hands. Barbie became Dr Beverly Crusher from *Star Trek* – someone who's worth admiring for both her beauty and brains.

My father would struggle to know which way to put my tights on, inevitably putting them on backwards before taking me to church. We created plays – with full lighting cues from torches – which would be ready when my mother came home on Sunday night. The travelling teddy that was rotated between all of us at school on the weekends would come back from my house, having written in his notebook about adventures my father and I had.

Most weekends held at least one birthday party, and every child in the class of twenty-eight made sure to have theirs. When my turn came, a student said that he wanted to buy me a present that would help me 'work on my hands'. He bought me a money box with a combination lock.

I had been successful in integrating myself with 'mainstream students', excelling at whatever the teacher asked. One day, the teacher and my aide started playing a game with the class; the winner would get to go on a trip to Disney World for the week-end. I quickly realised that the trick was to say you were going somewhere that started with the same letter as your last name, and that you were bringing something that started with the first letter of your first name. So, when my turn came, I was 'going to Sweden, and I was taking an aardvark'. I was the only one who got it right.

The teachers stopped the game immediately, praising me for figuring it out when no one else had. I waited that weekend to find out when we were going to Disney World, but the drive to the airport never came. When I returned to school on Monday, several of the other students asked me how the trip went. 'What was the teacher like outside of class?' 'Did you sit on an airplane?'

'It was nice,' I said, and left it at that.

Figuring out the game before any other students and forgetting to bring back a signed permission slip were the only two things I remembered that I did differently from the other children.

I was sitting at that plastic-lined chipboard table, looking under my skirt, my mother and seemingly every adult I had met at 'the normal school' were battling over my future.

The night before, my mother told me that, whatever happened in the meeting, I must not cry. If I cried, people in the room would use my tears against me.

I had no idea what that last part meant, but I knew to do whatever my mother told me.

Four weeks away from my sixth birthday, I sat for two hours while every adult I thought had liked me, who constantly praised my 'great attitude' and who called me 'a walking, talking dictionary', now listed all my failures.

I didn't walk, at least not without a walker. That would be a problem when kids got bigger.

Nobody really understood me when I talked.

I jumped at loud noises.

I preferred to play with dolls over blocks, apparently showing I had no interest in STEM subjects.

I constantly drooled.

'She cried a lot that one time she forgot to have you sign the permission slip for the trip to the zoo. A lot. It was inappropriate, Mrs Stevens, really.'

'And there's the fact that she can't use scissors and glue. Not even a glue stick, really.'

'We don't have a lift in the part of the building where we house the first-grade classes.'

'We could get past all that, were it not for her other problems.'

'She's crying, again. Mrs Stevens. Do you really think it's appropriate to have your daughter sit through her IEP meeting?'

The delicacy of the lacy slip began to blur in my vision.

They wouldn't make a decision that day. To me, this meant I had a few more weeks to prove to the adults around me that this was where I belonged. Then, three weeks before my sixth birthday, the teacher took me into the hall during storytime. She said it had been decided that I would not continue on with my class. I would return to a school where I would be separated from mainstream students; sent back to a class where children were not like me. They couldn't learn fast, they hit themselves, they yelled – presumably at the teacher, but it felt like yelling for the sake of yelling – they sat in the corner and rocked, back and forth, muttering and hissing to themselves over and over.

I searched back. If I thought about it, I always knew that would be how the school year ended.

But I'd hoped I could make my teachers like me enough to change the outcome.

My father said that the point of childhood was to learn and make mistakes every day. Yes, I had made some mistakes at school, but I thought my teachers had helped me learn from them. I didn't realise my teachers, all the adults in charge of me during what was dubbed my 'trial year', had been keeping a list of my mistakes as an armoury of reasons why I had to return to where students would sit on beanbag chairs for hours, with diapers on because nobody wanted to help us wipe our asses.

Mistakes cannot happen.

*

Within the safety of my London flat, locked down with The Little Girl watching *Peppa Pig*, I realise how cruel those twice-yearly IEP meetings were.

I picture all the adults in the flat extending the kitchen table to its full length and sitting The Little Girl down to rehash everything she's done wrong over the past months.

One evening, when The Little Girl should be going to bed, she puts the TV remote in my hand, points at the television on standby and says, '*Peppa Pig*! Three … Two … One … Look!' The conviction in her newly learned English commands me to oblige, the convergence of skills so impressive that I have no choice but to turn on the intolerable *Peppa Pig* for her.

As I pull back my white duvet, my mind can't help but think of how those adults, sitting around a flimsy chipboard table, would have twisted The Little Girl's achievements into proof against being able to keep up in a mainstream classroom.

'Miss Stevens either doesn't understand bedtime or simply doesn't care when it is. While we are impressed with her ability to mimic counting, several of our special-needs children are able to do this. Regardless, this behaviour shows a genuine lack of understanding and respect.'

Four hours later I'm woken up by a Covid Dream about Rishi Sunak running an American summer camp in the 1990s. The Flatmate is moving furniture in her bedroom at 2.15 a.m. Her wall backs up to where my headboard sits, so I can hear everything. It's one of those situations where it is absolutely pointless to ask what she's doing, because the answer is obvious.

She has decided that now would be a good time to feng shui her room.

She is stressed about the pandemic.

She's ruminating on George Floyd, and the reality that power sees what is convenient for itself.

It feels like the world is exploding and all she has control over is the position of the furniture in her bedroom.

She does not know, much like The Little Girl downstairs hugging her Peppa Pig doll, that we have always been in a world where power can rule over logic and morality. I have never had the privilege of seeing the world otherwise. But if I walk into her room right now and point out that the ongoing turbulence was never a question of 'if' but 'when', it would be a very cruel thing to do.

So, I listen to her dragging the furniture across the carpet, the NHS sirens wailing into the night, echoes of a protest playing in the next room via YouTube, and I come to the conclusion that is fundamental while living in this body: I would rather lie in silence than say something that, although true, risks a bad reaction because the other person doesn't want to hear it.

Chapter 5

I spent another three years sitting through twice-annual IEP meetings. The adults would run down every mistake I had made; most of which I remembered, but some of which didn't sound like me. I would say to myself every morning, 'Maybe if I'm smart enough, the adults will send me back to the good school.'

Unbeknown to my parents, I was illegally given yearly IQ tests in the hope that I would test below average and the school would be able to receive more government funding for a student with a certified intellectual disability. This only became apparent when a man with a briefcase and a degree in child psychology appeared to play 'games' with me one Saturday.

'Next, you're going to show me a picture of a duck and a bar of soap,' I told him three hours into our 'game'.

'How do you know that?'

'I've seen this umbrella before. Next, it will be a duck and a bar of soap, and they all have to do with water. That's what I'm supposed to say.'

'I'll be right back.' The man rushed out of our living room, leaving me locked into a wooden posture chair, pushing the cards he left on my tray table so they formed a straight line and were away from my drool. I knew a straight line would look smart.

He didn't come back for a while.

In the end, though, it wasn't the fact that my IQ was four standard deviations above 'normal' that proved I should be in regular education.

'This is our lawyer,' my mother said to those gathered around the chipboard table during my IEP meeting at the beginning of the third grade. 'This will also be the last year our daughter will attend your school. She will be in mainstream education. Whatever goals you want my daughter to reach, you have until the end of May for her to achieve them.'

That autumn, I became a fourth grader at Kildeer Countryside School. The kids there were kinder, nicer. They didn't hit the teacher. Or themselves.

The first sleepover I attended with the other girls from my class, I was amazed at how big the suburban house was compared to our apartment. The kitchen alone had twenty cabinets, painted in a deep-blue hue, with silver hardware on each of the drawers. The tiles weren't cracked. In fact, there were no tiles at all, but hardwood floors, plus a playroom and a study for my friend and her older brother, overflowing with toys, multiple computers, games and, more importantly, three American Girl dolls: Molly, Samantha and Kirsten.

In May of the previous year, my family had been due to go for a weekend camping trip that was meant to be my birthday present. It hadn't stopped raining since Friday night, so we went home by Saturday at lunchtime.

I sat in my bed, wet in the darkness – my birthday had not

gone according to plan. My father came in and explained that the camping trip had cost $200.

'There will be other presents, I promise.'

The next morning, there were three brown paper bags set on our wooden kitchen table. Looking back, I'm pretty sure he bought them that evening after I had fallen asleep.

Kirsten, the American Girl doll I now wanted for Christmas, was $80; $110 if you bought the accessories, too. The camping trip had been double that price and set my family back for months. So it was a risk, asking for her – a risk inviting the possibility of disappointment. But Kirsten was special. She looked like me. She had blonde hair and blue eyes, a pioneer girl who came from Sweden to the American Midwest, losing her best friend on the sea voyage there. My family came from Sweden long ago. In the absence of any doll that remotely looked like they had trouble walking, Kirsten was me. So, when Christmas rolled around, and I was finally back in a school with 'the mainstream children', I wanted to make sure that Kirsten was mine. I wanted her set under our tree, with her small box of accessories, waiting for me to begin our friendship.

That Christmas morning, I sat up and listened for my parents moving in their room. Just as I had hoped, there was the overly loud, monstrous snore coming from my father's open mouth; but otherwise, silence.

I pushed myself to the edge of my bed, slowly lowering my body in a dip, careful to avoid the metal bar supporting the mattress, until I was sitting on the floor. Then I crawled from my room, peering through the hallway at the Christmas tree standing at the edge of our living room.

My knees had become leather, like puppy paws that grow stiff with age and friction as they bear a dog's weight. Back then, my right arm moving forward to bring the left leg in sync, was completely automatic, soundless. I snuck up to the tree, as any kid would on Christmas morning, before Mum and Dad woke up.

The girls in my new school had American Girl dolls and *Sweet Valley Twins* books, access to computers, and art in their homes to a degree I had never seen. But it wasn't that I had less: I was already elected Class President at the age of nine. It was an inevitability that I would achieve and gain more. Teachers asked me what I wanted to be when I grew up. They never asked that at the other school.

So, I looked in silence, hope and dread at the Christmas tree that morning.

There was a twenty-four-inch-long box, wrapped in the maroon wrapping paper that showed the outlines of each of the American Girls when the light hit it, and the smaller square box, six inches by six inches, that held her accessories.

*

I'm curled up on my sofa, the grey of the fabric contrasting with the dayroom walls of yellow Farrow & Ball paint I specifically selected to colour the main room of my flat. My flat. I bought it four years ago. It is in the middle of Zone 1 in London, a twenty-minute walk to the National Theatre on the Southbank; another twenty-minute walk, twenty-five at a stretch, to get to Westminster. Both of my work spheres, politics and theatre, are close enough that I don't have to face public transport.

Performance is a high-risk, high-reward career. So is writing. So is politics. I have a three-ring circus of a career portfolio, which includes all of it. On paper, I have 'made it'. And just for this hour,

I am curled up in a tan velour sweatsuit, Netflix remote in hand. The flat is empty. I can curl up with my environmentally sustainable pillows and watch television by myself, as loud as I want.

Most people of my generation are decades off from owning their own home, if they ever can. A conversation with my friend, The Twin, several weeks ago was about whether I was doing 'adulting' right. Still living in a single bed and without a relationship makes me feel like I'm not doing Life right. I haven't met any of the milestones assumed by the generation before me, other than buying this remarkable flat, which was bought not with the money I earned, but with blood money.

The difference might be minimal on paper, but it's one I can't get my head around, particularly today.

Two years ago, when I was working in the West End, Toby Stephens said to me one evening, 'You live in a council-house flat, I'm assuming, right?' I had told him some weeks before that I lived in Elephant and Castle, a place where he admitted he used to knock about when he was young and trying to separate himself from his famous parents.

'No!' I said. 'I own a flat there. It's mine.'

Toby Stephens looked at me. Something really didn't add up.

I was the understudy for the titular character in *A Day in the Death of Joe Egg*. Most of the events of the play revolve around her moaning or drooling or having seizures. Ultimately, the father, played by Toby, is so fed up that he tries to murder his daughter one snowy night. It's the equivalent of understudying a lamp with a few groans chucked in on cue.

Most disabled people would like to set every copy of the script on fire and dance naked around the flames in celebration of its demise, but it's a play that is considered by the Theatre Establishment to be a British classic. It contributes to the complication of my life: that's how someone with cerebral palsy must be – drooling and groaning. The parents don't take action in the face of the doctor's 'mistake'. They live in a council house, barely getting by.

A Day in the Death of Joe Egg is the script my life is supposed to follow.

Still, being carried to one's death by Toby Stephens is no bad thing.

*

The February after Kirsten came, a Macintosh Quadra 650 arrived at our three-room apartment in Vernon Hills, alongside a printer and a flatbed scanner that was half the size of a single bed.

Three years before those boxes arrived, I wanted a computer. My parents suggested saving up for one, coin by coin, like the girl did in the book *A Chair for My Mother.* So, I had been putting my coins into an industrial-sized mayonnaise jar with a cutout of a computer from a Service Merchandise catalogue ever since I was in first grade. The coins went in the jar again and again and again. Anytime I received a nickel out of my ear at church, or a ten-dollar bill for my birthday, those went in there, too.

At one point, I had asked my mother if there was ever going to be enough. The jar seemed so big and the coins so small that this could go on forever. A jar full of nickels and quarters couldn't possibly add up to the thousands of dollars the computer would cost. We would need at least another jar of the same size. My mother said to keep saving, no matter what, and when that jar became full, I would have enough money.

But the jar had never been more than a quarter full.

Then came the boxes: monitor, CPU, disk drive, CD-ROM, printer/scanner, and a desk that had to be put together, which would supposedly fit them all.

'The jar wasn't full yet! Are you sure it's time to buy this?' I asked my parents in a nine-year-old's sensible voice. It didn't add up.

*

It has been a week of hell. I have three cases open with the Actors' Equity trade union, all of which revolve around mistreatment from professional colleagues due to my disability. I am fragile and on the edge of tears – trying to fight for justice and come up with winning arguments that will hopefully force the scales to fall from people's eyes.

So, this Saturday afternoon on the couch, watching a new show I've been bingeing, is just what I need.

'I have delivered over 1,200 babies in five years. I can handle your delivery now. All you've gotta do is get up and dance with me so we can get you dilated and that baby out.' The character who says these words is the good guy – he would be the kind of guy I would be thrilled to go out with. He works as an OB-GYN in a maternity ward, and on his days off, he manages a community clinic for lower-income women. The only flaw that the New York millennial woman on the show has found in her new boyfriend is that he prays before every meal.

It has never hit me before that ushering forth life and slapping the bottoms of fleshy, screaming human beings is a daily occur-rence. It is a job. I start sobbing.

Later, The Twin stands in front of our microwave, trying to

figure out how to set the timer to puff up the bao buns she has bought in the Korean shop around the corner. She's been out most of the day, while I've been on the couch supposedly enjoying the quiet flat and the big-screen television.

The Twin and I met at RADA when she was nineteen and I was twenty-four. I was dyeing my hair once every six weeks at that point to match the colour of a Dr Pepper can, while she had just begun to weave *Sweet Valley High* blonde extensions into her own hair. Together we played Juliet with our two co-Romeos. Mine was an Iranian woman, hers would someday become an LA-based fitness model – while pregnant.

Like twins, we bounced Juliet's monologues off each other with the ease and enjoyment of NBA players passing an orange ball back and forth. We climbed on silver metal ladders, her holding my waist from the next rung down, making the audience gasp. We called each other 'sister' in the dank caverns of the RADA dressing rooms, as we rolled on our artfully torn Marks & Spencer fishnet stockings, and tied our purple leather corsets too tight.

Thirteen years later, The Twin is still around, listening to K-pop and trying to cook bao buns.

'I had a breakdown when Ben on *The Bold Type* said how many babies he had delivered.' I tell her about the scene in the show I was watching earlier.

'Weird,' The Twin says, looking at the microwave, wondering if the setting is going to lead to the fluff of an Asian bao bun, or make the entire thing explode.

'Do you think so?' I wait to see if she can put two and two together; I stare at her in silence until she is forced to look away from the silver microwave spinning her plate at a consistent rate.

She tilts her head, trying to understand.

'Over 1,200 babies in five years? And I'm the one that got messed up.' My eyes stay dry just long enough to see her face melt with love.

And I am heaving all over again. The microwave dings but she walks away from it to sit on the couch next to me. Within seconds, I am crying so hard that I gag. I try to understand the complications of my week, and how it seems that I won some sort of twisted Birth Day lottery, which allowed for a flat in the middle of London, with Farrow & Ball painted walls, high ceilings and large-screen TVs.

Am I happy? Was it enough? Am I living this weird and impossible life 'right'?

The Twin just holds me, on a couch that I managed to buy with my own money and through my own work, and we rock, back and forth, saying very little, and yet somehow the lament feels like a release.

'Breathe in . . . and out . . . and in . . . and out . . .'

The Twin has the lungs of an opera singer, because she is one. So, when I break down and start to cry harder and faster, it is only because it feels like there's something else that I can't do right. Yet another thing affected by the day that determined everything.

'I can't even breathe right! It affects everything.'

'In . . . and out . . . in . . . and out . . . in . . . and out. And if you can't keep up with me, go for your own rhythm. In .. out .. in .. out .. in . out . in . out. There you go, there you go, good. Do you like breathing deeply? It gets oxygen into our bodies . . . it calms our heart rate . . . it gets oxygen into our brain—'

At this, I look up at her from her chest, and she understands the gaff.

'Sorry. Admittedly, wrong choice of words. I suck. Keep breathing. It gets oxygen to our . . . MINDS! Better?'

The Twin offers to put a Korean sheet mask on me and have 'Twin Time' that evening before she remembers that I'm due to go out and see a concert at Wigmore Hall. I wonder what it would be like to put on a face mask myself. Not having to wait to be asked or feeling like you're demanding to be spoiled.

*

We had our car parked outside of the Amtrak exit at Union Station in Chicago as we waited for my grandmother to appear between the glass doors. In my head, she would be holding a round hat box and wearing white gloves. That's what people used to do when they rode the train in my American Girl books. It was a six-hour train ride between Saint Louis and Chicago, and she was staying for nearly two weeks. My grandpa had died nearly two years before and I was told that she was coming now, near the anniversary of his death, to cheer herself up by spending some time with me.

My father switched off NPR. Terry Gross was reporting once again on the hostage situation in Waco, Texas, at the compound of the Branch Davidians – a religious cult. A week before, I had asked Dad if it was still happening, as it had been several days since I had heard about it.

'I think so, but that's a good point. They have seemed to go quiet on the news lately. Well observed, Puppy.'

Now the news story was back – for what reason I didn't know. The most important thing in my world right now was seeing Grandma exit through those glass doors, come home and play with me for as long as was fathomable for a soon-to-be ten-year-old.

'There! There she is! That's her!' I exclaimed from the back seat of our silver minivan. My father exited the driver's side in order to take her luggage. Then my mother got out, heading to the back seat with me, and the inevitable dance between daughter-in-law and mother-in-law started.

'I'll sit in the back.'

'No, I'll sit in the back!'

'No, no, no, don't be silly. You've had such a long train journey – I will sit in the back, Mary Lou.'

I could've told you that this debate was going to happen days ago. It seemed to happen every time I was anywhere near Grandma Stevens.

'Well, there's not much to tell,' Grandma said as we headed back onto the interstate to get home. She held just a common, everyday nylon bag.

For the next week, Grandma Stevens was home when I got back from school, rather than my mum and dad. They had meetings to go to.

'Teachers have meetings about every other month, but it only takes a day. Mum and Dad's meetings seem like a lot. I don't get it. Why do they have so many meetings right now? No, don't put the videotape in that way, Grandma! That's backwards!' I said, giggling at her. 'And it has to be on Channel 3, otherwise you won't see the video at all, and it'll just stay on Phil Donahue!'

The four of us would eat together every night. My father would say a blessing for our food, ask for it to 'strengthen and nourish us', and give thanks for the day. I kept my eyes open as I watched the thin, watery excess of tomato sauce start to seep out of the thick, rich sauce, ruining my dish. It was the most tragic thing that could ever happen involving a plate of pasta. I snuck a peek at Grandma, mouthing the words and nodding her head as she always did whenever anyone prayed.

What was she praying about before our meal of fusilli and Prego tomato sauce warmed up by my father?

Later that week, we watched the replays on PBS as the Branch Davidian complex went up in flames. David Koresh, a man who proclaimed to be Jesus, was dead, and now reporters were questioning who started the fire. What did the FBI actually do? The term 'tear gas' was being bandied about with such speed during the analysis that I wondered if it was the tear gas that caused the explosion.

Both of my parents looked at the footage while making dinner, my mother with a red plastic salad spinner in her hand and my dad waiting to flip the meat over. Grandma had gone into my parents' room for a bit to cry.

'Did Grandma know anyone there?' I asked, trying to figure out if she was sad because of the fire or because I had done something wrong that day.

My mother shook her head.

'So why is she crying?'

My parents said that they would tell me later.

'I'll tell you later' is always adult code for 'hopefully you'll forget'.

'It will take the focus off the case. We might get out of this lucky,' my dad said to my mum, his voice lowered.

'Do we know anyone there?' I pressed. If the man claimed to be Jesus, then maybe he was, and maybe someone at church knew these people.

Both of my parents shook their heads and went back into the kitchen to make dinner.

*

The Sunday before my tenth birthday, our church had a costume contest with a Wild West theme. I went as a cowgirl; I wore a blue-and-white blouse with a matching skirt that was part gingham, part cotton ruffle. I wore two plastic guns on either side of my hips, something that my parents debated about for hours that morning before church. But the guns were pink and plastic, and in the hands of a ten-year-old girl with cerebral palsy, and without the exploding caps inside, what could go wrong?

I sat on the corner of our wooden sofa with the cushions that were tied onto the rods of the seat and thought, 'This is my last day before I turn double digits. This is what I am wearing the last day before I turn ten. Don't forget that! Whatever happens, don't forget that!'

Being ten meant that I could have my ears pierced. Ten meant I could stay up until 8 p.m. and be a little bit closer to growing up. Ten was a step closer to PG13 films. I went to bed when the sun was still up that night, thumbing through fairy-tale books, wondering if it was all right to read them from tomorrow or if being ten meant that I was too grown up for them. All of my favourite books had at least one girl that looked like me and Kirsten – and who were always ten. Discovering secret gardens and hidden houses, a world trapped in a toy cupboard waiting to come out: none of that could happen until you turned ten. And that was going to be tomorrow.

My birthday party was at the end of the week, but on the actual day, Mum made a yellow cake with chocolate icing before I came home, and there was a small set of presents on the table, which was covered with a pink tablecloth. Five. *An improvement from last year,*

I thought, before berating myself. *What a selfish and greedy thing to say. Jesus wouldn't say that.*

Watching Mum bake, I realised it had been ages since I had seen the red box of powdered milk in the kitchen, my mum stirring it up in a pitcher in an effort to save money. And Mum and Dad had begun to smile a lot more after all their meetings and Grandma's visit.

I don't remember what the five presents were, but after they were opened, Mum reached underneath the table and pulled out a surprise. It was Kirsten's bed – something I hadn't expected. Her bed was particularly expensive. The doll alone was enough, and she slept with me, in my bed. But then another box came out, and it was her trunk. Boxes came out from behind the couch, holding surprises that I'd never dared dream of. New clothes, new dolls, the *Oregon Trail* computer game alongside *Where in the World Is Carmen Sandiego?* – all on the same birthday.

It felt as if Mum and Dad were discovering presents for me all over our small apartment for nearly two hours. When the sun went down, I looked on our kitchen table to see it entirely filled, saturated with pinks and purples, and a few blues to set it off for the sake of gender equality.

Then I felt sad. This cost way more than the camping trip last year. Something didn't add up.

It was another seven years before I learned that all those meetings my mum and dad went to would someday pay for a flat in Zone 1 of London. Learned why the sudden switch to pink and purple birthday presents hidden throughout our apartment's living room did not put us into debt. And how we could go from a three-room apartment up a flight of stairs, to a three-bedroom house lined by woods and an entire acre devoted to wildflowers. Why we could hire a lawyer to get me back into mainstream education. Why my grandmother came to stay, and that when she cried, it had nothing to do with what was on the news.

I slowly began to put together the bits of my life that had never really added up in the moments they were happening. The new computer and the mayonnaise jar; how a doll could go from being too expensive to being affordable along with her entire collection of dresses and furniture all in one go.

The day I found out all of these things, I received a rejection letter from Northwestern, the university I most wanted to get into. In the end, every single college that knew about my disability rejected me. All fifteen of them.

'Doesn't knowing you have this money make the rejection easier?' my mother asked, as she unbuttoned my French cuffs after our visit to the bank on Chicago's LaSalle Street that day.

'No. All it does is show the limits of what money can do.'

Chapter 6

When they said that the walker needed to be shipped from Germany, my nine-year-old brain thought it meant that getting it would be impossible. There was an out-of-date calendar taped to the floor-to-ceiling mirror of one of the treatment rooms of the therapy centre I'd been attending since I was eight months old. The hypercolour photos of Germany looked out of place next to the reflections of the room's blue mat and air-filled Swiss balls with varying colours corresponding to their sizes: perfectly pure yellow, green, orange, blue and finally red – the final size so huge it was hardly ever used in the paediatric therapy clinic, unless it was to allow a child with ocular nerve damage to follow it with their eyes.

There was no purple there, though. Nothing was ever purple in a disabled child's life. Just bright, simple colours – if you were lucky. Red, yellow, blue – at a stretch, green or orange. Mine was a world mostly filled with metallic silver and beige – an almost peach-like skin colour, which was meant to mimic 'all skin tones' but in doing so managed to match none. Small wonder it felt as if I would be better off if my disability was hidden. My impossible goal was to 'pass' as not being disabled – that would fix my entire situation. That pressure must have been compounded if you have skin that's anything more than about two shades darker than mine. Even as a kid, the weight of the expectation not to mind beige and chrome was suffocating.

You must be thankful for 'moleskin', the soft tape they made to soften the hard edges of orthotics against your overly sensitive, never-touched-the-ground feet. Act as if the fabric is exactly the same as your own skin colour, otherwise you'll upset the therapists, the doctors, the people who love you and are only 'trying to help'. Because collectively, that's the only story we can agree on as acceptable: the one where purples and pinks don't matter. Beauty and looking decent? Nice? Cool? Expressing anything about the essence of your soul from the inside on the outside? Why should you worry about a thing like that when you can't even swallow your own spit consistently? Now, as a feminist, I can't help but look back on these colours and ask, 'What about the girls?' as much as I ask, 'What about the people with skin tones other than … beige?'

There is a reason why we call the trauma and pain we don't want to think about 'unspeakable': oppression is dependent on silence. Oppression is dependent on colours like beige and metallic silver, while people insist it's the best they can do. Oppression takes advantage of the fantasy that if others don't look too hard, maybe they won't notice your disability. There's a reason why the moleskin padding was beige, and not glittery purple.

The walker I saw in the Chicago Disability Expo was made by Kindervagen, a German brand. It had its name written in pink across the back of the walker, and it wasn't just purple – it was lilac! Ask the majority of tween girls and they will tell you: lilac is a superior colour to basic purple. This was the only colour combination the company ever made. Maybe little boys in Berlin wanted lilac walking frames. Maybe in places with castles like Germany, the boys had enough sense to know that lilac was obviously a superior colour. But I really didn't care about them. This walker was for me.

The lilac object of my desire was a win, according to the physiotherapists.

After ten years of working in leotards with Swiss balls in front of full-length mirrors, and stabilising blue mats that were supposed to protect you when you fell, I was one of the lucky ones who could bear my own weight.

I used a reverse walker – not the type for old people which go in front of you and cause your back to permanently crouch. To this day, people set me up in a walking frame and immediately try to put it in front of me. People often assume that with a body like mine, I don't even know how to use my own equipment.

We decided to buy the German walker just before we moved into the house. 'The house' was the next big step in getting me everything I would ever need after Kirsten and the computer. We ordered the walker, and when we moved the first week of July 1994 into a real house – three bedrooms when we really only needed two – the walker still hadn't arrived. Germans, we were told, took the summer off, particularly August. So, we told ourselves the delay was inevitable and justifiable. International shipping was still functionally unimaginable.

The morning of our first day living in the house, I looked at the tiled floor outside my bedroom and thought, 'If I can't crawl here, that purple walker is exactly what I need. Once that comes, I can go anywhere I like, as long as I have my shoes on.'

I had started the fourth grade at Kildeer, introducing myself on the first day of class saying, 'Yeah, I use a walker to get around because I have a disability. That's my walker, but soon I will get a new one, a lilac one. And I can't wait.' To most nine-year-olds, 'soon' meant a few weeks at most. But I had lived enough of my life to know that 'soon' could equal agonising months of waiting.

'Soon' was when you ordered from catalogues and it took six weeks to get the parcel in the mail, eight if it was on special order. 'Soon' was Christmas after you saw Santa at the end of the Macy's Thanksgiving Day Parade.

We were told the walker would take ten weeks to arrive because of the reality of international shipping that came from sending a piece of equipment from Germany over to the US. It would be held up at customs, questions would need to be asked. But by Halloween, surely, I could be a princess in a purple walker and a glittery pink gown. None of the princesses in my books had walkers, but that's only because no one in America knew purple walkers existed yet.

I don't remember when the box holding the lilac walker of my dreams arrived from Germany. I know one day it did, and the next day I had the kids at school crowding around me, commenting on how much quieter this model was. How happy they were that after a year of promises, I finally got the one thing I wanted back in August when we first met each other. I remember hearing the exclamations of 'Cool!' or 'Awesome!' that are so common in fourth graders that are trying to grasp hold of adult sentiments. I remember thinking it *was* cool, it *was* awesome. In that moment, the frustration of chasing the package around various border agencies across the Atlantic was worth it. I had the walker I would use for the next phase of my life.

Within two years, using a walker full time would be replaced by using a manual wheelchair. It's too hard to explain to the able-bodied world why this is not necessarily a sign of a deterioration in your condition, but rather a change of lifestyle. I started to go to school with bigger kids, more crowded hallways and a more rigorous need for getting to class on time, instead of walking into one classroom for the day.

*

I sit on the London Underground debating which friend to call as I look for someone to grieve with me. At thirty, the pain in my left knee has become excruciating, and I can only blame myself.

My left knee has become capricious. I can feel it clicking and rubbing whenever I bend and straighten my leg, even while sitting. The inside tendon hurts without bearing any weight on it.

This is all my fault.

How many times had I heard from my army of therapists growing up that I would lose the progress I had gained through their hard work if I didn't exercise daily? That once I became an adult, my body would be my responsibility?

I had the tools to make sure my muscles and balance, the core of my body, the extraneous movements, were kept as physically normal as possible. Bodies of people with cerebral palsy age faster, I was told. I must actively combat that.

In college, taking movement classes and staying in shape for performances was easy. I was as motivated to perform well onstage as I had been to go miles in a lilac walker. But, throughout my twenties, I had settled. I used an electric chair to whizz around London. My choice. The right choice in order to save energy and be safe.

In my small, rented two-bedroom flat, I had not done the exercises to ensure I kept up the progress, hard fought for and sorely won from my childhood. Progress, everyone told me as a kid, which defied medical expectations.

Now I am on the Underground in my chair, looking at those around me, wondering what sort of ticking time bombs they have in their bodies, fused by their daily habits. Arthritis? That's what the doctor said I might be getting. Stroke? Brain aneurysm? Heart disease?

I had let it all spiral out of a thousand daily decisions not to do physio, not to walk, not to take the stairs in my flat on my own two feet, but rather scoot up them again and again. To sit in front of the computer day in and day out, typing blogs that no one ever saw in the hope that someday I could call myself an author. In the meantime, the sun passed outside the window of the train, reflected against the River Thames, and physically, I was immobile.

Had I gained weight? No. My metabolism works like a coal fire, my brain using up every spare calorie it can find so that I am able to put more of my thoughts on paper, key by key, working with one finger.

I texted my dad. The Tube had just got Wi-Fi service in certain areas, and I took the opportunity to send blue written speech bubbles eight time zones away in order to express how guilty I felt that I hadn't taken action, that this pain was my fault.

'How is this your fault?' my father wrote back, somewhere in between London Bridge and Waterloo station. I reminded him that I was an adult. I had made the myriad decisions that led to this pain now, but I was determined to do my best to fix it. I had no idea how.

'People with cerebral palsy get arthritis early. It's a fact. There's not much you can do about it.'

There might not have been much, but I hadn't done anything. I knew what could happen and I, by choice, did nothing.

*

In our old apartment, my mother would wake me up at 5.30 every morning, turn on the only show airing at that hour – re-runs of *M*A*S*H* – put me on a purple bicycle with adult training wheels so that the back tyre was not reaching the floor, and strap my feet in so I could pedal.

Riding a bike was part of growing up. Riding a bike counted as therapy to strengthen my legs. Riding a bike and balancing on a banana seat – although arguably ridiculous – strengthened my muscles.

We had found the bike in a Toys R Us store. It was lilac, with rainbows and stars. The design alone was worth waking up at 5.30 a.m. for. Sometimes I would imagine I was cycling through my SimCity, deciding to take right or left turns to go around residential blocks or to avoid the industrial parks that caused pollution for the game's fake citizens. I passed simulated commercial buildings that provided jobs and made the unemployment rate go down.

Combine fifteen minutes of SimCity bike rides with twenty minutes of ab exercises, another ten of weight-bearing on my hands every morning, and always more stretching. By 7 a.m. I had done the equivalent workout of a child who devoted their early mornings to becoming an elite ice skater – a routine that, I was told, would pay off in the end.

All those hours of early-morning therapy, the hour's drive to the paediatric clinic and the hour back, the thousands of dollars spent on improving my body and range of motion, I had let slip down the drain.

*

On the lift up from the Underground, I begin to search online for private health insurance. I want more than the NHS, or maybe I feel that I've failed myself so much, I don't deserve their help.

Two months ago, I was taking part in a reading at the Chatsworth House Estate when my knee pain went from annoying to debilitating. The auditorium of Chatsworth House is about three storeys up a stone staircase. The historical building has managed to invest in a slow-climbing stair lift that goes about the same rate as a beetle would travel up the same flight of stairs. They are proud of the equipment, as am I. At least they invested in something.

The organiser of the event demanded that everyone head downstairs into the ornate British gardens to take a group photo during the interval, only to come back up those three flights of stairs in that same fifteen minutes. The programme must restart on time, she said, or else we would hold up dinner. I wanted to throw a Victorian candelabra at the woman's head.

We had come into conflict the summer before about accessibility and access at a venue in London, and she had decided that I was self-centred. Yet here she was again, insisting that anyone who did not make it downstairs in time would be left out of the photo and arguably forgotten to posterity.

My father, visiting for the writing workshop attached to the performance, took my arm and started walking me downstairs. Within a few moments, Andre Dubus III, the writer and lead teacher of the workshop, was on my other side. No group photo would be taken without him.

Between my father and Andre, I rushed downstairs in a blue cotton dress, zipped up in the back and airy enough for a summer's day. With each step I took on the stone floor, I could feel my knee pain increasing, but I didn't want to slow down. I didn't want to ask for the photo to be taken somewhere else. I didn't want to put Andre in the awkward position of going head-to-head against the organiser. Andre had the authority to defy her wishes, but I didn't want to exploit that. And so, I made my way down, my father and Andre alternating between phrases such as 'We're almost there' and 'Take your time'. I said nothing about my knee.

The photo is beautiful. I stood next to a writer I respect and my father in the moment it was captured. It will be passed on and reflected upon when both men are gone, and I am still here. But coming from the Tube to my flat, I pinpoint the time leading up to that photo in my mind: when I should've said no; when I saw the warning signs and did not speak up.

I knew to behave better, and yet I still stayed silent. That was a mistake.

'Do you have a pre-existing medical condition?' the British insurers ask. I say that I have cerebral palsy – that isn't going to be hidden any time soon – but I don't mention my knee. After all, it has yet to be diagnosed. And without a diagnosis, it doesn't exist. To get health insurance is to be proactive just in case I need a knee replacement or, worst-case scenario, to have my leg chopped off immediately.

I find myself hoping that the hard work and smart living thrown at me as a child will still work as an adult. That I can undo the damage that I have brought onto myself. Neuroplasticity was how I was able to learn to walk in the first place, or talk, or swallow, or put on eyeliner and lip gloss, or any of the other things my parents had been assured would be impossible.

But neuroplasticity only works when you're a kid, I was always told. 'You can't rewire your brain as an adult.'

I find myself begging the God of Neurons and Dendrites to help me mitigate the years I have not done enough. I will work hard, I will 'get lucky'. Again. Through effort. *Please let me undo what can be undone.*

I have to wear my earbuds when I get an X-ray of my knee. I learned this during my growth spurts in school when my entire centre of gravity would shift, causing my almost-controlled limbs to go akimbo once again. During one particularly hormone-laden year, we visited A&E seven different times due to falls. The receptionists knew my mother and me by name.

Stillness is medically impossible for me. It comes with the constant misfiring of nerves and a fight-or-flight reflex that has nowhere to go. I have trained for years with The Movement Director and voice teachers how to rest and be still onstage. But the second you ask me to do it in real life – for example, 'Stay still, or else thousands of pounds of medical film is going to be wasted by an already underfunded NHS because the X-ray keeps coming out blurry' – I become as mobile as an over-caffeinated Freddie Mercury. The sudden whir of an X-ray machine coming on is my cue to shout, 'Ehhh-oh!'

Back in high school my mum would bring a Discman to drown out the noise. I was on an X-ray table listening to the album *Mad Season* the day Matchbox Twenty released it. This is still my medical soundtrack of choice.

I turn up the volume to 'If You're Gone' as the technician ducks behind the radiation wall. I try to ignore the connection between her walking away and the reality that her disappearance means she is taking the X-ray.

Be … Juliet dead in her tomb, I tell myself.

An hour later, the doctor is holding the image up to the light. He says it's a little blurry – thanks, Doc, any idea why that would be? – but he can tell that I don't have any real damage in my knee.

'You're probably going to get arthritis at some point soon, but that's just age. Happens to everyone eventually.'

'But I've done something wrong. I hurt and I never used to.'

'Can you pay a few hundred quid to see someone privately?'

I tell him I can. I will pay whatever I need to for my precious mobility. I have let this pain happen. I need to do whatever it takes to fix it.

The NHS doctor takes out a pad of paper and writes down a name alongside a telephone number. The sound of the note ripping away from its adhesive binding is like a zipper opening for my health and ability to walk.

'He'll fix you, but it'll cost you.'

At home I scoot up the steep stairs to my computer. Little Grey Cat follows slowly, resting on a step while I go up three or four. Then she bounds up the same distance I've just laboured up. On the top landing, made slick with old, polished wood, I roll my knees away from the staircase before bearing weight on them. Then I put my right foot in front of me and, swinging my left leg to do the same, I press my weight down to stand. The shooting pain in my kneecap nearly knocks me backwards. I have to grab the banister to keep from falling down the stairs. Even if some sort of angelic Fab Five keeps me safe, I need to keep myself healthy.

I hobble as best I can to my iMac. Hobbling is almost impossible when your walk is basically already controlled falling in a specified direction. Every time I put my left foot against the floor, I can feel my toes rotate inwards, my heel going out. This is not how I was taught to walk. And each step makes me want to collapse from physical agony, or the failure of it all.

*

Wet fibreglass plaster would be wrapped cold around my feet. The hands of The Woman Who Taught Me How to Walk would dip the roll of this magical hardening material into a bucket of warm water and then connect it to a new roll where the old one stopped.

The physiotherapists would joke that they were making us into mummies as an explanation for why we had to sit still all those hours, the material eventually turning warm as it was wrapped to knee level. With every layer, The Woman Who Taught Me How to Walk would put her thumb again on the arches of my feet, pushing them up. This made the plaster dry in the shape necessary to be a supportive orthotic.

This was my favourite annual activity.

The only scary part was when they took a box-cutter to slice the plaster off following the line of a black rubber tube, which ran from knee to toe as protection from the knife. I felt the pressure to be absolutely still, or else it would be my fault if I was cut.

Every time I changed shoe size, it would cost my family $800 in the 1990s. Inflation has doubled those numbers now. Within days, a pair of orthotics could go from fitting my feet perfectly to creating violent blisters following a growth spurt.

'That's it then, you have to wear your church shoes to school tomorrow,' my mother would say.

I loved wearing the shoes that looked pretty and fitted my feet without the thick fibreglass of an orthotic misshaping them. They provided less support for my walking, which equated to less pain.

My orthotics came to just below my knee in the beginning. Some years they were hinged at the ankle, other years not, depending on which part of my foot needed stability. The height and fit of the brace meant that when I sat in the plastic chairs during children's church and someone made a loud noise, my spasms would cause my legs to pinch themselves between the seat of the chair and the fibreglass casing.

When the pinching and bruises became more frequent, it was usually the first sign that a growth spurt was coming. We still waited until the blisters came, putting off the expense for as long as possible and bathing my feet in Lipton tea in order to turn inflamed skin into light calluses.

The knee-high braces eventually turned into calf height, ultimately retreating to ankle height in my teenage years.

'That's as low as I would ever be willing to make your orthotics,' The Woman Who Taught Me How to Walk said to me. The therapy clinic had just switched casting providers. This new company didn't use beige and white for padding and straps; they had options including lilac and, even cooler, lilac glitter camouflage. At age fourteen, I could finally make some fashion choices.

*

'Lie on your stomach,' the orthotist says to me. The look on my face must be extremely easy to read because he follows it with, 'I'm not nuts, just trust me.'

It has been ten years since I was last fitted for orthotics. The current ones are the only pair ever made for me as an adult. I haven't worn this pair enough, which is why I'm probably in this mess, I remind myself.

About a year ago, I was re-warned by my therapists about age and my body breaking down in time, faster than anyone else's. I was approaching thirty. I slipped the orthotics back in my Dr. Martens where they now sit at the bottom of the orthotist's table.

And, yes, I think this man is insane because this is not how you make orthotics for someone with cerebral palsy.

His walls are lined with photos and autographs – football players and runners, even a few MPs and other recognisable celebrities. So, the guy obviously knows his stuff. For normal people, at least.

What was this NHS doctor thinking when I was referred? Where are the Swiss balls and the people with crutches and unknown bone diseases that call for extreme footwear?

'OK, and that's it.'

Wait, what? He's barely covered the bottom of my feet, which are currently heels to the sky, to be clear, and it's taken maybe twenty minutes.

'I don't think you know what you're doing.' I figure I just may as well say it outright, because what do I have to lose? I'm trying to get my knee fixed, my body back into some form of stable shape, and what he has done is not exactly going to be a milestone on the journey, more like a pothole.

He laughs in such a way that makes him tilt his torso back. The movement of it somehow tells me this is fun for him, but he's not going to patronise me.

'They'll be ready in ten days. You pay £125 now and £125 when you pick them up. Is that OK?'

'You mean for each side? So, £500 total?'

'No, £250 in total. Both orthotics. See you next week.'

Ten days later I'm back on his table, sitting upright this time, which I suppose is an improvement.

'When you become famous in the West End, you'll send me a photo like the athletes up there, right? I don't have very many actors on my wall.'

'If these work, I will.'

My reticence is reaffirmed when he pulls out two flat pieces of plastic, which don't even cover half my foot. The arch is embedded, but other than that they may as well just be two small sushi dishes.

'You're going to need to get yourself some new Dr. Martens, these are too big,' he says as he slips the plastic inside my bright-pink shoes. 'Slips' is the key word here; not struggles. I don't hear the sound of the insoles being ripped out of my shoes, as was the custom growing up. They just slide in. And then he puts the insoled shoes on me, tying them up. He puts one hand towards me, palm up, as if he was Fred Astaire reaching for Ginger Rogers, and says, 'Come on. Stand up, now.'

When I do, I notice the searing pain that goes from the arches of my foot straight up to my knee. It turns my entire leg out straight, making it impossible to pivot in and have either leg fall lazily on the other. It hurts, but it is a 'good' hurt.

'This is right. This feels right. How can this feel right?' I ask the doctor. It feels like my feet have finally been stapled to the ground:

weighted, rooted in a way that means they aren't going to fly off and make me lose my balance. I can feel my calves and my legs relaxing on top of the weight of my foot as everything clicks into place, like the Tin Man in *The Wizard of Oz* figuring out how to walk again after being rusted through for so many years.

'You spun around so much in those old orthotics. They were too big for you. No wonder your knee was injured. It wasn't that you weren't working hard enough. Those orthotics made you work too hard.'

I think back to how my left heel would pivot every time I took a step, rotating my knee inward, and the self-blame and fear that came with that movement. Something wasn't right ... but it wasn't my fault.

The years of physio come back and remind me what needs to hurt in order to ensure that my body is working.

Not long after my new orthotics are fitted, I decide to get away for six weeks on my first extended writing trip. I have two screenplays to write, but more to the point, I need time to get away from the day-to-day. To not worry about where my next meal is coming from or the struggle of putting a bra on every morning. To just have someone help me when I need it and to leave the rest of the time for writing.

During this trip, I spend hours arranging story beats on Post-it notes. And with my new orthotics, I decide to try to start walking again. I pull up my laptop and look for a walker like the one I had as a child. Amazon sells them for £150 each. It is in bright blue chrome and still clicks, annoyingly. But other than that, it is exactly what I need. Looking at the price three times and trying to measure the size I'll need, I click 'Purchase Now', not really expecting what happens next. Somehow, in the middle of nowhere, England, the walker arrives at my door less than twenty-four hours later.

Chapter 7

'When I'm done having cerebral palsy, do you think I will have time to be both an ice skater and a ballerina, or should I just choose one?' The way my parents looked at each other as they tucked me in under the rainbow duvet that night was a look every child knows if they've been told by the best-meaning adults that 'anything is possible'.

'You won't ever not have cerebral palsy, darling. It will always be a part of your life.'

All of those hours of early-morning therapy, followed by the twice-weekly visits to the private therapy clinic; the inspirational posters; my mother's insistence that I was getting better; the new school; every effort I had made to be heard and understood, saying each word clearly, slowly, until my teachers swore 'her speech is really improving' – what was that all for? The endings of all the fairy tales I read were always happy. You work hard, you get better, you keep trying, you overcome: cerebral palsy becomes a thing of the past.

Sports came into my life when I was just coming to grips with the reality that hard work, a little bit of luck and a little bit of wishing on some faraway star wasn't going to change my disability.

The most it would do is give me the ability to stand up a tiny bit straighter, walk a few more steps, drool a little bit less. 'Pass' a little bit more.

*

'What do you mean, you don't run a marathon to win? Why else would you run a marathon?'

As I ask this, The Movement Director looks at me like I am a starfish that has just regurgitated its stomach out of its mouth in order to eat.

'You run it to finish the 26.2 miles. The number of people competing – wait, did you honestly think thousands of people ran the London Marathon with hopes of winning like some super-amped-up Hunger Games?'

As much as I want to answer, 'What would be the point if you didn't have a chance in hell of winning?' I realise that those words are complete nonsense. Statistically, she is right. I went to a university that boasted 'learning for learning's sake'. I have made a life out of doing things knowing that the odds of me coming out on top are slim, so I do them for the sake of doing them. I am the type of person who would say I want to climb Mount Everest just because it's there. There is inherent value given to your soul just by doing something. I don't have to win every time, as long as I simply invest all that I have in an activity. So why is any of this news to me?

*

I was first introduced to wheelchair track while lying on our living-room floor after a bike accident smashed up my face, breaking three orbital bones. As terrified and guilty as my mother felt, there was something comforting about it. Kids fall off their bikes; this was first and foremost a normal part of growing up.

The 1996 Olympics were in Atlanta and like every American child, I was glued to the TV screen; the only difference was that an ice pack was basically glued to my face.

'And now we have a very special exhibition sport, the 800 metres in men's wheelchair T1 track.'

Wheelchair track? What was this? Wheelchairs at the Olympics? This was amazing. Maybe I could go to the Olympics for cycling. A perfectly sensible thought for any eleven-year-old after breaking three bones by falling off their bike.

Scot Hollenbeck flew out in front as soon as the gun went off, the other five men quickly coming into line behind him. Draughting, I later learned, was how you relied on your opponent to break the air resistance, saving your energy until the final moments of the race. Second place was actually the best place to roll until the last straight, and then you could break off from behind with a burst of speed that came out of nowhere.

Not that that mattered for Scot Hollenbeck. By the last lap he was so far out in front that the air closed around him; there was no broken air by the time the person in second rolled by.

Within two years, Scot Hollenbeck was my camp counsellor, as was the Boston Marathon winner Jean Driscoll. My summers were spent with elite athletes because, like anything new, wheelchair athletics was a small community in the beginning. Three athletes in chairs might be in the Chicago Marathon, and I knew them all. They were only competing with each other, so one of them had to win.

My first time in a manual wheelchair, I was terrified of flipping over. My arms were unfit for propulsion, but I quickly pieced together that I could use my legs to propel myself backwards faster than my arms could push forward.

Mike Frogley, the Paralympic Canadian basketball coach, noticed the joy I took from moving fearlessly.

'Some people move their wheelchairs like that, too,' he reassured me as I kicked off from the floor and felt the glide of the wheels on the hardwood basketball court. 'That's OK for today. Until we get your arms stronger, at least.'

To my young ears, that felt like an implied contract – that I could use my feet now, but my arms would have to be stronger in order to become one of his athletes.

*

I sit on the corner of The Movement Director's guest bed, tucked underneath the staircase in the living room of her small but beautiful home. It is a daybed during most hours, and since the staircase in her home is generally considered to be 'lethal' – her words, not mine – the guest bedroom isn't really an option. If someone wants to watch TV, it is a communal activity.

I could turn on my headphones and play a game on my Nintendo Switch, but tonight my friend and her husband decide to watch *Tick, Tick… Boom!* And so, I choose to watch the musical interpretation of Jonathan Larson's life, using music from his first production. It is directed by Lin-Manuel Miranda and has thirty-nine-year-old Andrew Garfield playing twenty-nine-year-old Jonathan Larson.

At thirty-seven, I have already gone further than Larson went in his lifetime, cut short by an aortic aneurysm the night before opening his masterpiece, *Rent*. My most recent three plays have won awards – big ones. Best new play, best online play and an Olivier nomination. I am asked to judge competitions. At one point this autumn, I am judging four contests at the same time. And I can't figure out why I am struggling to write my own work. I am two years older than Larson was when he died. I think the twenty-nine-year-old presented in *Tick, Tick... Boom!* would be jealous of me. But when I was growing up, *Rent* and Larson seemed unreachable. The dreams in the back of my head of theatre, film and the arts were generally muted, either by myself or by well-meaning community organisations who insisted they didn't have the insurance to have a disabled girl in their dance classes. No matter. I was going to be a lawyer, a non-fiction writer or, if I wanted to take life at a bit of a different pace, a teacher at some university. But, unless I wanted to 'take it slow', politics was a better option. Teaching was something I could always do when I was old.

The Barnes & Noble website had digital radio stations on which I would play showtunes from their Broadway channel. Alone in my room, I stood up to dance with made-up moves that no one else could see but me. I could keep pretty decent time on a waltz – one, two, three ... one, two, three ... and adapt motions that would safely keep me upright but made me feel like I was at the edge of a theatre stage facing an audience of 2,000 people.

Watching *Tick, Tick... Boom!* from my little nest underneath the staircase gives me a growing disdain for this depiction of Jonathan Larson. The character sneers at his customers in the diner. According to him, they should be eating brunch from home, because it would be cheaper and result in reducing their very high cholesterol.

It is from this display of contempt onwards that the movie loses me. When I was in my twenties, trying to find my voice and figure out how to survive day to day, waiting tables was never an option. The entry-level jobs that most new adults have open to them are not available to those with disabilities. The only way I could successfully serve eggs on toast is if you preferred the plate to end up on the floor. Pouring hot coffee would be a health-and-safety hazard that would set the fire brigade running. It's not just the risk assessment for someone like me that makes jobs like table service difficult – physics makes it impossible. I would love to have a job that pays a consistent minimum wage. Because, even if everything else in your life is 'taken care of' – bills, accessible housing, heating, buying groceries, healthy people around you who understand the complex mechanisms that make up your survival – the world tells you at every turn that you only have value if you actually earn money.

Did Mr Larson ever consider that maybe it is better to be an able-bodied writer working in a café than an unemployed, disabled trust-fund kid with no professional structure? Larson, the character, doesn't see this, of course. Nor do my friends who are watching from the sofa. The protagonist doesn't see how privileged he was to be in *West Side Story* in high school. In the flashbacks of him and his friends at their inclusive and welcoming camp, he doesn't notice that there isn't a single person with a disability in his memory.

I have to walk out of the room during the footage of him in a community production as a kid. I remember the Children's Pastor at church who didn't want to cast me in a speaking role in the nativity play. He didn't want people in the congregation feeling sorry for me. And now the character of Jonathan Larson is feeling sorry for himself because Sondheim had his first play on Broadway at the age of thirty-two in 1962, and Larson thinks he is running out of time to write something great. Granted, by thirty-five he'll be dead, but he doesn't know that at twenty-nine. And so, this film, for me, perpetuates the myth of the troubled artist and the lie that creativity favours the young. When I was twenty-nine, I was still trying to figure out how to eat three meals a day, and which foods could give me the calories and protein I needed. Those that were easy to chew and swallow, yet enjoyable enough that I would eat a sufficient amount to ensure that I didn't pass out by midday. I was trying to figure out how to balance that 'independent life' the voices at those chipboard tables insisted I needed in order to 'overcome my disability', with the reality that if I don't eat enough, I can't think. And if I can't think, I can't write.

I find myself so angry that I have to leave the room, walk across my friends' kitchen, shut the bathroom door and gather myself in front of the sink. I am particularly angered by the assumption that people who live in the style of Larson's '*La Vie Bohème*' are somehow superior and living more authentically.

I try to exhale to the count of ten in my friend's bathroom. I remind myself that, given my life experience, I am allowed to feel anger towards this fictional character. Indeed, it would be irrational not to feel that and, perhaps more importantly, inauthentic of me.

*

I had geared myself up to wait for my own purple-and-blue sports wheelchair for at least as long as the walker, but it arrived within eight weeks. I don't remember the wait, which is probably significant in that it wasn't that long, nor do I remember its arrival. Like so much of my equipment growing up, it was just suddenly there one day, a part of me. Yet another bulky thing to somehow minimise my disability and make my life a little bit more fulfilling.

At that point, we had our own bolsters and Swiss balls at home and during this time of my life, when so much about my physical body was changing, growing, developing, there was a continuous stream of deliveries of new equipment constantly coming into our home – and in a pre-Amazon age.

Within a year of receiving the purple wheelchair, I had learned to push sixty metres without stopping and broke an international record at a competition in Canada for my classification as a junior female disabled athlete.

There were other events that people loved to see. The audience would plan their cigarette breaks around the races with the highest-classified athletes. Another preteen was one of these athletes who always had an audience. For our first two years together, we shared a racing chair. We had to ensure that our heats were separate enough that she could undo her straps and slip back into her everyday chair, and I had time to climb in and readjust the wheels and compensators to match my needs before heading off to the start line of my own heat.

The difference was that for her, as a paraplegic, the chair reached speeds that I would never make even with a decade of practice. All four limbs being affected meant that my classification was Cerebral Palsy Class II Upper – someone who pushed their chair with their arms – versus somebody who still used their legs (CP II Lower) and can only propel their chair backwards. My time of 29 seconds for a sixty-metre race was an unheard-of record for someone like myself. But my friend was a higher-class athlete than me: she could do a 400-metre race in the time it would take me to do sixty metres. Here's something no one ever talks about: every area of life has its own hierarchy and popularity, and adaptive sports are no exception. The Paralympics is presented as this great opportunity – an equaliser that means anyone can participate. But in reality, that's not how it is. Only the 'least disabled' get to compete. For someone like me who has all four limbs affected by a neurological disability – rather than a 'simple' spinal cord injury, for example – there are no events in the Paralympics.

Like the arts, like writing, like the Olympics, adaptive athletics has a hierarchy that serves the most able first. And no amount of hard work was ever going to make me the 'most able'.

*

The Children's Pastor asked who wanted to be Mary. My hand shot up like a comet. No other hand was raised, and yet he picked a girl who hadn't volunteered. Then he asked if he could have three wise men, and again, my hand went up. Let's be honest, I never lowered it. Three boys were selected for this, and I could see the point of that casting, even if it was unimaginative. A drummer boy? I could play a drum. Or a shepherd? My hand stayed up the entire time.

As the Children's Pastor went through the script, line by line, seeing what parts were necessary and handing them out, I volunteered for every single one, even the talking cow. And yet, my name never was called.

'Everyone else will make wonderful angels,' he said, after all the parts had been given out. This included kids who had expressed no interest in being involved, but whose parents had already signed up to make the costumes, so they were cast in the Christmas play by default.

The Children's Pastor later told me during my senior year of college that he had selected me to be an angel because 'it seemed perfect'. He thought so highly of me that an angel is how he saw me. But I didn't want to be a nameless angel – I wanted to act. I wanted to have lines and solos and to sit down at the breakfast table and memorise a script in the same way I had to with Bible verses.

I wanted to have a role that was written out in the actual Dramatis Personae, not the ensemble that would go on without having individual characters. How would an angel with a purple walker blend in with the heavenly hosts, especially when she never wanted to in the first place? How could a God that made me so individual expect me to be a nameless angel that somehow couldn't make her voice known? Why couldn't I get to play a character when I was the only one with my hand outstretched, literally volunteering to be a beast of burden, as long as I had lines?

I knew I could handle it, because after being in the same classes as the other kids in my neighbourhood, I was not only managing, I was thriving. No longer sat in a beanbag chair all day left in my own faeces, I was now included in all the classes I had always been taken out of for physical therapy, such as music and art. I was not just managing to get along with kids who were supposedly so cruel 'at this age'; there was no difference between what was expected from my academic outcomes and any other student's. For the first time since my trial year in kindergarten five years before, people were asking me what I wanted to be when I grew up. And I already knew the answer. I wanted to be an actress.

No, I *knew* I was going to be an actress, the same way I knew I wasn't supposed to be in classes with kids who groaned and repeatedly hit themselves; the same way I knew the boy with the football was going to kick over the sprouting potato in a glass jar; the same way I knew that my heats in wheelchair racing would always be the ones the volunteer coaches and audiences would choose for their cigarette breaks.

Trouble was, nobody wanted to see these truths about me, even if I was very clear as to what they were. Mum would spend her time while I was at school driving from one youth theatre to another. Meeting with the CEO, she explained that I really, really wanted to learn about performing, only to be told that they couldn't see how having me in their acting programme 'would work'.

At church, I was the superstar kid. I always had a smile on my face, a good attitude, I 'radiated God's love', and I was able to memorise and recite Bible verses way faster than any of the other children, who could, let's say, play video games and go outside of their own volition.

Why wouldn't the Children's Pastor let me finally get my big break on the stage as a talking cow?

*

At the age of thirty-seven, I push the LED light in my friend's bathroom again to turn it off. But the angle at which I hit it is bad, so it pops out of its plastic sheath and clatters onto the floor.

'Just leave it!' she shouts at me from where the movie is still rolling.

This is an act we've done a lot over the past month while I've been staying at her house.

The plastic clatters as I try to hook the light back in its place, held up by grip strips on the tiled wall. I don't want to 'just leave it'.

I want to put the light back for my host, the way any self-aware, able-bodied adult would. I want not to be having these feelings of very real resentment towards a talented, if unknowingly privileged, artist whose heart unfairly exploded two years younger than I am now. I want to look at pictures of nativity plays and sports days with happiness, not a sense of poetic justice.

After dropping the LED light several times in a failed attempt to put it back, I take another breath and remind myself that I don't have to keep watching the movie unless I want to. I have been systematically trained to smile at all times, to make other people happy, and share a version of myself that everyone else approves of.

My friend, I have to remind myself, isn't like that. I have found a small circle of people in my life who can imagine and see me with loving complexity. And she is one of them.

In the end, what gets me back into the little cubby where I have been watching Andrew Garfield complain about approaching thirty, is not that I am trying to be polite, nor that I'm trying to present a curated image of myself that will mitigate my complexity and put everyone else at ease. I go back because I want to.

Just like I went back to the local library with my dad, drifting into the 'Musicals and Drama' section every time I was overlooked for a performance at school or at church. My mother went back to community theatres and educational outreach programmes, asking why they claimed they could teach 'any child with imagination' but not teach me. When I realised there was no future for me at the Paralympics, I went back to my room and lay on my bed with my auto-reverse Walkman on loop, and listened until the battery died.

I listened to Donny Osmond in *Joseph and the Amazing Technicolor Dreamcoat*. I listened to Mandy Patinkin sing about Yorkshire in *The Secret Garden*. I listened to Madonna sing in *Evita*. In my bright-blue bedroom, under the rainbow duvet my mother had made by hand, again and again I turned on the Broadway internet radio station, determined to learn about an industry that seemed equally determined to shut me out. I made up dances and learned lyrics with as much devotion as I memorised Bible verses. I hoped that if I learned about what no one would let me take part in, then through my own initiative I would get the obsession out of my system.

One day, Jonathan Larson's *Rent* came through my headphones, and on my unstable, uncallused and underused feet, I choreographed my own version of his '*La Vie Bohème*'. I cast myself as Mimi, a young drug-addicted woman, desperate to be understood, though in my version she also had cerebral palsy. Surely Jonathan Larson wouldn't mind if I embellished his characters a little?

I have every right to be frustrated that Larson's privilege, arrogance, ignorance and self-righteous pity are commended in a Netflix film. But I also know that the little girl who only had the opportunity to dance in her bedroom and never got to play the back end of a cow would have done anything to see this film, be in this industry, be with these people, be here, now.

I watch the rest of the film for her.

Chapter 8

The first few years after I was back in mainstream education, life was uneventful. Fifth grade brought on what I thought was too much homework. I formally petitioned the teacher to give us less and had every student in my class sign it. I saw her read the petition and put it in her desk. She never brought it up.

I played basketball, tennis, track, field, and every other sport you can imagine at the local navy base on the weekends. I continued to break records, which my teachers at school knew nothing about. I eventually stopped competing. Every race either had no one in my classification, or winning against them wasn't rewarding.

My new school district was over 60 per cent Jewish. Most kids were second-generation American, if that. One girl left Russia with her family after Chernobyl and spent the first four years not saying a word. She was brilliant at maths, so they kept her in classes, counting on the day that she would pick up English.

In my school, kids weren't bullies, because bullies were the reason that Aunt Golda didn't make it out of Europe alive. You spoke up when you saw something wrong, because if you didn't, you could be complicit in political evil, sending millions away in cattle cars. You held yourself to the highest standards because you were capable of achieving greatness; you needed to work all the time, because life was a blessing. Man and woman were made equal in the sight of God. The same God whose name was never written down on a piece of paper. The same God who knitted you together in your mother's womb and created you to be fearfully and wonderfully made.

There was an underlying expectation from the moment anyone entered my home district that we were going to be the next leaders of the world. Most families held the shadow of sorrow in their grandparents' eyes at Thanksgiving. So, we'd better listen up and fly straight now. There wasn't time to waste. Victory and justice were inevitable, as long as we kept working.

Stevenson High School was one of the best schools in the nation and considered the best in the state of Illinois – unless, of course, you went to its rival, New Trier. Each year 1,200 students would enter the school as fourteen-year-old freshmen. They would come from three district schools, equal in size. The school boasted four theatres, two swimming pools, multiple orchestras, dance studios and, of course, every sports field you can imagine. It was essentially like going to a fully-fledged university at the age of fourteen, and Stevenson loved its reputation for excellence.

Up until this point, I had been placed in the classroom with a one-on-one aide to help me take notes, fill out worksheets, write my name on papers, and basically, as the IEP document put it, 'act as her hands due to her fine motor difficulties'. Having one assistant for everything worked pretty well. She would go off for lunch and another assistant would step in to feed me. She sat in the back of the classroom and read fantasy novels as lectures were taking place. I never quite realised how extremely cool this woman was until now, at the age of forty, when I too prefer to sit at the back of rooms and do very much the same.

At school, I had a desktop computer, a full printer and a scanner put onto a wheelie desk. In between classes, everything would be unplugged and moved from classroom to classroom. This is why I have an extraordinarily high tolerance for embarrassment. After having a middle-aged, well-meaning, smart woman follow you around in junior-high hallways pushing a giant table of electrical equipment behind you, nothing can compare in rank humiliation.

She had offered to come with me to high school, and my family and I assumed that this would be the case. One less transition to make when jumping from pond to ocean. But when I arrived on my first day of high school, I was met by a new woman, Stevenson's Woman. In second-period maths class, our teacher had written some very basic algebraic equations on the board to test how much we remembered after the summer. I leaned in to my assistant for her to start noting down my work as I whispered, 'Right, so, we need to use $y = mx+b$. Y is a slope that has been decided as one over four. It crosses the x-axis at two.'

I looked down to see what she was writing.

'No, no. You need to use numbers. Like maths. You know, like the number ½.'

She wrote, 'One o-v-e-r two.'

'No, like a fraction!'

It was in my third-year Spanish class that I found out that she had never taken a foreign language, and by advanced accelerated English, I learned that her education had ended in the 1960s.

'But I'm looking forward to learning Spanish,' she told me at the end of the first day. We were already learning present perfect verb forms that needed two years' worth of knowledge just to communicate. Our teacher said that all answers must be in Spanish, and no answer could ever be, 'Yo no sè.'[2]

'Say, '*Mis zapatos son azules*,' or, '*Yo quiero flan*,' or, '*Señor, me encantan los dinos*,' but never, ever – and this is the last time I will speak to you in English – say, '*No sè*,' in my class.'

I was the one who had said, '*Yo no sè*.' I was too busy thinking about how I was supposed to navigate this classroom with someone who hadn't taken the first two years of the language that we were obligated to speak during that class period each day. I told her I didn't need her at lunch, and hid in the bathroom during the thirty minutes we were supposed to be eating, trying to wrap my head around what was going on.

The second half of our lunch as freshmen was spent with our guidance counsellor. This would be a daily occurrence, as, apparently, we were not to be trusted with a full lunch break until our second year at Stevenson.

'You need to start working towards college admissions now. I know that seems very far away, but the grades you get now, when you're fourteen, matter. They look at the full transcript; this is not like your parents' generation. Colleges are competitive, so don't waste any time goofing off and getting bad grades. You have to graduate at the top of the class to go to a good school.'

That afternoon, when my mum picked me up, I explained the situation.

'She uses words in maths problems!' My mother was keeping

---

2   'I don't know' for those who *no habla español*.

her eye on Butterfield Road with her hands at ten and two, shaking her head. That night, she called the Special Education advisor at Stevenson, to ask why my former aide wasn't with me this year. She was told she didn't qualify for an interview.

'Well, you know, Spanish and advanced accelerated algebra are not required to graduate from high school, so technically we're not required to provide your daughter with any assistance in these classes. To me, it's a matter of good, better, best, Mrs Stevens, and what we are providing for your daughter is good. If she wants to excel beyond that, that's wonderful, but we are not required, by law, to give her any additional help beyond the basic curriculum.' Professor Umbridge was based on a real person. She worked at Stevenson High School's Special Education department during the 1990s.

*

It was clear that Stevenson's Woman wasn't going anywhere, unfortunately. Three weeks into high school, she got the giggles and gingerly passed a worksheet of the human reproductive anatomy to the next person. 'Can you spell that?' she asked when I said the word 'ovary'. Looking back, and for a multitude of reasons, I wish we were taught where the clitoris was.

As the semester progressed, my confidence in this woman deteriorated faster than I could lower my standards.

'We can put you in lower-level classes if you're struggling,' the Special Education head said to me.

Exasperated, I arrived at 7 a.m. one morning to talk to my maths teacher. I asked him to put me next to some girls that I'd noticed were smart. He said he wouldn't rearrange his classroom for me, and why was I coming in at seven in the morning to talk about what clique I wanted to be in?

'It's not about making friends or wanting to be popular. It's that, well . . . How do I say this without being mean? The woman hired to help me isn't at the level of maths that we are working at.' I directed him to the notebook in the backpack on the back of my wheelchair labelled 'Advanced Accelerated Algebra 2'. He opened the black-and-white composition notebook.

By second-period maths class, I was sitting in a new cluster of students.

'I can help you,' the brown-haired girl with the purple twinset cardigan said. She looked like Belle from *Beauty and the Beast*.

We were two months into high school, and a temporary respite was given by our second-period maths teacher. We had to solve linear equations, plotting points onto gridded paper that inevitably made the shape of a jack-o'-lantern. It was easier than the work we usually got, but we had to check all our plot points before we could take out our coloured pencils.

Belle was beautiful, and from one of the other feeder schools that went into Stevenson High. She had been added to my cluster table. Stevenson's Woman tried to jump up when it was obvious that another student was marking on my paper, but I made eye contact with her and shook my head.

My mum and I talked during our car conversations, both staring at the road, about how unfair this situation was to Stevenson's Woman. I dwelt on that and tried to ignore the fact that the situation was most unfair to me.

The teachers handed down grades like judgements from the gods on Mount Olympus. So far, I had done a decent job of keeping them happy. Their ability to understand my situation, and my ability to navigate the situation so I didn't appear to be slagging off an adult, was key to my success. But I was very quickly drowning in eight hours of homework a night, not eating lunch, and wanting to get perfect scores for fear of being sent back to 'good', or, even worse, lowered into a classroom where Stevenson's Woman would have been comfortable.

'I don't think the stem should be green. I think it should be mostly purple,' I told Belle. And she smiled.

'Brilliant idea. Let's do mostly purple, with a few green streaks in the stem. That's how they look in real life. I love the colour purple, don't you?'

Belle and I were in maths and science together. They were two out of my five classes, but the two that required equations rather than words. The other three I could type my notes at six words a minute.

'My mum uses this stuff that's really old-fashioned. Maybe you've seen it; it's like this sheet of paper that you put in between pages, and if you push down hard enough when you're writing, you make a copy of what you're writing on the next page. I bet we could do that, and you could have a copy of my notes for class.'

*

One of my employees has gone rogue. Usually I have four, but we are in production, so there will be twelve pay cheques that need to be cut at the end of the week. I am unsteady about my new play going up. I know it's not at its best, but the depression I have felt for the past three years has been weighing on me to the point where I need to do something, even if it's not my best work.

Right now, it's my backstage PA who is the problem. The woman is helping me through six different costume changes in a two-person show. She is adding at least five minutes to a play that is overwritten by the playwright and slowed down by one of the actors having cerebral palsy and inconsistent speech patterns.[3] The last time I ran backstage during the dress run, I found her asleep on a theatre seat.

'What can we do to make these costume changes quicker? Have you thought about maybe having the costumes preset backstage?'

Me and the backstage PA are driving home, and I am trying to delicately balance the reality that she is slowing the show down, while still giving space for her to feel comforted, useful and liked.

'Really? Do you think it's a problem? I don't think it is. No one's actually going to take this play seriously because they can't understand you.'

I try to compute if she has actually said what I think she's said, or if I have misheard. Either way, it's not a particularly good sign for our working relationship.

'Well, the last play I did was really well received in the press. No one ever mentioned my speech.' I feel like I'm trying to make small talk, while holding back the desire to rip her face off. Actually, that's not true. I know I have almost every right to rip her face off, but I don't want to. I'm scared. The only way I know how to deal with incompetence is to carry the debilitating person on my back, while I move forward.

'Do you think you have it within you to go even a little bit faster? Is there anything I can do to help?' In the back of my head, there's

---

3   (It's me. Hi. I'm the problem. It's me!)

a voice telling me that I'm not doing this right. I need to make myself clearer. If she's in the wrong, I owe it to her to explain why, to give her the opportunity to change. But I am also aware that most people would kick her out of the car at the next stoplight.

It is the last dress performance before press night. Two minutes are added to the run time. Usually run times go down or stay pretty much the same during previews, unless drastic changes are made.

The backstage PA took two minutes to find my shoe. I only wear two pairs of shoes throughout the entire production, so the heels that I wear in the final scene could have been on set at some point during the previous 110 minutes.

The next morning, I call the stage manager, who tells me, 'It's press night! You will make this worse if you get rid of her now! Just wait, and we'll figure out a solution after this evening.'

But what about the reality after press night, when the entire London theatre industry will have written reviews?

After confirming with The Lithuanian that she is able to help me for the remainder of the run, I grab my phone and send an overly saccharine text to the backstage PA. I tell her I don't think it's working out, I take the blame for my lack of leadership, I say it's too much of a cultural difference, I say I found someone else to help, so don't worry about me.

'Just so you know, I don't like the decision you've made.' The stage manager is blunt, and I appreciate her honesty.

Most people are able to say, 'This is my choice and if you don't like it, that's just too bad.' I'm not. If people don't like my choice, they leave and I'm stuck. If I don't appear grateful enough, I know able-bodied people who will take away technology, computers, wheelchairs, food and drink in order to reassert their dominance over me, to make me learn to behave. I know this logically – but I also know it first-hand.

During the press run, we shave eight minutes off the running time, coming in just under 105 minutes. The Stage Manager shakes her head in disbelief and congratulations. 'How did you know?!'

And as much as I want to tell her that it was bleeding obvious who the problem was, I have to play it down.

'Lucky gamble, I suppose.'

*

Assistive technology was making strides in the late Nineties, and I was told during a private assessment that voice activation might help save time on my homework. I was suffering under the weight of the hours that it took me to do written work. My father became my hands for maths and science at home, filling out worksheets after he returned from his banking job, taking dictation from me while he had dinner simmering on the stove.

When she could, and when I allowed it, my mother sat in front of the family computer and typed as I dictated book reports, history papers, written responses, journals and, as the teachers liked to call them, 'check-ins' to reinforce what we had learned from that day's class. I went to bed later than either of them. Rare was the night that I didn't see midnight or 1 a.m., before waking up at five to complete my physiotherapy before school. I was always sleep-deprived; I was always wondering what it would be like to have fun again.

I was always hearing the words spoken to me years before by that teacher who I thought liked me: 'We decided it would be best for you to go back to a special school next year, rather than stay with the class you are in.'

'We don't use Windows machines in this school, so Dragon Dictate is out of the question,' the head of Special Education announced at my end-of-year IEP. 'I've been telling you she can just submit her essays on tapes, and if she feels like she has too much homework, she can go down a level in all of her classes except history.'

Everyone took the same level of world history when they came into Stevenson. Mr Odysseus was known as the most difficult world history teacher in the school. He was my favourite teacher and was pushing me to take my first university-level class next year: advanced placement European history. I couldn't go down a level in world history, nor did I want to go down a level to regular placement maths or English or science.

I wanted to move up a level in Spanish next year so that I could be with Belle. She and I had made it through to the end of the year with her taking notes for me, and grabbing my hand, pulling me in my manual chair to navigate the hallways, especially during the unreasonably short five-minute passing periods between classes. She and I had a system that allowed her to twist and turn my chair, weaving me in and out of high-school students who had little awareness of their own bodies.

In between the classes where Belle was not with me, I pushed myself slowly in my chair. Calluses built up on my hands and small cuts appeared on the knuckles of my thumb. A hangnail would send me to the nurse at least once a week, because if it was not cut immediately, it would snag and ultimately bleed.

But by the time eight hours of school were done, my day was only half over.

'You can't possibly think that writing an essay is the same as talking into a tape recorder. How is my daughter supposed to edit her work?'

'Hit rewind and tape over it, of course.'

'The technology is available for her to see what she is writing as she writes it!'

'I'm sorry, Mrs Stevens. The technology is only available on Windows computers, and we don't use Windows in this school. We are a 100-per-cent Apple-education school.'

As an appeasement, or maybe just out of a shrewd underhanded play, the Special Education faculty agreed that I could try voice-activation software on an Apple computer. The system for Apple was not nearly as good as it was on a Windows machine. On Apple, you had to say each word individually, so I would probably only get about twenty words a minute with my talking speed. Supposedly, Dragon Dictate on Windows would allow you to speak full phrases and sentences, thus enabling me to type up to sixty words a minute. But twenty on the Apple computer was better than six on my own, and thus my laptop was sent to the computer lab and the software was uploaded.

I was not given time to train on the software, and my workload at home was so laborious that it was impossible to put in the extra hours, endlessly repeating, 'Alpha, Bravo, Charlie, Delta.' The military alphabet was key to navigating the system software. When all else failed, maybe I would be able to spell the word faster than typing.

My eighth period, the final hour of school, was spent in a study hall. A free period where I was supposed to sit in a room and complete my homework with forty other students. It was, of course, impossible to use voice activation in the presence of forty other students. Frankly, it probably would have been possible; it would also have been yet another layer of embarrassment and shame that I would need to take on board at the age of fourteen.

There was an airlock between the side door of the school leading to Parking Lot C and the door to get into the hallway that held my locker. I had Stevenson's Woman move a desk and set up my laptop in this tiny six-foot-by-six-foot 'fishbowl', as I called it, so I could use the voice-activation software in private. The parking lot was for faculty use only, with the exception of my mother, who came to pick me up right outside this door after eighth period.

For weeks, faculty and students peered through the glass windows of the fishbowl as they walked past, watching me correct words. It seemed like every word that was spoken, I had to correct. And then I had to correct the command to correct, because the computer didn't understand that either.

Several English teachers stopped by and knocked on the window and waved. My own seventh-period teacher often popped her head in, incredibly friendly and encouraging. 'You've got the software. You can do this!' But I could tell every day that something wasn't right, and I started to fantasise about the Windows system being better.

Another teacher, whose class I wasn't in, would often stop by.

'Sounds like that computer is really frustrating you.'

'Yeah, it is. I get one sentence right, and then it completely messes up the next one. But I'm trying my best. I know I can get this to work if I try hard enough.'

'How long are you going to put up with that program?'

'Well, I'm taking Government this summer. It's only one class over eight weeks, so I can really get to work on it then.'

'I've got to run out the door today fast, but it's really great seeing you …'

'And you, Mr Varian!'

'Are you sure you're getting enough to eat?'

'Yeah, I don't want to depend on other people. But SlimFast shakes are food.'

He would nod, smile, take it in and not argue before putting his weight behind the clanky push mechanism that opened our school's security doors. Once he was through, Varian would inevitably fling his cloth briefcase over his shoulder and walk out to his car.

I knew Mr Varian was gay from the convertible Mazda Miata that he drove, looking so out of place inside a teacher's parking lot. The Miata itself wasn't the indicator, nor was the fact that it belonged to this young teacher. The indicator was the rainbow America sticker on the back bumper. This was 1999. Matthew Shepard was murdered the autumn before, and rainbow flags and stickers were popping up occasionally among members of Stevenson faculty.

Little did I know that people in my family had prayed for years for me never to encounter a gay teacher in school.

Mr Varian always spoke to me. At the end of freshman year, I requested that I be put into Varian's English class, as well as every possible class I could take with Belle. I felt like a 'bad girl' asking for either.

*

'Tell me honestly, have I just got stupid?' I look to The Movement Director, who I am proving to be overly reliant on during this production for some unknown reason. We're in tech, and I can't seem to remember how to direct an actor, or a technician in the box, while keeping some sort of thematic consistency throughout the entire production.

'No, you're not stupid. You're just trying to do the impossible. Nobody rehearses a show and techs it at the same time.'

That is what I have been asked to do. Most shows are short on time. Then there's this project, the performer of which is also the producer and the writer, and has never been onstage before, but has received Arts Council funding. They are an accomplished poet. They have in them the ability to hold an audience and dramatise their struggle, which needs to be told. They are brilliant. They also have no idea of what goes into a theatre performance.

I knew this when I agreed to go from the R&D phase to a scratch night up in Manchester. One look at the schedule, and it is clear that nobody with a theatre background was involved in the planning. There's a gap of three weeks between when we tech in London and when we take the show to Manchester. We are to tech on a different stage than we are to perform, and with only half the cast. We have three days to load in the show, no days to rehearse it, and after spending a day travelling up to Manchester, we get thrown straight into dress.

I am doing the impossible.

Still, my reflex is to say I can make this work.

I huddle with The Movement Director backstage as we try to take on some sort of risk assessment of what can be done to fix tonight's performance. Our main performer's wheelchair has decided not to go above 0.2 miles an hour.

'Even if it were possible to re-block the entire show this late in the day, we would have to rehang all of the lights as well, and that's not feasible.' After I say this, the lighting designer pokes her head out from behind the production manager, nods, and gives me a thumbs up. She didn't want to have to point out the obvious, so I did it for her.

'So, what are we going to do if the chair doesn't get fixed?'

'If the chair doesn't get fixed, we don't have a show. The best we can do is play a video of the production we have on Google Drive. It's still out there, right?' The production manager affirms that it is, but I take out my iPhone and get on Google Drive just to be sure.

I can make it work.

I realise for the first time in my adult life just how big of an impact Stevenson's Woman had on my thinking.

I turn to The Movement Director backstage.

'You know, I hate the line, "It'll all work out in the end."'

'I know. You have good reason to, Athena.'

'I do know this performance will be brilliant.'

'I'm also not going to say, "It will work out because it has to,"' she says to me.

'No, it doesn't have to. One of these days, a performance is going to fall flat on its face because the expectations are too high, and we haven't been given the right tools to meet those expectations.' Am I saying this about the performance, or the unfairness of inequality as a whole? It doesn't particularly matter at this point.

A text comes through confirming that the performer's wheelchair is fixed and everything 'can now continue on as planned'.

Chapter 9

'We hold these truths to be self-evident, that all men are created equal, that they are endowed by their Creator with certain unalienable Rights, that among these are Life, Liberty and the pursuit of Happiness.' Thomas Jefferson's promise was scrawled across the whiteboard in Mr Odysseus's distinct, all-capital letters.

'What does this mean?' He tapped the cap of the marker on the dry erase board, drowning out the tapping of the August rain outside momentarily. In particular, he had circled the word 'men'; all *men* are created equal.

'I want to come back to this word in a moment, but first, what is "Life, Liberty and the pursuit of Happiness"?'

Mr Odysseus was a master at getting to the nerve of such questions straight away. 'Life, Liberty and the pursuit of Happiness'. If we, as American students, driven back into the classroom by both the calendar and the summer rain outside, were going to excel in life, we had to know that the Declaration of Independence was written for us and how the gears of American history fitted together.

'Men. Let's talk about men. During this time, the colonists decided that only white men over the age of twenty-one who owned land would be allowed to vote. What kind of American Dream allows for only 6 per cent of the population to vote?'

It kicked off another round of ideas from a room full of sixteen-year-olds. The world opened wider every day we were in high school, allowing us more potential, more opportunities and more confidence to pursue what we desired.

Teachers and parents reminded us daily that we were privileged to go to school at Stevenson. Forget all the snobby rich kids at New Trier or across the sea at, say, Eton. We were the ones who worked hard, and the world was at our feet.

I was comfortable in Mr Odysseus's class. Because he'd taught me world history the year before, I knew I didn't have to strain my mouth any more to be understood.

For two years in a row, I had again failed to get a role for any of the autumn productions that the theatre teachers oversaw. That summer, I found out the musical was *Hello, Dolly!* and despite practising the same sixteen bars for an audition again and again, my name did not appear on the cast list, or understudy list, or any list at all. I thought maybe I had a chance when I was allowed to complete the full sixteen bars during the audition.

I knew I didn't sing my best. I never sang my best when other people were watching, but I did the best I could. During this time of my life, I would routinely lose my voice every two weeks. I was working so hard to be clear and climb the ranks of 'good, better, best' that it was inevitable my body would demand I stay quiet every once in a while.

Walking through the glass double doors of Stevenson's new atrium for a new academic year meant going back to late nights looking at homework, eight hours at a time, and lunches that often ended up in the bin because I was sick of SlimFast and either didn't want to or didn't know how to ask anyone to help me to eat. It was disordered eating, where it was easier to say, 'I'm not hungry,' than to invite the awkwardness of needing to be fed.

I was better off sitting and listening to a teacher and logging notes in my head, rather than writing them down at six words a minute on my school-bequeathed laptop. If a teacher saw me typing, they would smile and nod at the inclusivity of it all, not knowing that I was actually secretly writing poetry in Microsoft Word. Outside of Belle, it seemed like the animated Microsoft Word paperclip was my best friend in high school.

Back in Mr Odysseus's classroom, he re-circled the word 'men' to punctuate his question. 'Who are the men in this sentence? Why didn't they say "white men over the age of twenty-one who owned land"? I mean, I know it wouldn't make for a particularly concise sentence, but they could have done it. They were creating a country, after all.'

After a back and forth between students as to 'what extent' Thomas Jefferson, a slave owner, could ever see his slaves as 'men', I tentatively raised my hand. The teacher scratched his goatee, then pointed to me without saying my name, as he always did.

'Maybe that's what American history is about: defining what "men" are and redefining it when we need to do so.'

'Explain.'

'So, it started with white men who owned land, right? And then it turned into white men, and then it turned into Black men and white men after the Civil War. And then, like in the 1920s or something, it became all men and all women. Maybe the story of America is the story of us opening up the definition of "men" to become more inclusive so that all people, all humans, are created equal.'

The teacher nodded, considering my point, and then put his hands down by either side of him, taking a step back to the whiteboard. 'Good,' he says. 'I like that. Well done.'

It was going to be a good year.

*

The night encroached on the room from about 2.30 p.m. The room itself was so small, it was honestly about 90 per cent bed. In addition to being further north than London, Edale Valley, where I sometimes come to write, is surrounded by mountains, causing the sun to go dark before it sets over the true horizon. It is now 4.30, and I lie in the pitch black playing a YouTube video to keep the sound of my tears from my assistant in the next room. If they were to ask what was wrong, I would blame it on Trump being elected president the week before.

It is an easy excuse, but not the truth.

Two months ago, British Airways destroyed my $35,000 wheelchair, leaving me with next to no mobility. But even this isn't easy to explain, nor all that is making me ache. I am in Edale to write. But I'm not writing. I want to die. I shouldn't want to, but here I am. Privileged, yet wanting to end it all.

Recently, people I love keep following a pattern: they love me, and then I disagree with them, and I am trash. It's a lather, rinse and repeat loop that I can't seem to get out of, or even find the words to explain properly. The idea of more intimacy, sharing with someone everything that is going on in my head – that is too much. But there isn't really a good way to end myself in a tiny cabin in the middle of nowhere with my 'carer' in the next room.

I have promised myself that tonight I will take the half-hour train journey to Manchester, despite only having a rental wheelchair that feels very unsafe to drive. It is the first ever Women's Equality Party Conference, a political party set up by Sandi Toksvig, Catherine Mayer, and Sophie Walker in the name of, well, what it says on the tin, basically: women's equality. The emails have promised an open-mic night the first evening of the conference, where anyone can address the party and say whatever they want.

There is nothing in my body at this moment in time that makes me want to move out of my bed and into the cold.

I sent in an application the week before to be the party's Spokesperson on Equality in the Media. There was a niggle in the back of my head that said if people see me talk, maybe they will elect me to that position. It is a long shot, but the only thing that seems worth trying.

'Are we going?' I say in a wobbly voice to the person in the next room after turning off the YouTube video.

'Are we?'

I lie there. The least I can do is this. And if it doesn't work, I don't have to do anything else ever again. Truly ever again.

'Yeah, let's go.'

*

Public speaking is often referred to as the thing people fear more than death. As Jerry Seinfeld used to joke in the Nineties, that means that most of us would rather be the person in the coffin than the one giving the eulogy. Actors are no different, but they do it anyway, and the reasoning they give is that they can be someone else onstage. But being themselves and expressing their ideas? No way.

I don't really understand the differentiation, but then again, public speaking was my high-school extracurricular activity of choice.

The root of the word 'forensics' is the Latin word *forensis*, which translates as 'public forum' and means 'to explain'. The forensics department in the police seeks to examine a body or a crime scene in order to explain what happened. Forensic speaking comprises speeches to explain, but for the Forensics team in high school, other events included verse reading, original comedy and duet acting. Leave it to the Americans to take an activity that is supposed to be fun and subjective, like stand-up comedy or poetry readings, and turn it into a competition to be judged objectively, and leave it to Stevenson High School to make it a varsity sport, rather than just an extracurricular activity.

From dramatic acting to improvisational comedy, radio broadcasting to extemporaneous speaking, there were twelve events you could compete in for our Forensics team, ultimately leading to the state championships. An individual was allowed to compete in two events per weekly competition.

The notion of not needing to audition in order to have a chance to put in some hours of experience for the dramatic arts and communication seemed too good to be true.

The actors who were lucky enough to be cast in the school's production of *The Man Who Came to Dinner* swore up and down that they didn't like the competitive aspect of the Forensics team. But what, exactly, did they think auditions were if not a competition?

*

'Sandi is going to say something and then there'll be the first speaker, but you're on second,' a member of the party tells me. 'Just go up the ramp and we'll bring you on when it's time.'

As I lean forward to go up the steep incline, I wish I was in my own chair. This one moves by shifting my weight, there is no joystick, and while it is marketed as keeping the user more active in their core muscles, it just makes me feel unstable. I dub it 'the suicide chair', which is apt, all things considered.

Maybe I should've stayed home. Try, just try, I remind myself. It beats the alternative – at least for the moment.

Sandi Toksvig talks about how no other political party would let any and every one of their members speak on the opening night of the conference, or any time for that matter. The Women's Equality Party is going to be different. We are going to build it from the ground up. We are going to take small steps, the way women always have done, to achieve great things together. She sets a green Lego base on the table in the centre of the stage, takes one small Lego brick from a box, and places it on the bumpy green plastic.

'I want each speaker to add a Lego brick when they're done speaking. I don't know what we're going to build, but we're going to build it together, and this will be a representation of our party, built together.'

I don't remember the first speaker, which should cast a light on just how self-centred my political ambitions can be, but now she is gone, and the party's policy secretary looks at me from across the stage. With a bit of apprehension, I lean forward, willing and initiating movement in my 'suicide chair'.

The first thing I notice is that the lights aren't nearly as bright as they can be – a good sign. Either my eyes have biologically adjusted to shrinking their irises quickly, or the event's lighting designer knows what they are doing. As much as I want to hope it is both, I don't feel like it is. In my mind, it is the latter, it having been four years since I was last onstage.

'Lego's not really my thing when I have cerebral palsy.' I look at Sandi.

In America, such a line would be taken as defiance. But I know enough from past shattered relationships here in the UK that I need to say the line in a small way that could only be interpreted as self-deprecation. The British way.

I walk out of the Friday-night opening event of the first Women's Equality Party conference pretty quickly after my speech. On the way out, three people stop me to ask my name. I tell them.

'Athena Stevens, I want to vote for you for the policy committee when we cast our ballots tomorrow.'

It is nice to be wanted, even if by a few people, but the odds of me winning over a group this size are slim. I never do well in large groups, which is part of what made Stevenson so hard. My introverted personality and slow voice often get lost around people who are able to speak louder than me.

Maybe I would get a few votes in the election, but I never seem to win the top prize.

Without being able to plan my life much further ahead than the end of the conference, I don't think about it too much. I will decide what needs to be done after the weekend. I have done my bit and spoken. I miss speaking in public.

When Sunday morning rolls around, I come in late. A full day of conference activities on the Saturday in a cold warehouse meant that I missed the train I wanted to catch and laid in bed a bit later than I should have. The combination causes me to walk into the main conference room at 11 a.m. while motions are still being voted on publicly. The ballots for the Policy and Steering Committee have already been cast, counted and announced.

I wait at the back of the dark room in a corner, not feeling anything like myself.

'Congratulations,' the policy secretary whispers in my ear.

'What?' I say.

'You missed it because you came in late, but they announced the first Media Spokesperson for the Policy Committee. And it's you.'

*

The sound of teenagers yelling and clapping was stimulation overload when I stopped my comedy routine and headed back to Mr Varian, who sat in the front row of the auditorium. It was the first standing ovation I had ever received, and the energy of 400 students in a Peoria high school watching the original comedy finals nearly blew me back to the walls of the stage. When I turned around to face the performance area again, there was still clapping.

Mr Varian put both hands on my shoulders and shouted in my ear, 'I have never seen a Friday-night audience respond this way. People don't clap for Stevenson Forensics. What's wrong with you?!' I looked at him and saw him smile. This was better than any state championship I could receive.

I had transferred from oratorical declamation to verse, deciding that year on original comedy. Integrating material about parking spaces and wobbly handwriting, autographs that were twenty pages long, and being low enough to look up and assess people's nose hairs while remaining seated: these were jokes I was making at the age of fifteen.

I was outdone by a boy whose comedy routine included a full rendition of 'Happy Birthday, Mr President' as a pitch-perfect Marilyn Monroe impersonator. He didn't even need a wig.

The Monday after the state championships, Belle and I made our way through the halls, and I couldn't wipe the grin from my face.

'Not that any of us are surprised. Impressed – proud – is a better word, but not surprised,' Mr Odysseus said when he congratulated me as I walked into the classroom. As I took off my wheelchair gloves and Stevenson's Woman put my Apple laptop in front of me, he knelt down at my desk, putting his chin in his hands.

'Don't worry about second place,' he said. 'This is only the beginning. Longevity is key, and we'll all be hearing about you for a very long time.'

My homework load as the years passed didn't grow. In fact, one could argue that it hit pinnacle level in my freshman year and never dropped. The difficulty was that I had begun to outstrip my parents' university-level education at the age of fifteen. This made maths and science impossible to work on at home.

Mum and Dad had to hire a tutor. Every second or third day, I would stay after school to get my maths and science homework done with the help of teachers taking on the homework their colleagues assigned.

Halfway through high school, I still had that Apple computer. Its voice-activation system still did not work – it could barely pick up one word at a time. Even if I had perfectly clear speech, the reality of saying every word in isolation was not as fast as my peers could type.

We hired a lawyer to come to my twice-yearly IEP hearings,

much as we did years ago, but the lawyer sent a paralegal instead. One day when my mother was out doing errands, she found the paralegal and the school's lawyer laughing over drinks and lunch.

She promptly called the lawyer and told them not to send the paralegal to the next meeting. If he didn't show up himself, he could forget about getting paid.

'I can't believe the head of Special Education just won't do the obvious,' Belle said as she stabbed into the hardboiled egg of her Caesar salad. It was the only choice of protein in the cafeteria and the dressing was legendary.

I once tasted the dressing on the tip of Belle's fork. After that, I stopped bringing SlimFast shakes and started bringing lunch money. The days that I could manage it, I would turn a fork upside down in my hand, use it to stab a boiled egg and dip it in the salad dressing before taking it to my mouth. It was delicious. Sadly, the leaves, by and large, were a lost cause for my flighty fine motor skills. On the days I couldn't manage it, I gave my lunch money to whatever charity the students had set up a table for in the cafeteria. On those days, I would get in the car after school and beg my mother to take me to McDonald's for a snack before dinner.

'It's like they're waiting for you to just graduate so they can argue that they ran out of time to get you the equipment you need. What more do you have to do to prove your need to them?' Belle continued.

I thought of my grades. I thought my A-/B+ average was mediocre at best. The fact that I still hadn't persuaded the administrators to give me an upgraded Stevenson Woman, or upgraded equipment, was proof that I wasn't good enough.

'I wish I could just die,' Belle said abruptly. 'Wouldn't it be great to just fall asleep and not wake up and not have to deal with this at all?'

'I would appreciate not having to deal with the ineptitude that is the Special Education department,' I shot back. 'A very long nap would make that happen.'

We were teenagers, and where most teenagers would sulk and act surly, our way of mitigating everything we were navigating was to talk jokingly about the desire to cease to exist. Life already felt overwhelming. If this was high school, the time that our parents swore up and down was 'the best time of your life', what the heck was the rest of life going to look like?

The same day that I had returned triumphant from my placement in the state forensics championship, someone from the school administration team delivered me a pink slip after lunch.

Pink slips were notes direct from the administration. They could be as threatening as 'you've missed too many classes and now have detention', or as minor as 'your mother has locked herself out of the house and you need to drop off the keys at the principal's office for her to pick them up'. They were a way for the administration to communicate with us without having to disrupt our education. You could still go to class upon the receipt of a pink slip – you just might not want to.

I had a sinking feeling of dread as my hands shook to open it. I must have done something wrong while in a fugue-like state (something we'd just learned about in psychology class) and now had detention. Instead, the pink slip was a printed letter telling me when my spring IEP meeting would take place: one month from now, during the school day.

'You're kidding me!' Belle exclaimed over my shoulder as she looked at the pink slip. There were no secrets between someone you depended on for your notes and yourself. What affected me affected her, and so she didn't hesitate to read what was printed. But Belle had noticed something before I did.

'That's during our English class. Mr Varian won't be able to go to your IEP meeting.'

I was so busy imagining what horrible thing I must've done while in an altered state of consciousness that I didn't bother to look at the time printed on the meeting notification. It was right as fourth period started. The teacher I knew would advocate for me the strongest was intentionally excluded from my IEP meeting. All my teachers for that year were invited, but Mr Varian, my most outspoken ally, was intentionally double booked.

Mr Varian had tenure – something several of my teachers, including Mr Odysseus, did not have – meaning that the school couldn't fire him. Because he had a permanent job until he retired, he was in the most strategic position to say the unpleasant things that needed to be said. He was my best in-school fighter, and he was excluded from coming to my defence due to my own class.

The school newspaper had wanted me to finish lunch slightly early so that they could take my photo with the second-place medal pinned on my still-undecorated letter jacket. I had been told that the coveted gold 'S' for Stevenson was to be presented to me at the next school pep rally. I stepped outside the classroom where the school photographer was waiting and sheepishly smiled, wearing the jacket. I held the pink slip flat on my lap so it didn't appear in the photo, an invisible weight that pushed me down no matter how much I accomplished.

*

The assistant head of Special Education was seven months pregnant at the time of the meeting. She walked around the school's chipboard table distributing agendas to all of us. It was 11.34 a.m. Fourth period began at 11.35 a.m., and although several of my teachers had given up their early lunch period to be at the meeting, Mr Varian was nowhere to be found.

I pictured Belle sitting in his class, the sheet of carbon paper still under her notebook and above mine, pen poised to take notes, while they watched the digital clock above the television. Only once it hit the designated start time would he begin.

'We are here to discuss the plans for Miss Stevens's education next year. Agendas are being passed out. We will have ten minutes to hear from the teachers. I do hope that this meeting only takes one class period so we can all get back to our day.'

'It will take as long as it takes,' my mother clipped.

This was already off to a fine and amicable start.

The two teachers in attendance were my science teacher, Ms Up/Down, and my maths teacher, who was wearing his green-and-yellow braces as it was game day, and he was the head baseball coach. Ms Up/Down noted that they could only stay for half a period, then they had to slam down some lunch before meeting with students who needed help.

'Good, good. We're thankful you can take the time at all. I'm sure you'll have lots to say about Miss Stevens's progress.'

I started to mentally flip back to that time I shouted out an answer without meaning to in physics class, then clasped both hands to my mouth in regret. Did she log it? Or the time I was caught writing a note to Belle on my computer in maths. Mr Game

Day had said, 'I let you two girls get away with a lot of fun . . . don't push your luck,' when he walked behind us.

I could feel every muscle in my body uncontrollably tightening and I wanted to sit up straight to appear more alert, to minimise my disability, to become engaged. Anything to make it more difficult to deny me the computer system I needed.

As the head of Special Education started talking, Mr Game Day put his thumb in between his braces and his shirt and started rubbing one of the badges that weighed upon two strips of elastic. He collected pins of all sorts, but there was one button he was stroking across the table while looking at me.

It was a yellow smiley face, inconspicuous against his school-spirited yellow-and-green get-up. It said: 'You're My Hero'. When he saw that I had seen it, he sighed and then took his thumb out of his braces, leaning forward as if to catch every word the head of Special Education was saying.

It was a message. And I got it.

At that moment, the handle on the fake wooden door turned down, causing it to fly open, and there was Mr Varian. He passed by me and put both of his hands on my shoulders as he did during the Friday-night performance of the state championships. And then he pulled a chair from the corner of the room, sat down at the table and said, 'Right. We need to talk about this computer system. It is a disaster. It's quicker for her to type with one finger than to fight with it. If the Windows system has a chance of letting her write more, then she has to get it, and the school has to pay for it.'

To the best of my knowledge, here is what happened: Belle told me that Señor Yo No Sé from freshman year had suddenly walked into English class and said, 'You have a meeting to go to. Get going.'

Mr Varian turned around to the rest of the class, asking them to pull out their notebooks and write a response to last night's reading assignment of *Death of a Salesman*. He then ran out the door.

It was Señor Yo Ne Sé's planning period, and he had always made it his business to know where I was in the building. Señor had taken it upon himself after the Columbine school shooting to know my class schedule. During fire drills, he would suddenly appear if I was not on the ground floor and offer to help me down the stairs. So, when he had somehow obtained a copy of my IEP pink slip, Señor had looked at the meeting time and my class schedule, realising it alienated the person I needed most. He took it upon himself to relieve Mr Varian of teaching my class that day so that Mr Varian could make it to my Special Education meeting.

Chapter 10

'Athena, you don't have to go on any roller coasters. I won't be disappointed if we don't.' As The Twin says this, I think of all the responses I can come up with to tell her she's got the wrong end of the stick. I *do* need to go on the roller coasters. The opportunity to ride one doesn't come along every day, and fortune favours the brave. What exactly is the point of going to Disneyland Paris if you aren't going to ride any roller coasters?

One of the qualities I treasure most about The Twin is that she gives me peer pressure and entitlement in all the right ways. Rare is the person who doesn't demand that I work hard and always keep a good attitude. Rarer still is the one who does demand that I stop working so hard and take a break, or buy a nice coffee, or just stay home every once in a while and have a duvet day with K-dramas or video games. These are the things that The Twin gives to me. Sometimes. When I let her. Other times, she'll stand in the door frame, stomp her foot and say, 'Damn it! Why can I be a bad influence on all of my other friends, but not you?'

This form of strange and rather wonderful peer pressure is what got me on a Eurostar train to Paris. She offered a trip for five days, which I whittled down to three, and then finally 36 hours. I had too much writing to do, meetings that presented themselves as once-in-a-lifetime industry conversations and, ultimately, a women's march to attend.

So, we are at Disneyland Paris for one day. And aren't you supposed to ride roller coasters at Disneyland? What else is there to do if you're at Disneyland and there is no Hall of Presidents?

Indeed, Disneyland and disability is a pairing as legendary as peanut butter and jelly. The legend and the lore from the Make-A-Wish Foundation where the 'wishers' get to skip lines and are treated like Disney royalty for the day, is the ultimate concession that is supposed to make being disabled 'all worthwhile'. But in addition to all the social expectation of Disneyland being the 'happiest and most accommodating place on Earth' for the able-bodied and those with 'special needs' alike, there is another reason for the expectation that Disneyland is meant to be a place where I go on roller coasters.

*

'On a roller coaster, the first drop will always be the biggest. After the initial descent, momentum and therefore velocity will have to decrease.' Ms Up/Down drew the opposing vector lines along the gridded slopes, plotted out along the X and Y axis to mimic the trajectory of an amusement-park ride. The path began high on the Y axis, the next hill not even half as high as the first, and the one following it being half the height of the second, and so forth.

'That would be the dullest ride ever,' the boy one row in front of me shouted out. 'There's no way they're like that.' The eyes of Ms Up/Down flashed, and I saw the muscles in her jawline tighten.

'If you are within Planet Earth's gravitational field, this is how roller coasters are designed. The problem is, Mr Silvers, your emotions are so shaken in terror by this' – Ms Up/Down circled the first hill, – 'that you have no idea what follows.'

I really liked Ms Up/Down's class, but I never felt as if I was on stable ground with her. It felt as if the rules were always changing. One day she loved when we'd shout out ideas and would rush to write the litany of numbers on the whiteboard. Then, within the same fifty-minute class, she would throw a face-melting look to the kid in front of me for not raising his hand.

I looked away from both teacher and boy. When Ms Up/Down became like this, it felt as if entering her force field, even with an outside glance, could set her up for combustion.

'As I was saying before I was interrupted . . . If you don't want to be reduced to a screaming coward on a roller coaster, remember: all tracks are essentially the same. After you go down the first hill, the ride can't go any higher, and the friction of moving means you cannot go any faster. Ever notice that roller coasters just slowly come to a stop, Mr Silvers? This is why.'

Every action has an equal and opposite reaction. Forces come in pairs. An object at rest will stay at rest and an object in motion will stay in motion unless acted upon by an external force.

It was in Ms Up/Down's class that I was taught to draw every force acting upon an object, to ensure that none were forgotten in the calculation of how to overcome inertia with motion. She demonstrated with gravitational experiments off the school mez-zanine, or by pulling a tablecloth from under a place setting without moving a single piece of cutlery.

One day Señor Yo No Sé found me in the halls. As well as teaching Spanish, he was also the school's wrestling coach. 'I heard you're taking physics this year with Ms Up/Down.'

'*Sí, señor. Soy entusiasmada.*'

'Good. Physics will serve you well. If you pay attention in that class, you'll be able to outlift any of my wrestlers by the summer.'

Ms Up/Down's was a far more enjoyable method of teaching science than the previous school year's biology teacher. Mr Bio picked names out of a hat to assign us into pairs for the anatomy unit, which consisted of dissecting fetal pigs. This yielded a collaboration between me and a boy who kept kosher. We looked at Mr Bio, who said, 'You're going to have situations like this all the time when you're adults, so you might as well learn how to navigate these issues now.' For the record, I've never in my adult life had to navigate pig dissection with a man who keeps kosher. Given Mr Bio's ferocious argument, I was expecting it to happen at least once a week.

Anything was an improvement on Mr Bio, so we put up with Ms Up/Down's mood swings. She looked at the boy in front of me. There was a charge in the air around her, as if she was ready to pick a fight with him.

'And if you're really scared, remember that everyone on that ride is going at the exact same decreasing velocity with the exact same force on the exact same track. So, stop being scared and just think of the physics of it.'

The idea that roller coasters took me on the exact same track as everyone else on the ride, that there was no special seating or access door, stuck with me. Now, in Disneyland Paris, I find myself thinking about Ms Up/Down as I step off the manufactured wooden dock and into the hyper-realistic pirates' boat that will carry us through the foreboding mouth of the ride's cave. The smell of chlorine is pleasant, clean and comforting to my nose. But the feeling quickly turns to panic as I sit. The boat's metal bench gives me no support as it doesn't contour to my body at all. The sides of the boat are too low. How are kids not falling overboard daily?

As the boat lurches forward, I can't find stability at all. My feet don't touch the bottom of the boat, and the fabric of my trousers slides on the bench, making my hips move. As my body jerks, looking for its centre of gravity, the situation worsens exponentially.

And then the darkness of the cave swallows us. The laughter of the gnarled pirates chasing each other around a wooden barrel looms overhead. The cacophony of irregular voices makes me jump on repeat. In my head I tell myself that all the other people in all the other boats are experiencing the exact same stimulus that I am experiencing. And it doesn't appear that anyone is falling out of their boats. This is a homogenised experience, and it's only going to tame itself as the ride proceeds.

I know that the pirates' guns aren't going to fire and shoot me. This is Disneyland. I know in my brain that the fears of my body are utterly without reason. But no part of my body is getting the message.

*

I had rarely done it before, maybe only once or twice over my first years in high school. I knew it was OK. Those who sat around the chipboard tables promised me that I was allowed an extension on any homework assignment. Any class, I didn't have to ask the teacher. I was sceptical of Special Education's offer. I wasn't exactly on trusting terms with them by that point. The previous summer, the head of Special Education called in my GP without consulting my parents, to ask if they would change my prescription from a manual to an electric wheelchair to 'address access issues within the building'. Not only did homework extensions feel tied up in their proposals to 'drop down' a set, but also, as far as I could see, handing assignments in a day late didn't solve any problems. If I didn't finish an assignment on Monday night, then I would have to do it on Tuesday, which would push back Tuesday's homework to Wednesday and so on, until I spent my precious weekend catching up on everything else.

But the night before I had struggled. I don't remember why but there was little choice; I needed extra time on the previous assignment. I would double up on work and have both assignments ready by class the next day. I didn't beg or ask. It was a statement. The people who made choices about my life assured me I could have extended time.

I explained to Ms Up/Down that this time, I was going to have to turn in my homework late. She tightened her jaw muscles. The charge of the air around her changed, too.

*

'OK, all right. So, Pirates of the Caribbean was a disaster. But if you want to try again, maybe the *Star Wars* ride will be a better fit. You don't actually go anywhere. It's like a big box that moves. So, the floor and the chairs shake, and you watch a 3D movie with Jar Jar Binks leading a spaceship.'

'That sounds like something I can handle. Let's go on that.' This is new technology. Not the same as the promises that Ms Up/Down made about the first slope of the ride being the steepest. The *Star Wars* ride must have some sort of motor inside it, so the biggest drop could be at the end or, if the ride designers are following the rules of storytelling properly, the biggest motions will be three-quarters of the way through. But that's all fine, I tell myself, because there's nowhere to fall into and there's no actual travelling.

We enter the space-themed waiting area, and it feels more like Samsung or Apple HQ than Disneyland. Blue LED lights reflect themselves off the walls and the floor. Life-sized statues of stormtroopers stand at the ends of the hallways. And the air feels like it's been breathed and recycled several times over by those who share this spaceship. By the time we take our seats, I've nearly forgotten that an amusement-park ride is involved. Rather, we are a crew waiting for our captain to appear and tell us that our fleet is in their safe and capable hands.

I look around the room and it's a normal movie theatre. Perhaps there's a bit more formality than the screening rooms that I am used to. The chairs are wider, with PVC leather. But unless the floor suddenly opens up and swallows us whole, I don't see us going anywhere.

This will be less like a roller coaster and more like a rocking chair, or at worst a jittery carousel. Not a problem.

Taking advantage of that fabled Disney privilege of getting to skip the queue in this scenario means that The Twin and I are the first to take our seats, which I notice are firmly bolted to the floor. We talk about nothing as the able-bodied holiday-makers file in. All the while I tell myself that this ride will be fine. It's a chair that moves. I live my life in another chair that moves, so what's the difference?

'The emergency stop button is just there. If you need me to, I will jump up and push it in a second,' The Twin points out. I look at the now rather obvious red button on the side of the wall.

'The fact that you can leave the ride, even if it's to press the emergency stop button, tells me there's not going to be an emergency.'

I put on the 3D glasses as a full stop to end the conversation as the 'ride' begins. There's no harm that can be done to me. Everyone in this room will have the same experience and, this time, there's no creepy, creaky boat to fall out of.

The blue neon lights dim and C-3PO enters to give us an attempt at basic health and safety, rules and regulations during our short time with the Starfleet. So far, so good. Let's get to the part where we lift off and explore the wondrous galaxy.

Jar Jar Binks crashes in and shoves C-3PO out of the way. As he does so, he slams into the control board, making the spaceship lurch back.

The Twin takes one look in my direction.

'Oh, God! This was a mistake!'

She full-body tackles me in an embrace as our spaceship shoots off the launch pad.

*

I had snapped at my mother for three nights in a row when she suggested I go to bed before all my homework was finished. I double-checked my history and American lit homework, looking up precise definitions of words I already knew. Those subjects had to be done as soon as I came home. As horrible as it was falling in Ms Up/Down's estimation, to do so with Varian or Odysseus would be devastating.

When the autumn rain drove us into the classroom for the start of school and every teacher said they did not accept late assignments, that included me. The safety net of extended time discussed around the chipboard table at IEP meetings was a ruse. I had been foolish to trust that Special Education could offer me help with anything.

When my mum pieced together what happened, she immediately called Ms Up/Down.

'Your daughter inspires me so much, Mrs Stevens, I would never do anything to harm her.'

'Well, right now she's terrified of all her teachers and staying up until two or three – I don't even know – checking her answers over and over just to keep you all happy. Do you know my daughter has to get up at five-thirty every morning to do therapy, so she can sit upright in your classroom? Did you know that, Ms Up/Down?'

'Gosh, I had no idea. She's so amazing. I'm so sorry, Mrs Stevens. I forgot. I won't let it happen again.'

'You don't need to apologise to me. You need to apologise to my daughter. Tomorrow. During class. Be sure to make it a "teaching moment".'

'Of course. I will do that, Mrs Stevens.'

*

My quest to curate an experience that is exactly like that of the able bodies surrounding me daily would not be thwarted by Jar Jar Binks crashing our spaceship. Throughout the ride, The Twin asks me, to the sound of rockets exploding overhead, if I'm sure I don't want her to push the emergency button. It leaves me raw to other people's feelings. There is no way I am about to ruin everyone else's perfectly choreographed intergalactic space journey. During those minutes, there is no emergency. But my body feels like it's going to die.

'Do you really want to try again? OK, well, Buzz Lightyear Laser Blast doesn't have any drops. Everyone's literally just on a loop track trying to shoot Emperor Zurg and help the Little Green Men get power.'

No drops, maybe a little bit of spinning on the track – I can handle that. It goes without saying that I was not going to get a winning score when it comes to the laser-gun shooting, but nobody really trusts those numbers anyway. 'And the ride literally falls under the classification of omni-mover,' The Twin adds: the designers created a ride that controls every rider's line of sight, so everyone sees the exact same thing at the same moment throughout. This is exactly what I want. Nobody has died on this ride. There is nothing for me to be afraid of.

However, when I again find myself sitting on a hard plastic seat, it's difficult to find support for my feet or waist. For a children's ride, everything here feels hard, slippery and unsafe. I pick up my 'blaster' in an effort to divert my attention.

My life is stressful enough. Why on Earth – or, in this instance, not on Earth – have I signed up to join Buzz Lightyear's intergalactic space troop to help defeat the Evil Emperor Zurg? This is supposed to be a holiday.

We roll away from the boarding point and I see my wheelchair drift further from me until our pod turns a corner. We are whipped around to be in the eyeline of a plethora of Little Green Men begging us to help them. Buzz Lightyear is over twenty feet tall and his voice bellows instructions to us in the darkness – 'Shoot here!' – as UV light reveals a glowing target. 'And here!' Another target bursts forth in the darkness and the Little Green Men groan, in stifling unison, their pleas for help.

Just as I have found my stability and can send the signal for my arms to unglue themselves from my chest, the space pod spins around again, causing me to flinch back into my chest. If the laser gun were real, I'd be dead.

I hear laughter around me and I think there's no way all of us on this ride are experiencing the same thing. How can everyone on the ride be having the exact same experience and not find the whole thing miserable? I hate not having control of my body. I've spent years in therapy ensuring I never felt that way.

*

My mother told me to expect Ms Up/Down's apology the next day in class. By that time, I had caught up with the assignments and even worked ahead a little, too, in case I wasn't reading the syllabus properly. Or that I wasn't good enough to stay in my classes and Ms Up/Down suggested I drop down a level in science. Or if I suddenly became ill and I couldn't do my homework one night, I'd at least have cover.

Ms Up/Down walked in between the rows of lab tables and handed back graded homework assignments. It was the assignment that I had turned in a day late. When she reached me, she bent her knees so that she was on my level.

'Now, we all make mistakes,' Ms Up/Down said to me.

'Yeah, it's fine. Don't worry about it, please,' and I flashed a smile. I had been wrestling with the anticipation of the apology all day, wanting to be gracious. I wanted to note that she was a teacher, but also a human being. I wanted her to believe that she didn't hurt me, because it would hurt her to know that she had. Harming Ms Up/Down because I was hurt wouldn't solve anything. Indeed, I had seen through her actions that students were either on her good side or not. Ms Up/Down didn't do well with complications.

The fact was, how the remainder of the class went was reliant on my response in that moment. I had to forgive Ms Up/Down in the brief time available for the apology. To take any longer would risk setting our entire class's learning behind. Even when wrong was admitted, the weight was still on me to fix the situation. And I wanted to be a good victim and forgive in the allotted time.

'What I should say to you is—'

'Don't worry about it, Ms Up/Down. I've forgotten that it happened,' I said, taking my assignment from her hands. I received a ninety-eight.

'You are such a good girl,' Ms Up/Down praised my lie. After all, it was exactly what she wanted to hear at that moment. And I had learned that whenever someone harmed me, it was up to me to balance out the universe again.

The easiest way to ensure that everyone was at ease was to minimise the force of the impact on me.

*

'Before you get on, I need to ask – in the event of an emergency, can you use a ladder?' I look from the ride's host to The Twin, remembering our days as Juliet at RADA. We could do ladders. Not a problem.

'There's always a super long line for Peter Pan's Flight. It's really cool because the track is above you, so it feels like you're in a flying ship. And it's a little kid's ride. The scariest thing in it is the crocodile with the ticking clock. This is an entry-level Disney ride,' The Twin says as we cross the Magic Kingdom. 'But really, Athena, if you feel like it's too much, we don't have to—'

'No, that sounds fun. I want to be on one ride that's fun, and I'm not going to stoop to the level of It's a Small World or the Teacups.' Between working in theatre and my scientific education, I knew more about how these amusement-park rides worked than most people at Disneyland. My mind knows that the fourteen-foot drop down the waterfall in the pirate's cove wasn't that big, or that the Emperor Zurg wasn't going to jump out of his intergalactic station and yell at me. So why can't my brain tell my body of the scientific safety of it all? I should be able to enjoy this experience the same as any other body. Disneyland is the happiest place on Earth. So why is this experience being tinged by my brain injury?

I sit on another ungiving and slick seat, this time in a boat that flies rather than one that drifts through overly chlorinated water. But I still worry about sliding out, falling down past Wendy putting her brothers to bed and the dog, Nana, overseeing everyone's welfare but mine. Or, at least, that's how it seems. As we fly out of the bedroom window, the ship feels like it's accelerating into the black night, lit only by pinpricks of white starry light.

Without having my feet on the floor, and without any idea of where I am in space, I am lost. To look down gives me the sensation of tumbling headfirst into an abyss. But I am only oriented towards the pull of gravity and 'down' is the only direction my brain understands in this boat flying through the air. And 'down' on a ride that needs a ladder to rescue you is not a direction I want to go.

Passing over the tiny models of Big Ben and Tower Bridge, I can feel my heart catch on a latch in my throat. The old song of 'You Can Fly! You Can Fly! You Can Fly!' cycles around the hidden speakers coming at me from all directions.

No, I can't fly. No one can.

More to the point, I can't even find a sense of stability on this hard metal boat. There's nothing for me to hold on to, nothing to help me know where my erratically moving body is in space.

I've been rock climbing and ultralight flying, water- and downhill-skiing many times in my life. Adrenaline rushes are not foreign to me. But I don't understand how people can find these manufactured fantastical experiences fun. I don't understand why this is meant to be the happiest, most accessible place on Earth for people like me. And I don't understand how anyone could see a ship sailing in space and not be terrified.

*

Never again was I willing to lean upon the accommodations promised in my IEP meetings as a disabled student. Even though things were technically made right with Ms Up/Down, it wasn't worth the risk of another teacher forgetting the reasonable adjustments I was entitled to. The risk of a fallout would, ultimately, only hurt me. Ms Up/Down didn't feel an existential threat to her job by making a mistake with her student, but I had every reason to worry that Special Education could get wind of my late assignment. The rift between student and teacher could be enough to suggest that I move down to a 'less rigorous' level in classes. To stop all possibility of this occurring, I doubled down on homework assignments even more.

By the time summer break came, I asked my parents not to share my grades with me. The cycle of staying up until 3 a.m. to triple-check my answers wasn't a set-up for success. I was upsetting teachers if I didn't stay up until all my homework was completed, but I was upsetting my parents when I stayed up past their bedtime to ensure that I finished my assignments on time.

I grew increasingly frustrated by the presence of Stevenson's

Woman. She carried my laptop from classroom to classroom, but otherwise received a paycheque for being a millstone around my neck, rather than assistant. Still, I was expected to be polite, to navigate the emotions of the able-bodied adults around me, rather than indulging in my own adolescent moods.

My success at school felt very much based on how little I rocked the boat, and how much I kept everyone happy. And I was doing a very bad job at both.

'Hey,' said my mum, 'I think Señor Yo No Sé is down in the wrestling room. Should we surprise him?' My mother and I stopped by Stevenson at the end of summer break to pick up the next year's course schedule and books. Without the school's 4,500 students filling its halls, the air conditioner on full blast made the building feel like a bit of an ice box. The wrestling gym, which was about seven steps below normal classroom level, was particularly cold. Somewhat understandably, the school had made no attempt to make this room accessible. So, I left my wheelchair at the top of the steps and took my mother's hand as she supported me for what I thought would be a summer pop-in visit with one of my favourite teachers.

There were no wrestlers in the gym. Señor Yo No Sé sat alone in a folding metal chair. As we walked in, me with a huge grin on my face but unsteady on my feet, he got up and set out two more folding chairs.

'Have a seat. Your mother and I are worried about you.' Señor's voice was usually a bit gruff, thanks in large part to his own injury sustained on the wrestling mat in his youth. But there was no joviality in his voice.

'Worried about me?' A high-school kid could go off the rails with drugs, alcohol, getting pregnant and self-harming. But my stress levels were the pleasant kind of teenage destruction. I was the 'pleasure-to-have-in-class' sort of teenage miserable, not the 'hurry-up-apply-yourself-please' teenage miserable.

'You are defining yourself by your grades. You've made an idol out of your report card.'

'I need good grades to get into a good school. You're one of the teachers who is saying that the most.' I looked at my mother, tears in her eyes as she was looking away from me. Suddenly it was very clear that I had been lured into this conversation, and with my wheelchair sat outside on the steps, I had no way out of it.

'Your grades will be good enough to get into plenty of universities—'

'But not the top-tier ones everyone wants to get into.'

Nothing about this made sense. Señor Yo No Sé was the most demanding of excellence among the teachers at Stevenson. Any whiff of not performing your best sent him rattling off in Spanish about how this was our one life, how privileged we were to be at that school, and how time wasted was potential lost.

What was he doing saying he was worried that I defined myself by my grades? Since the moment my kindergarten teacher pulled me into the hallway and declared that it would be best if I didn't continue with my abled-bodied classmates, everyone else defined me that way, too.

'You'll get into the school you're supposed to go to. You need to also take up the responsibility to stay healthy and get enough sleep.'

'I tried doing that in Ms Up/Down's class and she—'

'The fact that Ms Up/Down forgot about your reasonable adjustment is her problem to deal with.'

Really? Because it didn't feel like her problem to deal with when the full force of her anger landed on me in front of twenty other students. I was very clearly left to pick up the pieces after the destruction of impact, simply because she 'forgot' I was disabled. Ms Up/Down made the mistake, but the momentum of that error disproportionately affected me.

For every action, there is an equal and opposite reaction.

Forces come in pairs.

An object at rest will stay at rest. And an object in motion will stay in motion unless acted upon by an external force.

For over two hours, Señor and I argued about my approach to school and, in turn, life. I wanted to be living in the world he offered, but my lived experience had clearly taught me that I did not. When it was all over, I felt betrayed by a teacher with such high standards, he would never allow English to be spoken in his classroom.

It would be decades before I would have language to explain these unwritten rules and realities to him or anyone else.

Chapter 11

I keep my forearms on the black leather tops of my chair's armrests. In the baking July sun, if I remove them for too long the material becomes so hot that I am likely to burn myself. I hopped back from Paris earlier this morning after the overnight trip to Disneyland, and I am driving my chair from King's Cross to Oxford Circus in order to get in front of the Women's March that is being led that afternoon.

I say 'led', but I am in the front row. I am one of the leaders.

A few weeks ago, the leader of the Women's Equality Party, Sophie Walker, emailed me and asked if I would be the party's representative on the front line of the march. Not only that: 'Would you mind speaking in Parliament Square? I'm racking my brain to find a speaker, and I know you can pull it off. I'll make sure that the stage is accessible.'

In the air-conditioned coffee shop where I read that email, it seemed like the answer was obvious. *Yes. Yes, of course, I would love to. No problem.*

Then her reply came in: 'Oh, and by the way, I told them that you would be doing spoken-word art because they don't want anything political in nature onstage.'

Cue the sound of a record scratching.

I wrote back, 'Poetry. So, basically, you want me to write poetry that is spoken out loud. Is that what "spoken word" means?'

'Sure, I guess. The entire "no politics" thing is completely ridiculous, but poetry seems to fit the bill.'

I listened to recordings of The Twin speaking my poem into my AirPods the entire Eurostar journey to Paris and back. Once at King's Cross, The Twin and I went into an accessible toilet, and I took one of my jewel-toned spandex and neoprene dresses out of the rucksack looped across the back of my wheelchair.

The Twin swiped a NARS red lipstick in the colour 'Don't Stop' across my lips. I looked in the mirror for a few minutes to let it dry before The Twin took the rucksack off my chair and swung it over her shoulder to take home herself. She would return it to me in the next few days.

Now we are at the starting point of the march, a famous poet, an actor, a lawyer, myself and another party member who has agreed to help me during the event. I raise my new wheelchair, the iBOT, up to standing level, thankful that finally I have settled with British Airways.

The gyroscopes in my wheelchair shiver back and forth as I can feel the momentum of half a million women, and probably a fair few men, becoming a mass behind us.

There are so many details that go uncaptured whenever you see a political protest in movies. One of which is the waiting. The waiting for the press to get their shot, the waiting for the police to get their OK so we can start moving. The waiting as everyone hits their stride to keep the mass whole, to not allow anyone to fall behind; to pace oneself and become a single entity that is able to stop and change direction, then go again at a consistent rate marked out by the beat that the ground shakes, a common step acting as a metronome.

*

Mr Varian wrapped his arms around me, coming down to the level of my wheelchair – something he never did. Patronising was not his style. But now I needed a paternal something – a patron, a pater – because I had just told him the reality. That despite applying to seventeen universities, I had only got into two of them.

The previous summer, we had travelled all over the US looking at Vanderbilt University, Emory University, Stanford, Pepperdine, University of California – every good school my mother or I could find that had a prestigious name and was south of the Mason–Dixon line. The last part was key in my mother's eyes. Having lived for eighteen years in Chicago, she was convinced that life would be a lot easier if I didn't have to worry about snow. I was not so convinced and, at the last possible minute, started saying that the university I wanted to get into most was Northwestern. Forty-five minutes away from home, I could come back and visit on the weekends.

I had begun to tell people: 'I really want to be an actor, but since that's impossible, I'm going to be a lawyer.'

After Mr Varian made his appearance at my IEP meeting, essentially demanding what my mother and I had been saying for years, Stevenson offered to pay their people for an assistive technology assessment. Stevenson's 'people' wrote the four-page recommendation that cost the high school $2,000. It said I needed voice-activation software, specifically that available on a Windows machine. And all of a sudden, I got it.

Stevenson counsellors made it very clear how to apply strategically for colleges. You applied 20 per cent for stretch colleges – ones that were just a little bit outside of your grade range – and then 60 per cent in the range that you fell into statistically. Knowing that statistics and dreams didn't always work out, the final 20 per cent were those below your grade range. Still good colleges, as there was no such thing as a 'bad' school.

This meant that out of the seventeen schools, there were three stretches, three safety colleges and ten that fell within my grade range. I had noticed a growing confidence among teachers leading up to my applications in January.

'Even the stretches will take you. Don't worry.'

'They'll be thrilled to see you on their application stacks!'

'People in college admissions know that Stevenson High School is really difficult. They adjust your grade point average accordingly.'

'You tick so many boxes. Don't worry about not being the perfect match.'

'Writing a letter of recommendation for you will be so rewarding. Will you let me do it?'

And now, I was sobbing in the closet-turned-meeting-room of the English department, Mr Varian kneeling on the floor, wrapping his arms around me.

'I did everything right – I don't know why I didn't get into Northwestern or any of the other schools.'

'I don't know. It doesn't make sense. I don't know what happened. But listen to me … OK, just listen.' He rolled me back from him and looked me in the eye. 'I know everyone at Stevenson has made getting into the right college the only happy ending possible. That's not true. And I'm sorry we didn't tell you the whole truth. But life can be complicated and still turn out OK.'

'How can you say that? I've just spent four years doing everything that anyone asked of me. I did well at the state championships. Was I just not trying hard enough?'

'This is what you will do, OK? I promise. You'll go to one of these two schools for a year, and then you'll reapply somewhere else. I promise you, a year from now we'll be having a different conversation. I promise it.'

*

When we finally start marching, I am surprised at the choreography that is put in place to keep us safe. A row of young women in bright-orange traffic vests march backwards a metre and a half in front of us, acting as a barricade between us and whoever might get strange ideas to obscure a march of half a million women.

I know they are younger than me, both in age and experience, because of their fear, evident in the way they link arms with hands entwined, knuckles going white. At one point, a police officer tries to come in between this phalanx of women moving forward, and the ones in fluorescent vests set out as a thin line of protection.

'Hey! Leave her alone! That's not fair!' my friend screams at the officer who is using his stick as a stencil to keep the security marchers in a straight formation. 'He shouldn't be doing that. He's got all the power in the situation.'

A trans woman with a Vegas-style burlesque feather fan in hot pink comes between the officer and the protest marshal, tickling the officer's nose in a not-so-subtle way of telling him to back off. She is towering over everybody. The height of a human being who once had male hormones now in five-inch heels is formidable.

On a typical day, I can make it from Oxford Circus to Parliament Square in just under twenty minutes. Now it is taking five hours.

There is ability and safety in speed, but there is also ability and safety in numbers. Sometimes for change to happen, things go slowly, and numbers create their own inertia.

*

'It'll work out,' Mr Odysseus said in his usual clip. From him, that gave me comfort, as opposed to the more florid nature of Mr Varian. 'I know at seventeen a year of your life feels like forever, but it really isn't. If you hate it, then there are other options available to you.'

He sat, perched on top of his desk in the empty classroom, hands on either side of him, like wings.

I was more worried about telling Odysseus than Varian about my college application status. He was a minimiser – not in a bad way, just in a matter-of-fact, 'this-is-going-to-hurt-but-we-have-to-do-it' sort of way.

'Athena, the big ideas and questions will be the same wherever you study. You will write brilliantly no matter where you are. *The Iliad* has the same words printed in it at Harvard as the community college I work at on weekends. Don't confuse colleges with country clubs. The big ideas, and old friends like Walt Whitman, they will give you peace wherever you go.'

When I finally decided that I would go to Davidson College, my mother called the Dean of Students and mentioned that I was disabled – something I conveniently left off the application because deep down I knew the world we were living in.

'But we already accepted our disabled student for the class of 2006,' the Dean of Students said over the phone to my mother.

'What does that mean?'

'We only have space to take in one disabled student a year. We've taken one in – we've never had more than one disabled student in a graduating class.'

'Well, now you have two. I suggest you figure out what to do about it.'

*

Turning off Whitehall onto Parliament Square, I expect there to be a lot fewer people in front of us. But in reality, a multitude of others are already, strategically, there.

'Speakers, she's a speaker!' my friend says as I wave my speaker badge in front of another marshal, this time an older woman.

'Everybody on the lawn, except speakers.'

'But my friend is a speaker.'

The woman with the clipboard takes a closer look at my badge.

'Oh. Right, you're a speaker. Well, over there by the stage, I guess.'

The doubt that I am there to perform happens so often I have almost become immune to it. When I was at the Olivier Awards, one marshal did not believe that I was a nominee, insisting that I could not get on the red carpet and that 'people from charities go over there'. Backstage at Shakespeare's Globe Theatre, I have often been blocked from my starting position. 'Accessible seating is right there – you don't need to go that way.' At another theatre, I took a copy of the poster with my photo on it out of the usher's hands as she refused to let me go onstage for fight call. 'See? It's the same person. Look at what you're giving out and look at people properly,' I told her, in a rare instance of losing my temper.

Discrimination rarely comes in the form of a bullet. Usually, it's in the form of a cheese grater to your soul. Slow. Meticulous. Constantly irritating, and often going on for years without drawing blood. A cheese grater can do as much damage as a bullet; it just takes a lot longer.

As I head to the designated speakers' station, I begin to regret not taking the sunscreen with me after The Twin applied it back in the King's Cross station loo. The three-mile walk that has taken half a day has made me sweat, and I feel the sun break through the SPF protection.

In Parliament Square, I look at the statues of men Mr Odysseus taught me to see as 'old friends'. Winston Churchill. Nelson Mandela. Maybe more specifically, Abraham Lincoln. Old friends in a world where all humans are created equal. During this speech, I am able to sit beside my old friends. But first I have to get to the stage, which has been blocked by a giant orange balloon of a baby Trump in a diaper, crawling on all fours. This blimp, full of hot air, has been positioned by its four guides right in front of the wheelchair ramp leading to the stage. My scepticism of Trump is suddenly superseded by my absolute hatred of things standing as obstacles to what would otherwise be an accessible path.

When I ask the hot-air Trump guides to move, they look at me like I've just popped their balloon for no good reason.

'I need to get up there. I'm a speaker. Why do you think there was a wheelchair ramp even built here if there wasn't going to be a wheelchair speaker?'

'Moving this is going to be really hard.'

'I'm sure it will be, but I wasn't the one silly enough to decide to park my Trump in a pathway that was clearly going to block a speaker. Seems like you didn't think this one through.'

'OK, OK, give us a minute and we'll figure something out.'

All the handlers are looking at me at this point. It makes me wonder if the people that the real Trump surrounds himself with might have seen this coming. During a march that is supposed to promote equality and call into question the reigning privileges of men like those in the US White House, why is the wheelchair ramp blocked at all?

By the time they get Baby Trump out of the way, I have sat and watched the handlers begin to fight among themselves for about seven minutes. They throw looks back at me that seem to suggest the expectation that I should say, 'You know what, never mind. I don't need to speak in Parliament Square today. This piece that I have been working on for the past month (that's not in the least bit political, mind you, so I don't know why there is a Baby Trump balloon that takes four people to handle it tied to the stage), it isn't that good. I can just go home and let you put your Trump wherever you want.'

'Thank you,' I say instead. I form the words at the front of my mouth, with an edge of irritation that is sharp enough to slice the blimp open with just a graze. I am not thankful. I am following the script to appease a bunch of able-bodied balloon-baby handlers.

*

By my second semester of senior year at high school, I had full-blown senioritis, the name given to many students' inclination to start coasting once they got into their selected university. My senioritis was different, though. I wasn't slacking off because I was assured of my position in life; I was a combination of burnt out and disillusioned.

'If someone is in the wrong and you love them, according to Plato you have a moral obligation to tell them what they are doing is wrong.' Odysseus wrote on the whiteboard in his chicken scratch, all capital-letter handwriting. 'You don't do this,' he said, tapping with the end of his capped pen, 'then you rob someone of the opportunity to grow. How can you say you care about someone if you do not give them that opportunity?'

I have outgrown world history, European history, US history, and have come back, yet again, into his classroom, this time to study philosophy.

'This is going to be something that you will face increasingly often once you're out in the adult world. Who do you care about enough to point out their mistakes in hopes that they will grow? And who do you allow to continue acting in ignorance?

'Relationships, how you navigate your relationships, are as much about your philosophy and your approach to life as they are about your psychology. The way you approach human beings as either tools to use, or people with inherent dignity, will make more of an impact on what your life is to become than anything biological.'

I stopped typing, trying to undo the knot Odysseus had just put in my brain. So, if I believed that people had inherent dignity (all men were created equal and endowed by their Creator ...), then I couldn't decide to ignore anybody out of convenience or wanting to dismiss what they were saying. No matter how broken they were, I had to listen to all of them, because all of us had a piece of the Divine inside our souls.

I looked around to understand the inherent dignity of my classmates, the ones that I barely had time to look at under the weight of college applications.

Other than Belle, Plato and the Microsoft Office Paperclip, I wasn't particularly great at having friends in high school. Everyone seemed to have a lot more energy than I did. We all worked hard; there wasn't a single one of us who was able to go to bed before eleven at night, given the mounds of homework that were notorious for screwing our backs if we didn't carry a well-balanced rucksack. But my peers didn't lose their voices every fortnight from trying to be loud enough to have clear speech. They didn't come home with blisters and bloodied hands from having to push up ramps that were too steep to be compliant with legal building codes.

I knew everyone's name, though. I smiled at people, and they smiled back, either out of reflex or because they actually meant it. We would build on each other's arguments in class and laugh at each other's sarcastic takes on what was obviously a rogue answer doused with a heavy bit of teenage angst.

After Varian stormed into my IEP meeting, Belle was taken out of my classes, which in a school the size of Stevenson essentially meant that we may as well have been shipped off to different planets. I went back to hiding in the bathroom during my lunch break because the idea of finding a new table to sit at seemed so overwhelming.

*

The adrenaline from fighting to get onstage is higher than the adrenaline of performing. Now, I know I am where I am meant to be. Now, I can do my job well. My chair balanced on its two wheels with all three gyroscopes working, the Women's Equality Party logo emblazoned on the back of my chair, I unfold the piece of paper that I have been carrying since this morning in Paris and begin.

Even with the muffled, hypo-nasal sound of cerebral palsy, I have trained to speak with a giant voice that is equally qualified for Shakespeare as it is for my own work. The microphone is just a bonus, not something to be reliant upon.

'They told me not to be political.'

It's a force of habit, but one I'm rather proud of, that I pause after the first line.

I wait, holding on to this moment and turning on the flash of my mental camera. I am here. Now. I am aware of all the forces that have got me up onstage, from my friend who keeps my tyres inflated to my voice teacher making shapes with her mouth in the mirror. I think of Odysseus and Varian teaching me the value of every human self, and I know I have a right to be on this stage in front of Parliament speaking my words. All nervousness ran out once access was permitted to that ramp. And I want to take my time reciting my piece, not so that I will be clear, but so that I can enjoy it, like the forces of buoyancy in a pool of water holding me.

*

Senior year sped towards an end with what was called the 'Operation Snowball Retreat'. I had never considered myself someone who was going, having not been invited to a sleepover since grade school. I was content to stay in my shell of work; there was no time for fun. But the revelation that came with more colleges than not rejecting my applications made me want to have at least some memories of being social while in high school.

From March, a school counsellor I had befriended two years prior during an educational trip to Greece insisted that I eat lunch with her once a week.

She wanted me to talk about my feelings.

I insisted I didn't have any.

It was she who arranged for me to attend the Operation Snowball Retreat.

'But how will I eat or get dressed?' was one of the myriad rejections I threw out. She had an answer for everything.

Realistically, these were conversations that I was having with myself about life once I left for college. *How will I get my shoes tied? How will I get three meals a day? How will I stay hydrated? How will I do anything resembling any sort of independence if I haven't already mastered these skills in seventeen years of physical therapy?*

'You'll stay in the same cabin as me and we'll work out meals. There will be loads of help – don't worry.'

I decided that, for at least this one weekend out of my four years of high school, I would be with the other students of my class.

The social workers at Stevenson made the Operation Snowball weekend about reflecting on your self-worth as an individual, your ability to make change just by being who you are, and the fact that individuals are needed to create mass movements that forever alter the world. Anyone had within them a 'snowball effect'.

When the bus rolled up to the campsite and we were given cabin assignments, I felt in over my head. To make things even more overwhelming, there were twenty-one girls and two faculty members – now turned mentors and operating on a first-name basis – to a cabin. The School Counsellor who fed me lunch once a week was in my cabin. I started to hug my rucksack, set on my lap and densely packed, close to my chest, balancing it on my knees whenever I had to push my chair forward.

Our teachers, now in shorts and Operation Snowball long-sleeved

T-shirts, yelled out our names as we clustered into the cabin. The rest of the girls briefly called out top bunks or bottom bunks. The counsellor looked at me and put my pillow on the lower-level bunk.

'This looks like a good spot for you. I'll be the top one above your head.'

'Yeah, yeah, that sounds great, thanks.'

Dinner was our first activity after the three-hour bus ride north. The School Counsellor slipped in next to me, holding my plate as she dished out the spaghetti bolognese without skipping a beat. I reminded myself that she had seen my parents do this before, and she had done it every week, so I was lucky.

I needed to find her for the next six meals.

*

'You and your Women's Equality lapel are on the cover of the front page of every newspaper in the nation! I couldn't be more proud.'

Sophie Walker touches the back of my shoulder as she walks behind me, reminding me who I am. In this moment, it feels like I am serving the purpose I was created for: to be a voice for change. I don't believe it, and do a quick online check myself. The *Guardian* – there is the front of the march, of course. The *Telegraph* – yes. The *Daily Mail* – holy cow, this is getting bizarre.

A few months later, an Instagram-loving friend is working for my company and finds a picture that a portrait photographer took of me that day in front of the microphone. It is fierce. It is a moment that obviously captured his imagination. When I receive the grainy black-and-white image, my mouth in a position that is overly wide for most people to speak with, I am amazed at the interconnected-ness of the world. A silver-lining moment where a body that was damaged by another person was able to speak louder than the thousands of able bodies in front of her.

*

That weekend, we could call our teachers by their first names and acknowledge that they were people, not just animatronics that got deflated and stored in a closet at night. In the cavernous meeting hall supported by wooden rafters, we listened to speakers who, six months before, dropped everything they were doing and ran to New York because they were firemen and wanted to help the rescue effort of 9/11. We listened to people who had suffered from abuse and the inevitable complications of life that somehow we, as seventeen- and eighteen-year-olds, still thought we could avoid.

Each speaker told us that life had a heavy dose of inevitable suffering. But as one of them put it, what mattered was what you did in the face of impossible situations. Did you stay home, safe, with your family? Or did you drive to New York, knowing that you had the training and education needed to help in a crisis that was unfolding there?

That afternoon, after a fellow student fed me lunch, we were told to all sit down in a space on the floor and count off by twos – 'one, two, one, two, one, two'.

I was a Two.

'Will all the Ones stand up and come over here to this side of the room. Twos, stay seated and put your head in your hands and shut your eyes.'

My manual wheelchair raised me above the rest of the group, making me feel out of place. Not elevated, just different. So, I collapsed my chest into myself and bowed my head, as I had so often done in the hallways as I was left to navigate my chair, on my own, through a mass of developing teenagers. My eyes were shut, but I could see the shapes and outlines and colours that so often showed up when I wanted to look at nothing.

'OK, Ones. I'm going to give you a description, and I want you to go around the room and tap everyone on the shoulder or head who this statement represents to you. Got it? Twos, you don't have to do anything. Just pay attention to what you feel.

'I want you, Ones, to go around the room and touch every single person you have laughed with at lunch while you were in high school.'

Belle wasn't at the retreat, so I knew I wouldn't be touched. There was an air of distrust in the room as the One group went out from where they were all congregated and touched a few heads.

'I want you to touch someone who really helped you in a class during these past four years.'

I was barely good enough to keep up with my own homework. I never received a call asking for advice on how to do a maths problem. I was not going to be touched.

'OK, now go around and find someone who consistently makes you laugh and touch them.'

Fine, I got a touch or two here. I had taken second place in State in original comedy.

'Now, touch people who have inspired you over the past four years.'

Touch.

Touch.

Touch.

OK, so I was inspirational. That was my job. That was the adjective stuck to every single student like me who ever existed in an able-bodied world. Of course I would get tapped on the shoulder here.

'Now, I want you to touch anyone who you feel grateful for every time you see them.'

Touch.

Touch.

Touch.

Touch.

Touch.

Touch.

'How about people who make you feel like they know the world is going to be OK just by their smile.'

Touch.

Touch.

Touch.

Touch.

Touch.

Touch.

Touch.

'Now touch someone who you know has it rough – harder than you – but still reminds you that there is good in the world.'

Touch.

Touch.

Touch.

Touch.

Touch.

'Someone you wish you knew how to help and couldn't figure out how.'

Touch.

Touch.

Touch.

Touch.

Touch.

Touch.

Touch.

Touch.

Touch.

The water from my eyes spilled over onto the cotton leggings I was wearing underneath an oversized sweatshirt, the liquid turning from warm to cold as it began to rest on my quad muscles. How did I always wind up in the bathroom at lunch, rather than asking someone for help? How could I have been so smart and not noticed the obvious – that there were people around me who saw me, who cared, who would have helped? Belle was only the beginning. How did I miss all of this for four years?

Touch.

Touch.

Touch.

Touch.

Touch.

'Someone you wish you knew better.'

Touch.

Touch.

Touch.

Touch.

'Someone you will remember for the rest of your life, even if you were never to see that person again after today.'

Touch.

Touch.

Touch.

Touch.

Touch.

For years, I clung on to grades in an effort just to survive until I could get out from under Special Education, and go to a school where everyone would immediately know my intelligence simply when I said the name of the institution.

Touch.

Touch.

Touch.

High school could have been totally different, if only I had known that the strength I needed to fight the impossible was the vulnerability everyone had seen, despite my best efforts to keep it hidden.

Touch.

Touch.

Touch.

Touch.

Touch.

Touch.

Chapter 12

'Good morning!' I said as I stepped out into the dormitory hallway wearing a matching skirt and blazer, with a black turtleneck underneath. I pivoted at my dorm-room door and jumped into my electric chair, switching the toggle to turn it on. I waved goodbye to The Tuesday Morning Girl, a fellow college student who had taken it upon herself to dress me on that day of the week. I bounded out at full speed, as quickly as my electric wheelchair could go, to the front door of Belk dormitory, hitting the wheelchair access pad and enjoying the sound of the door flying open at my command. The Student Union President walking by dodged out of my way.

'Woah! Athena!'

'Sorry! Good morning!' I called out after passing him, turning right out of the door and zigzagging down the ramp that was built long after the building itself.

If it is possible, over two years, to make up for a childhood lost because of disability, that is what I did at Davidson. Knocks on my door at ten o'clock on a Saturday evening to suggest that we play a spontaneous game of capture the flag with friends; climbing up the college bell tower; sneaking up on someone in the cafeteria to whisper in their ear, only to have them turn and plant their lips on yours, laughing because, for both of you, that was your first 'kiss'.

My first semester at Davidson, a dean recommended a college senior and a new graduate help me for thirty minutes each in the morning and getting ready for bed, respectively. By the next semester, I lost the morning help. It was suddenly left up to me to find help getting ready for class and making sure that I got breakfast. Lunch was covered by two girlfriends who lived down the hall.

Dinner was Russian roulette at first, but after approaching cafeteria tables of people I knew and trusted, who happened to eat at the same time as me, I had multiple people to turn to for my evening meal. There were many people on campus who enjoyed my company and recognised my needs.

After that first semester, The Tuesday Morning Girl, The Photographer and The Crew Gal put a calendar on my dormitory door. It listed out morning help – 'girls only in the morning, please' – lunch help, dinner help, and people could sign up and help me with every activity of daily living.

The boys added a second list, for people to spot me while using the campus gym.

If someone pulled an all-nighter studying, they would approach a mutual friend to cover them the next morning so they could sleep in.

I had worked hard in high school to ensure that nobody knew what I needed. But the switch to becoming vulnerable, honest and open about all the pieces of me that needed to fit together in order to function settled inside of me a new golden seam of belief that the need for independence was a lie, and had to be changed to an interdependence between equals for any person to survive this life.

I made my way down Main Street, the single street that ran through the town of Davidson. The autumn colours were already turning, highlighting the red brick that had been taken from campus and made a part of the town itself. I ducked behind one of the buildings and into the new hair salon that opened three weeks before the start of my freshman year. 'Davidson Hair Studio', the A-frame board said in Papyrus font.

'Good morning!' I said as I came through the door of the salon, passing the multicoloured bottles of hair products neatly aligned on the shelves. Most people came into the salon a maximum of once every six weeks, but I was there three times a week so that I could keep my waist-length hair clean, braided and out of my face. In the four years I was at Davidson, my hair stylist would never do the same braid more than twice. I went to classes with elaborate crowns and weaves made from my blonde hair, which we turned Moulin Rouge red at the beginning of my junior year.

'Good morning,' the hairdresser said back, turning her salon chair around to face away from the mirror so that I could access it more easily. I parked my wheelchair in between the seats of the waiting area and a shelf holding hair gel. I was perfect at parallel parking, a skill I'd had to master quickly when I transitioned from a manual to an electric wheelchair in college.

This far into the semester, the salon staff had wised up to the fact that they didn't need to make jokes or compliment me on my driving skills. The merit of being a Davidson student, a school that is often cited as 'the Harvard of the South', was that I had a title that finally screamed, 'I am smart!'

I had decided to make college about relationships – friendships – becoming a mixture of easy to be around, charming and fun. I was going to use these four years to catch up on all the things I'd missed out on as a kid. During my first week of class, I bought a sketch pad and a box of 112 Crayola crayons, telling myself that I would draw and colour during my spare hours of the day.

Now that my commute to class was literally twenty-five metres away from my dormitory, or fifty max if I was going to theatre class, I could sleep until 7.30 a.m. and still make the 8.30 class. With a population of only 1,600 students, I'd gone from being a tiny fish in an ocean to a koi in a pond. By the end of the first semester, I had the highest class ranking in my freshman hall.

'What classes are you taking?' my father had asked as we were going through the bookstore stacks to find the reading lists.

'Spanish 250, Greek History 101, Aristophanes' Plays … and Acting 1.'

'Acting 1?' my father said, stopping to look at me. 'Why are you taking Acting 1?'

My logic was simple: I was at a private school, and I was paying full tuition. I could finally take an acting class. There was no, 'I'm sorry, Mrs Stevens, we just wouldn't know what to do with your daughter's disability,' or, 'Is this a realistic expectation to put on our teachers, who are using their spare time to teach children theatre/dance/music/visual arts?'

There was no saying 'no' to me this time.

'I just have to try, just once, just to say I've done it and got it out of my system.'

*

'You're in fluffy slippers, you're dyspraxic, and this is a particularly slippery floor,' I tell my actor. 'I want you to take the time now to make sure you can do all your moves without falling.'

The Sam Wanamaker Playhouse is, for all its charm, probably the most impractical theatre ever built. I'm glad it exists. I'm thankful that we have it. The world doesn't need another one.

Producers at Shakespeare's Globe Theatre had written into its bylaws that this tiny little Jacobean reproduction would only be lit by 'natural light sources'. For the third year in a row, I find myself working there, this time as a writer, actor and director.

I am at the helm of the Globe's biggest new works festival to date: directing twenty new plays, written by twenty women, all of which are twenty minutes long and about various women that history has forgotten or conveniently brushed aside.

I am sitting on one of the yellow wooden pews, and my butt hurts. I have spent the past two hours in near darkness, save for twenty lit candles on the stage reflecting off the mirrored floor. I have been doing the equivalent of ab exercises trying to keep my balance while sitting, perched on a seat that is not only as hard as wood, but a few inches too high for my legs. It is impossible for my feet to rest firmly on the floor and find a point of stability.

I am sweating, and I am also totally lost when it comes to my position in time or space. Rehearsals cause the former no matter the venue. Rehearsing in the Sam Wanamaker, where I'm out of my wheelchair – 'because the wheelchair seating is a terrible seat to direct from' – does the latter.

'Babe, I got it,' the actor shouts back at me in her fuzzy slippers and nightgown. She not only looks out of place, but the Eighties child in me reckons she is highly flammable, too, given her flannel pyjamas and the candlelit atmosphere. The reflection of her body on the floor shows the immense thumbs up she gives to convey that she is set for her performance.

This new actor – I've never worked with her before – is a ticking time bomb of talent.

'Great, you're all set. Everyone ready to go back and get some dinner before call time?' The other three actors are in agreement. 'Tech, are we ready to be done?'

The candle master says he wants to put in a few fresh candles but everyone else can leave. I watch the women shuffle out of the arched back doors, knowing that they are passing through a system of levers and pulleys, digital screens and people in headsets backstage.

I know I need to open my script and look ahead to tomorrow night. I am performing the last piece of the festival, a play that comes in at just over twenty minutes. It fell out of me on a cold January weekend. I've been too busy directing the nineteen other plays to even look at mine.

But then I close the blue binder, look up at the candle lights, the ornately painted grey, brown and gold ceiling that holds stars and cherubs on it. I take one of those moments that I must constantly remind myself to take, otherwise I miss the reforming that is my life. I acknowledge who I am, what I've become, despite so many broken shards and so many fractures.

*

I approached my Acting 1 professor during office hours with trepidation and a written-out list of apologies. He was a bald man in his sixties, known in large part for playing King Lear for a North Carolina theatre troupe. He sat behind his desk in his office, always refusing to turn on the fluorescent overhead lights, so the upright floor lamp in the corner of the room cast a yellow glow and strange shadows against the back wall.

'I know I don't speak clearly and I'm willing to work on that. I've always thought that if I could get a theatrical voice teacher, maybe my articulation would improve. And I know you don't have time for that – you've got your own classes – but I will try my best to be clear during scene presentations. And it's important to me that I use my manual chair in your class. I've done a lot of movement, a lot of physical therapy, and I think I can express myself better if I'm moving on wheels that I propel myself, rather than this electric chair. Can I keep it in a store cupboard of the theatre building? I've always wanted to take a theatre class, and I know this will probably be my only one before I go into my profession. What should I be reading to get the most out of it?'

My three-page list of questions had taken me seven hours to type.

Fifteen weeks, I kept reminding myself. One of which had already passed. Fifteen weeks to get this theatre thing out of my system. I would give it everything I had: read it all, chew it up, spit it out, from Stanislavski to Meisner and any other book I could learn about acting from. Then I would be done. I promised this to myself, and to the logical brain inside my head, which told people, 'I really want to be an actress, but I know that it's impossible, so instead I will be a … blank.' The blank changed to whatever was expected of me.

'Teacher' had become as far afield as I was willing to stray. It was liberal and not well paid, and it provoked sighs from family members who swore up and down that I could change the world as a lawyer; that I would be bored teaching. Law, maybe even medicine, the State Department – all these things I was capable of. But I knew teaching the best; it made sense to me.

'Was that good enough?' I asked the professor after the class. It was a random scene of thrown-together words, an exercise rather than an excerpt from an actual play. The words themselves were not meaningful unless one took the time to imbue them with some sort of intention. I was so worried that I would miss a line in the ninety-second exchange that I seriously thought about writing the words on my hand. The preparation that morning had made me nearly sick to my stomach.

'Yeah, you'll get an A, don't worry about it.' But even I knew that an A didn't mean 'best'. An A meant that I had done my work; it didn't mean that I was brilliant. It didn't mean that I was really understanding what this theatre thing was about.

*

The phrase 'in the bleak midwinter' takes on a whole new meaning during December 2020.

The theatre industry is dying.

We need to go back to work.

Nobody in the arts wants to say it, but I know. Another lockdown is coming.

Tonight, I am sitting in the Actors' Church as a Hollywood Star stops singing Joni Mitchell's 'River' for the sixth time in a row.

I hit send on an email to a director at Shakespeare's Globe as soon as the cameras stop rolling.

'No, no, no!' says The Hollywood Star. 'Can we cut the smoke machines? I'm really struggling up there as it is – the haze isn't helping.'

I have never seen a professional suddenly stretched to the end of her rope by nothing but nebulised molecules thrown forcefully in the air. I say 'nothing but', yet I know, in all of our minds, those molecules carry moisture, and anyone who took basic biology or has watched the news in the last nine months knows that moisture is where germs and viruses breed.

'Of course. Sorry!' a familiar voice from the darkness shouts out. I was scheduled to be taping fifteen minutes ago, and we have spent the past hour on this performance.

As usual in filming, things aren't going to plan. Which means, on some level, things are going exactly to plan if you have the humility to recognise that what you intend to happen rarely follows the schedule. This is why you always bring something to do when you're on set. In this case, I have written a response to a florid email about 'green shoots' of hope coming during this Covid winter. The writer of the email ended with a parable about the Japanese custom of kintsugi: how gold paint is used to repair broken pottery, highlighting the reality of the cracks and making the piece 'more beautiful than it would have been otherwise'.

It's a rank, Westernised oversimplification of trauma that I can't let go of. There's no mention of the fact that the original piece of pottery upon which kintsugi was applied was only broken because of a man's arrogance and temper. The author skips over the reality that the gold lacquer used is toxic to humans, and that the pottery shattered in a second can take decades to mend. Ensuring that no piece is lost over years of waiting is as much part of the healing process as waiting for the glue to dry. And, of course, the original email doesn't state the reality that the mended vase was never supposed to be broken at all.

To me, the email from the Globe seems like cheap holiday optimism in the bleakest midwinter – like the Christmas cards about Jonny's first steps thrown in the trash by my father. The cheap platitudes of misunderstood kintsugi sent in this email neglect the complex fortitude of waiting in hope, which personifies this season. So, I felt bound to share these intricacies in an email (to which I would never receive a response). The orchestra starts up again with the introduction to Joni Mitchell's song, and I sit in the darkness holding the script I've written, commissioned barely ten days ago. My five-minute piece from the point of view of Scrooge's ex-fiancée is blown up to size-twenty bold font so that it can be read at a distance, because writing at such speed left no time for memorisation.

The director, who concedes to the singer's requests from the darkness, knows me. He commissioned this piece urgently, and I have already gone through in my mind where the pages will be sellotaped so that I can see them without breaking eye contact with the camera.

The Dresser holds the oversized roll of Sellotape in her hand, playing with it, back and forth, finding the end that needs to be pulled in order to access the sticky bit. She stops as the cameras roll once more.

We sit on the back pews of the Actors' Church. I am keenly aware that this is a place where Dickens himself could have visited at some point. I look around to see plaques for Noël Coward and Charlie Chaplin.

I suddenly feel this well of energy rise up from my diaphragm into the middle of my chest, forming a knot that puts pressure on my eyes, causing them to water. *Don't make a sound, they're filming,* I tell myself.

And then there is silence in the church.

The Director looks at me, and I have worked with him for long enough to know what that look means. It's a look that he and I can give each other because we trust each other's work. A look that says, 'Do you think you can pull this off in one take and get us back on schedule?'

Yes. Yes, I do.

The Director cues for my performance to have the fog machine.

I have got over the tears that I shed in the back pew while I was waiting for the Joni Mitchell song to end; the tears that came because, once again, I am alone at Christmas, seated next to an empty chair that I wish was filled. This is my annual season of sadness that comes at the end of yet another year of being a single, disabled, immigrant woman.

The difference is that this year, 2020, many more empty chairs will be set at tables than any of us expected when the year started.

'Don't start crying. It'll run your eyeliner,' The Dresser whispers to me, slinging an arm over my back.

'We're in Covent Garden,' I hiss back. 'There's a Bobbi Brown store right round the corner.'

There is a sense that, not only do I need to get this monologue absolutely right in one take, but that perhaps today is the last day that any of us can meet inside again for the rest of the year, if not longer. Time is precious. A moment stolen in the back of a church, sitting on a wooden pew, laughing with a friend, seems like the closest thing we will receive this Christmas to some semblance of normality.

I deliver the first line with the cameras rolling, seated in an evening gown that strangely mimics the attire of the Victorian period: 'Nobody ever told me that Christmas was so wrapped up in grief.'

*

I marvelled at the ability to drive an electric wheelchair, still a new phenomenon in my life, down the paths of Davidson. I was heading nowhere in particular, but doing it at full speed, enjoying the wind on my face and the smiles I presented to my fellow class members.

I hadn't been in a theatre class since my first semester, but somehow, I was the assistant sound designer for the upcoming production of Tony Kushner's 1991 play *Angels in America*. I knew nothing about how it should sound.

The entire production was shrouded in whispers around the mostly conservative Christian campus. The design professor had worked on the original production in Charlotte, North Carolina, which was shut down by the authorities for being 'lewd' and advocating homosexual behaviour.

The day before, we'd had what I learned was a 'production meeting'. The director was presented with samples for every single costume. She felt the materials, rejecting or accepting the possibility, commenting on the design boards, and working with the dramaturg to make sure that the production would somehow fit into Davidson's educational curriculum. Every detail was considered, thought through, talked about, debated, laughed about.

By my second semester at Davidson, there was no one who did not know me.

Every once in a while, an alumni weekend would be held. An older couple would be strolling around their old haunt, see me and, often using a false baby voice, say, 'Are you a student here? How nice they let people like you in now.' A student the year ahead of me, whose dad was a firefighter on 9/11, saw the encounter from a distance. He jogged the thirty feet between us as the elders walked on.

'Man, I saw that bullshit!' The Fireman's Son bounced on his feet as if he wanted to go after them. 'Do you want me to—'

'It's fine. You've just gotta smile through it. Happens all the time. People don't know better.'

'If they're old enough to do it, they are old enough to be told it's wrong.'

'No, let them go about their day. I don't want it to be a thing. Let's be kind,' I say to The Fireman's Son. Though I considered it. *Maybe we should tell them, otherwise how will they change? Maybe they would listen to The Fireman's Son if they couldn't listen to me.*

'They probably thought the same thing about Black folk when they saw me.'

'Wait until they meet The Student Union President tonight.'

'You going to the library?'

'Yeah, I need to return a few scripts.'

'You just be you, baby girl. You don't need to be anything else. We've got your back.'

Going into the brown and dusty theatre building, I thought about the level of care and intelligence I had seen during the production meeting the day before. I didn't want to leave this world of imagination and reality meeting onstage.

I considered what I should do. I thought of the majors I went on insisting that I would study: history and philosophy. I was also taking metaphysics. The German-born professor drawled on and on about how the existence of possible worlds meant opportunities were infinite. There was a possible world out there where the sky was green, or I might not have cerebral palsy. There was a possible world out there where, when someone asked me what I wanted to be, I could end the sentence with: 'I want to be an actor.'

There was a possible world where I was my authentic self. The entire thing seemed far-flung from the lessons of Kierkegaard and Plato that Mr Odysseus had taught me the year before.

The metaphysics teacher claimed weekly that there was a possible world where anything was possible. I thought that was called imagination, not philosophy. But what about this world? Why can't this be the possible world where I am in theatre? Why submit to what is called impossible after a lifetime of making the impossible things – walking, putting on eyeliner, sitting up independently, learning not to drool – possible? How can I say that all people have dignity, that all men, all humans, are created equal and are worthy of this dignity, if I'm not willing to give it to myself?

'I want to major in theatre,' I said as I walked up to the professor/scenic designer who was currently wielding a circle blade in his hand. He stopped building the set for *Angels in America*, took his goggles off and looked at me. I could see the outline of dust and sweat that covered the rest of his face, his eyes clean.

'Well,' he said. And then a long pause. It was something that we all made fun of him for and a trait that he had, as a result, owned. His slow starting and stopping of speech gave the impression that he was a very careful man who thinks about his words. 'Have a think about … who you want your advisor to be.'

He put his goggles back on, and I immediately blurted out: 'I want it to be you!' He stood upright and put down the saw, looking at me. 'I like you. I like the way you talk, and you don't rush things, and the only teacher I've had is my teacher for Acting 1, but he doesn't have tenure so he can't be my advisor. I like working with you on this play – I think we would work well together.'

The silence of my last words hung in the air with the plywood sawdust. Now, I wished he wasn't quite so slow to speak. He nodded. 'When does disability kick in for you?'

I was confused by the question. On the surface, he seemed to be asking when my disability had started. But that was nineteen years ago. Then I connected that he might be thinking about money; like there's some special pot of gold that people get if they're disabled in America.

'What I mean is: when do you start getting government cheques to take care of your disability? Because that's the only way you'll survive while working in theatre.'

Chapter 13

The Super Genius of Davidson, who had her own disability, decided to graduate early. She was a junior when I was a freshman, and she already had all her courses lined up to graduate with honours before immediately going into a philosophy programme at St Andrews in Scotland. At first, I assumed she wanted to leave early because of her health, but the PhD programme halfway across the world suggests otherwise.

My first year away from home, feeling so liberated and enjoying the warm weather, left me baffled at her decision.

'Davidson is like a womb. It's all soft and squishy and warm while you're growing. But sooner or later there comes a day when you feel cramped and it's impossible to move. All you can think is: get me the fuck out of here.'

It took two years, but I got there, too: the fact that my world ended when the Davidson community pavements stopped and turned into grass, ultimately following an off-ramp onto the highway; the fact that, despite having declared my major a year before, I still had yet to be cast in a mainstage production; the fact that the Christians on campus started to ostracise me when I would hang out with gay students, and not evangelise on the beach. All these details, which in isolation could be ignored, started to feel like the walls were closing in on this North Carolina campus.

'I have to go to London this year. Not giving me a grant is not an option. It's the European Year of People with Disabilities and I have a voice teacher lined up who said she would help me with my speech. I don't know when she'll be available to work with me again. It's such a good opportunity!'

In the Davidson cafeteria, I begged the dean in charge of foreign study grants to reconsider his decision. At $4,500, the cost for me to go abroad was higher than for most, but I wasn't including the fees it would cost me to take two personal assistants with me. Three students on one student's foreign study trip, and he couldn't seem to get the mathematics of the bargain I offered.

'Most students are capped at $3,000 for a summer grant.'

Of course, I'd read that figure and, as I'd explained in my application, $3,000 was not feasible for me. I had to live next to a Tube station. The two Davidson students-cum-personal assistants would cost me about $1,500 each. I would pay for this, so surely they could stretch the budget a little given my disability?

For whatever reason, this 'no' as I asked for a grant to study disability in theatre seemed louder and more unfair than any 'no' I'd ever encountered in my life. But I pushed, and I got my way.

Soon, I was buying tickets for myself and two graduating seniors for six weeks in London, followed by three weeks backpacking throughout Europe. I assumed that I was not going to make it to the other side of the Atlantic ever again, so I figured I'd better get the whole backpacking and Euro-rail pass thing done. *Then I will settle down*, I told myself. *Then I will go back to becoming a teacher, and live the life that makes sense with the forces of momentum I have been given.*

*

When I arrived at the immigration desk at Heathrow Airport, I was too exhausted to go on.

I tried to speak to the immigration official, but between my lack of sleep and my disarticulate speech, he found it difficult to understand me, which was embarrassing. It made me wonder what on Earth I was doing even setting foot in this country.

I turned to one of my two personal assistants to ask for help in answering the questions posed by the intimidating officer in uniform. This proved not only to be my first mistake, but also to set the tone for the next six weeks: a deferral. Me not wanting to get into trouble; afraid that the fragile construct of our trio would topple over if I were to breathe the wrong way.

We stayed with a family in Hounslow who offered two rooms – a downstairs annex for me and my female PA, and an upstairs bedroom that used to be their son's. At about £30 a night, it was a good deal when you're travelling with multiple genders and need three beds. Hounslow, Zone 4 of London, though, was far enough away from the centre of the city that, in the back of my mind, I kept thinking, *This is nice. When are we going to get to London?*

Hounslow East was meant to be one of the rare Underground stations that is accessible, except the only lift in operation was for the journey on the way into town. To come back home, there was no working lift yet. So, on our return each evening, I would get out of my wheelchair and walk downstairs with the support of one of my assistants, while the other one carried my lightweight, yellow manual chair behind her. We looked like some sort of odd, limping parade that was once meant to have stature, but was now beguiled by the complexities of the lack of accessibility.

The resentments of life being difficult began to pile up. I was groomed to take those resentments onto my shoulders. It was my fault life was complicated. But my ability to slap on a smile and minimise the difficulties for the sake of protecting my own mental health, and holding this fragile threesome together, was proving to be impossible.

'I don't think London is the problem. I think I want to come back to London, but with one other person instead of two,' I mused as we made our way down Hounslow High Street, the female personal assistant pushing my chair.

We got along somewhat better without the guy in our midst.

The guy and I got along fine without her in our midst.

'No. Absolutely not. Athena, that is a terrible idea! The only reason we've been able to survive this trip is because there's two of us. I am telling you right now, do not put another two people – do not put *anybody* for that matter – through the hell you've just put us through. Enjoy the fact that you got to travel to London and Europe once. But I am telling you, it is wrong to attempt anything like this ever again.'

She had told me the first week we got to London that it was wrong to spend money in an effort to create equality for myself. Doing so was 'operating under a wildly capitalist system'. It was wrong for me to expect them to be willing to take my manual wheelchair up and down stairs for weeks on end. Even travelling was wrong, and I needed to make my world smaller.

Back at Davidson after London, I struggled to write up the academic side of my journey, asking again and again for an extension on the document I was obligated to create as part of receiving the grant. The shows I watched blurred one into the other as I spent hours staring at the wall. I would become alert at three in the morning only to find myself sat in a bathtub full of tepid water, not really sure how I got there, but marvelling at the fact that I did. Cerebral palsy usually made every movement conscious.

The promises made to me that I would have a place in this world, and that I would be able to shape whatever environment I found myself in, suddenly rang hollow. If all 'men' were created equal, and 'men' had been redefined again and again over the centuries, then why did the female personal assistant insist that I had no place in Europe? Why did the male personal assistant refuse to let me borrow his books when he was done with them, saying he didn't want them torn up by my hands?

What was my role in changing this world if I could not change these two people? What had I done wrong that made me fail to do exactly that?

The psychiatrist at Davidson asked, 'So this was the first time in life you really ran into obstacles?'

I knew that wasn't true, but it was easier to agree.

*

'Whatever you do, in the next two weeks, you need to make yourself indispensable. You don't know what doors are going to open up.' My singing teacher at Davidson took me by the shoulders and looked me dead in the eye as she said these words. This is what we had been waiting for.

Time with the Royal Shakespeare Company, a residency that I was promised I would witness during my junior year, was about to start. The company were flying in during spring break, while the campus was empty, to load in and do their technical rehearsals for *Two Gentlemen of Verona* and *Julius Caesar* on alternating nights.

After the fiasco that was my summer in London, I struggled to get back to Davidson. I had even debated with my parents whether I wanted to return to Davidson at all. The six weeks abroad had exhausted me, making me erase myself and question my place in the world.

Just before Thanksgiving, the school psychiatrist had put me on antidepressants after declaring that the trip, and specifically the behaviour of the two people my family and I had chosen to be my companions, had given me PTSD. What use was an education from a facility where new graduates only resorted to bickering and rolling their eyes due to the 'inconvenience' of it all? We had even looked at the drama department of the University of Nevada, Las Vegas over Christmas break, while on a family holiday to the city where what happens there stays there. I had decided to stay one more semester at Davidson because of the Royal Shakespeare Company.

I went into an overpopulated and hot room, full of loud actors laughing and holding their drinks and taking turns on the piano. I still remember the smell of my lipstick lingering on my lips, thinking about how I had just put it on moments before in the dorm room, not wanting to go to this welcome party for the RSC. The combination of slightly floral but mostly mineral scents hung in the air as I steadied my hand and retouched the lipstick.

How was I supposed to smile and say, 'Welcome to Davidson'?

'Have you ever been to London?' The actors at the party opened with this. It's meant to be an innocuous ice breaker, of course, and so I smiled and nodded and explained that I was there just last summer seeing productions to study disability in theatre. 'Oh. That guy over there was in that. See him? The bald one?'

As I named productions, they pointed out who auditioned for what and who I would've seen onstage. There were about four such actors in total.

I walked back to my dormitory smiling. I had dreaded this evening and almost hadn't gone at all, but I liked these visitors from the UK. More than that, I was already feeling something different than the basic pull of affection: I connected with them. I communicated with them. My heart beat to the same iambic pentameter as this group; an ensemble where everybody, in theory at least, should be welcome. A group where there was no awkward small talk, or people patronising me for my presumed lack of intelligence. I didn't just want to be part of their theatre world, I felt like I was supposed to be. And that evening, I felt like I was.

A few days later, I found The Leading Lady perched on a high chair, checking her Hotmail account at a computer kiosk in the Student Union.

'Tell me how I can become like you.'

The question came out clumsily. I didn't want to be like her – I couldn't be like her by any stretch of the imagination. I wanted to be an actor. I wanted to be in theatre. I wanted to do whatever she had done to get to where she was now.

'Drama school,' she answered with two words. 'You have to go to drama school. I went to RADA – that stands for the Royal Academy of Dramatic Art. That's, like, the classical one, but there are others. There's LAMDA, there's Guilford – do you want me to write these down for you?'

Twelve days into my relationship with the Ensemble, and The Leading Lady knew that I can't write things down for myself. She reached around to my lilac backpack hanging off my electric wheelchair, unzipped the largest pocket and took out a notebook. 'Is this one OK?' I nodded.

She swung back around and perched herself on the high chair again, logging out of her Hotmail account. And then The Leading Lady started writing, talking me through five or six various options, circling and making notes of what might be a good fit and how to choose two monologues (one classical, one contemporary) to use for audition pieces. I wanted conservatory training – real artist training. Not a BA in a subject that colleges regard as a 'break' from the real purpose of going to school: to advance to either business school, law school or medical school.

The Leading Lady invited me to visit her, as would every person who put their phone number and address into my notebook the night of their leaving party.

'Come to London!'

'When you get there, call me.'

'We'll have a great time eating at Wagamama on the South Bank.'

'Come to London!'

The world as you want it to be is maybe in the place where you never thought it was.

The Ensemble told me to put on as much theatre as possible for my last year and a half or so at Davidson. I had been debating whether or not to create my own show for the mainstage for months. Past graduates had done it, and I was eager to find something that would give me hope and get me out of my post-London depression.

The head of the technical team of the performance hall had blocked out a weekend at the end of April long in advance with my name on it.

'Nothing else is going on that weekend, so if you want to, you can have the theatre.'

Having worked as a lightboard operator earlier in my Davidson career, I sat in the technical booth and helped the lighting designer do a cue to cue. I managed the sound and selected the actors out of a pool of Davidson students who were looking to do something fun for a few weeks.

Then my advisor invited me into his office, his voice sounding out from the hallway and causing my motorised wheelchair to stop and turn into the room where he sat behind his desk. I expected him to give me the passcode to log in to the system to arrange my classes for the upcoming fall semester.

I could hear the other students' laughter outside dim as he shut the door behind me and locked it.

What followed was two and a half hours of verbal assault. I had upset the theatre department by putting on my own production. I hadn't been cast in anything because my B+ grade point average wasn't as high as it should be. My writing was shit. I had gone over their heads and done something insidious. I had embarrassed them by paying more attention to the RSC than I ever did in their classes. I was a disappointment. I was not good enough to be writing anything that was fit to be in anyone's mouth at this point in my life, and it would be a very long time before I had the skills to do so, if ever. I was deceitful, dishonest, and never told them the full truth about my plans for the April production. The Fireman's Son would later remind me that my name had been on the Union's production calendar for that weekend since October. But that was little comfort to me.

For two and a half hours on that sunny spring day, I sat in front of yet another chipboard desk as my advisor rattled off again and again all the ways in which I was a disappointment to him.

The only thing I can remember saying to him was at the end of his tirade. I did not cry, nor did I gasp or scream. It was a first in what would eventually become a pattern in my adult life: 'informal chats' behind closed doors to mask the sound of a verbal battering.

I remember how it ended.

'I always considered you to be like a daughter to me, and I am very disappointed in your behaviour.'

'I already have a father, and he's a really good one,' I replied.

Chapter 14

I didn't want to live on campus my last year of college. Frankly, my last 'year' of college would be a semester. Any semblance that had remained of Davidson being a safe place was gone. I turned cold every time I saw my advisor in the hall.

'Do not apologise to him,' my father instructed. 'Don't apologise because you don't feel sorry. If you do, any apology for the rest of your life will mean less after faking one.'

There was a new teacher, a visiting professor who was only there for two years. When I said I wanted to do another play in the black box theatre, I was told that the new professor would supervise me.

I was now the problem in the department.

I took refuge with the English department, who were excited that the RSC would be returning in the spring, for a much smaller teaching residency.

My private singing teacher and I decided that this year, rather than worrying about what would or would not please the Davidson theatre department, my main focus would be preparing for drama-school auditions.

The fracture between myself and my professors, as well as my shift in focus, might best be exemplified in the fact that I was suddenly thrust into the chorus for the college's musical during parents' weekend, yet, due to what I justified to myself as a drama-school recce trip to London, I would inevitably miss the first rehearsal, which fell on the Sunday concluding fall break. I was due to land right as the rehearsal was starting, making it impossible to get from the airport to Davidson before the end of the session. For once, I was breaking the rules. I was putting myself first, and the theatre department was going to have to deal with it.

During that trip to London, I ran one of my audition pieces for The Leading Lady – a monologue from *Julius Caesar*. I had worked on it with my singing teacher. We sounded out the articulation at 25 per cent speed, and attempted to get my resonance as strong as I could, while still not knowing how to move my soft palate.

I looked up, having finished my monologue, which ended on the floor as Portia begs Brutus to tell her the truth. I looked at The Leading Lady, and she had tears in her eyes.

I watched her swallow; the bump in her throat moved down in order to make room for her voice to come out. Then she put her hands together as if she were praying and shook them towards me.

'This is going to be a long, uphill battle, but you have to do it. You have to pursue acting. I don't know if you will get into drama school, but I do know this: you're a fucking good actor. And it's going to take your fire to blaze a trail.'

I quickly reminded myself that this only meant as much as the one person it was coming from. It didn't guarantee me anything. But the thing I most picked up on was that my acting wouldn't be the issue. The struggle for me to stare down ableism in the industry would be intense. I would be the one given that task – at least, according to The Leading Lady.

*

Our budget is out of control. Our producer has quit after weeks of goading me to fire her. Everyone else expected me to make amends, but I wasn't sure she was worth the effort.

Admittedly, I had seen this coming, but each time, I folded my hands and shut my mouth in the hopes that it wouldn't happen. *Maybe this time it will work out*, I told myself.

The final straw came when I noticed that everyone, including my male counterpart, was being paid, except for me. According to the budget, there is no money for me. The difficulty is that being a spokesperson for the Women's Equality Party means that equal pay is put on my agenda in a rather large way.

'This isn't a commission. There's no room in the budget to pay you!'

Actually, there is room in the budget: the money set aside for my wage as a performer is now placed in the column of what we will pay the male actor. His fee rose to be exactly and conveniently doubled, while my fee was eradicated.

It feels as if everybody is getting a free ride, holding on to me.

When the producer leaves, I refuse to make a scene. Inside, my heart is cracking. I have not done well enough yet again, and things are falling apart.

*

'What do you want to do?' My roommate had blonde hair with curls that fell down past the middle of her back, the kind of hair that Shakespeare would have written about. That day, it was tied back in a ponytail.

She had several days 'off' while I was in London. I covered her rent that year in exchange for her helping me get out of bed and ready for Davidson each morning, or to act as a personal assistant in random situations, like a pick-up from Charlotte Douglas International Airport after returning from clandestine recces abroad.

'Go to the theatre building. I should try to make it to at least part of the rehearsal if I can.'

'You sure? Wouldn't it be better if you just made a clean break?'

I don't know.

To not go to the rehearsal would be straight-up defiance. To go would make for a very uncomfortable few days.

As we took the exit towards Davidson, my pulse started to race, and I tried to suppress the horrible feeling of oncoming conflict.

We pulled into the car park next to the theatre building. It was completely dark. We looked at each other. Before going through the trouble of taking my manual wheelchair out of the trunk, she went up to the double doors that led into the building.

They were locked.

I gave her the plastic key that was meant to open every door on campus. She swiped it. The doors were still locked.

Was I locked out?

The headlights of another car illuminated the car park and pulled into a place a few feet away from us. The new Davidson theatre professor jumped out.

'What are you doing here?'

I felt morally obligated to come clean. 'I'm trying to get into rehearsal for the musical, but the doors seem locked and I know I—'

'That's odd. Let me get in with my faculty key.'

Shakespeare's Blonde took my wheelchair from the trunk of her car. I edged towards the door, pushing the rims of my wheels, while the professor flipped the switch, flooding the building with fluorescent, shadowless light.

I listened to nothing but a deafening silence in the building as I walked around to where the call boards and rehearsal schedules were. There, posted in the middle of the call board, was a new rehearsal schedule. Sunday evening was … blank.

*

The night before load-in for *Schism*, I am at the Aldwych Theatre for a fundraiser.

I am to sit in a box with celebrities while Richard III is being put on trial. Was he a monster? Or is he unfairly framed for history's mistakes and miscalculations? It's a fun way of raising money, and each of us as 'jurors' have been given a packet of information to help inform our verdict. Having written my verdict last week, I made sure it was less than the limit of twenty seconds. A few carefully placed words, a laugh or two, and that would be me out.

When it comes to be my turn, I start to give my spiel. I'm cut short.

'No one can understand you. Just a simple "guilty" or "not guilty", please.'

I am stunned.

I don't remember my verdict. I say what I say and exit the box as soon as possible, making a beeline with my date towards the taxis.

The words 'no one can understand you' keep me up all night. The notion that they didn't want to understand me never enters my head.

In the back of a black cab the next morning, I start sobbing.

By the time I get to the theatre, my eyes are bloodshot and my throat is raw. Three times the cab driver offers to pull over, but I don't want to be late. I don't want to be a burden. I don't want to make the whole precarious production – which has already been shaken by me not chasing after our producer – fall apart.

*

My last semester studying at Davidson passed by in a combination of lightning bolts and sludge. Moments of working, against times of procrastination.

The lightning-bolt moments were when I worked on my audition songs one-on-one with a pianist for half an hour every day. I spent hours in the voice studio going over the syllables of Shakespeare again and again; Saturdays were spent organising applications, traveller's cheques and audition monologues. I devoted myself to preparing for my auditions with the same intensity as I did physiotherapy every morning during my childhood.

Then, one lightning bolt flashed unexpectedly. The theatre department offered for me to put on my own production in their small black-box theatre, the proposition tinged with an air of, 'No harm done, don't worry, let's just brush everything under the rug. We all get along here, don't we?'

The weeks passed on, and I promised myself that I would finish my script for that production that weekend. And then the next. And then the next. Five weeks away from the show, it still wasn't done. So, for the first and only time ever, I did what every American kid stereotypically spends their college years doing: myself and a friend, who had a paper due the following Monday, each got a pint of ice cream and a bottle of wine. We sat down at the little mosaic folding table I bought when I moved into my off-campus apartment. We ate, we drank, we wrote, we laughed when we noticed the effects of the drink, and then we wrote some more.

The sludge of not-writing shifted and morphed into a landslide of words as dialogue hit the page, moving the story to an end.

Throughout the writing process, I had flashbacks of being locked in my advisor's office, and I realised that my instability didn't come from me, or my lack of talent, or an insecurity about what I was capable of. Rather, this sense of instability came as the inevitable consequence of feeling like the sword of Damocles was constantly hanging above my head. My professors had shown that they could withdraw their support any time they wished. With those I was dependent on to graduate, I had no autonomy, only the obligation to keep them happy. My grades that semester were stunningly low.

This time, when the play finally went ahead, the entire theatre department did indeed turn up and gave me rousing applause. This, I was thoroughly sure, was unwarranted. After all, I had written the play largely in a weekend, with the help of Ben & Jerry's, and a bottle of Yellow Tail wine.

At the end of the second night, which was also the last night of the run, my advisor appeared in the dressing room right as I was putting my street clothes back on. In his hand, he held a single red rose. It felt like an olive branch, but the rose's head was already beginning to droop from needing water. I plastered a smile on my face because he had one on his. This was the expected response. As I went to take the rose with my full hand open, throbbing with inconsistent movement, he yanked it away.

'Careful, there are still thorns attached.'

I looked at the stem of the rose, and it was covered with not just a few thorns, but hundreds of tiny barbs. I had worked with my advisor for over three years, and he still didn't know enough about me to notice that I couldn't isolate the movement of my individual fingers.

That January, with my grades completed and my play done, all I had left to do was focus on my voice and body training, and in March, three people from the previous RSC Ensemble would be back. These two factors were enough to give me hope at Davidson. For the first time in my life, my every action wasn't being dictated by a bell or a timetable. I had my daily appointments with the pianist, and my now-twice-weekly appointments with my singing teacher, but that was all. We went over the monologues and songs again and again. Like building an Italian repertoire, one piece could take months to perfect.

This time, the RSC would be directing Davidson students, not their own actors. Because I was no longer a student, I could not be considered as a possible casting option for their educational production, but I still had hopes that I would learn from the residency.

*

The education head of the RSC agreed to let the two actors in residence run a mock audition for me. I needed to prepare as the tour of British drama schools was quickly approaching. The actors were the understudy of The Leading Lady and a man who looked like a wolf. One was dark, the other had silver-grey hair.

By the time I finished the Shakespeare piece, I was again on the floor. The Wolf rolled my chair to me and held it as I got in.

'Good,' he said. 'Can I just try something right now?'

'Yes, absolutely.'

'I want you to pretend like I am Brutus. And I want you to respond to how I am reacting to your words.'

I went through my lines again. This time The Wolf stepped away from me, turned to look at me again, and took a breath like he was going to interrupt. This caused me to put more force behind my words. And then I was done.

'Thank you. That is all.'

The head of education had joined the two actors, forming an auditioning triumvirate. When I was done, the understudy to The Leading Lady peppered me with questions. Then I was sent backstage so that the three of them could talk.

Time stops when you can no longer see the seats of the theatre, particularly if you're waiting to be judged. At that moment, you run through all your rehearsals and your notes, trying to do calculations in your head of what was expected of you, what resources you had and the effort you put forth leading up to this moment.

Then I heard my name, and I rolled onstage to face the three panellists.

'Well, if any of us worked on a drama-school auditions committee, we would be telling them to take you with flying colours.' I can't remember who said this, the rush of it being said at all overriding the details.

'So, why Portia?' The Wolf asked.

'I related to Portia,' I replied. 'She thought her husband would listen to her, and he didn't. So, she was reduced to swallowing hot coals in order to prove her strength.'

That night there was another party, but the professional actors retreated back to the Davidson guest house for quiet drinks in the small library with some of the people they had become close to the previous year. I heard some of them laughing as I was waiting for the Shakespearean Blonde to pick me up.

'Where's Athena?' I heard The Wolf say.

The now-graduated student sitting next to him said, 'She's outside in the foyer running her lines.'

'Oh, good for her. Although she doesn't need to.'

I knew what The Wolf had said was genuine, and I was grateful he had said it out loud. Years later, I would learn from The Wolf that the theatre department had specifically requested this mock audition from the RSC. The trio were asked to dissuade me from auditioning for drama schools.

*

'No!' The Dresser and I say together as the door tries to eke open, The Dresser slamming herself against it for the umpteenth time. I am in the middle of a quick change, naked except for my bra, and once again Mr Bumbling wants to 'just sneak through' my dressing area.

The five-year-old, multi-million-pound theatre lacks an accessible quick-change area. There is a small, soundproof breezeway in the space between the offices, the flight of stairs leading to the dressing rooms and the auditorium itself. Six feet by four feet, maybe. And it is here that I carry out five of my eight costume changes, the other three taking place onstage, assisted by The Male Lead.

We have been in performance for over three weeks. Despite the addition of a 'Do Not Enter' sign to the door, as well as an email expressing our frustration about the situation, Mr Bumbling and his staff continue to ignore our demands. He always opens the door saying, 'Can I just sneak through?' sounding flaccid and harmless. Later, I would learn that there had been other accusations about this man and his inappropriate behaviour towards actors.

'Go away, now!' The Dresser bangs on the door so loudly that I am afraid she will be heard in the auditorium. Like any pest, assertion is sometimes not enough to get rid of them entirely, but at least it will assuage conflict momentarily.

'Fuck me! What is it going to take?' I say, as I put the bathrobe onto my shoulders, holding it as she tightens the belt. She takes a pail of water and draws two duck-shaped sponges out of the lukewarm liquid as I put my head into the bucket. It is a sort of theatrical baptism of convenience to make it look as if I have been freshly yanked out of the shower. The Male Lead enters backstage, to the sound of my voice screaming via a recording on the auditorium's overhead speakers.

'Calm down,' The Male Lead whispers, seeing our rushed move-ments. 'Are you guys—'

'You don't know half of what we've been through back here,' I say, as he picks me up and The Dresser holds the door open for us to return onstage. I flop over in his arms to appear as helpless and feminine as Mr Bumbling assumes me to be.

These are the realities of what too often occurs backstage, out of view of the audience, only this time, the audience consists of forty Year Nines; thirteen- and fourteen-year-olds whose teacher has decided that a play written and performed by a disabled woman 'would be a wonderful learning experience about disabled people'.

The play is about a fourteen-year-old who is groomed by her high-school teacher to become dependent on him for twenty years. He sticks her up on a pedestal when he needs to feel good about himself, only to tear her down and abuse her when her light begins to eclipse his. The play's climax comes when she begins bleeding out onstage from a botched abortion, and he proceeds to beat her unconscious in her bed. I had begged the theatre in pre-production to put trigger warnings and age advisories on the publicity pack sent out to schools and the press.

As soon as I learn that a school is coming for the matinee, I don't want to go onstage. After the interval, I want to return even less, knowing the inevitable fallout that is about to occur, complete with vaginal haemorrhaging.

'Maybe there's a boy out there who will find himself in love with a disabled woman, and maybe he won't hurt her like other boys have hurt me. Maybe this play will stop that. That's all I can focus on right now.'

This type of justification is one that comes so easily to me in moments of crisis, and The Dresser knows it. I look at her and she pulls the pyjama top over me.

'Yeah, that's a good way of looking at it,' she says calmly.

'Or maybe one of the students has a family member that is going through something similar, and seeing this will give them a language for their trauma.'

Keep focus on the good that can come out of doing this very nearly impossible thing. That is all that matters right now. I'm willing to go through the humiliation onstage if it means that one disabled person somewhere, somehow connected to these students, doesn't have to go through the ableism that I have gone through. One person – that's all it takes to justify this painful performance.

The door to the office starts to open again.

'Go around!' The Dresser shouts as she kicks the door closed.

Both myself and The Male Lead are in position on stage at the end of the interval, before the audience re-enters.

I sit at my desk and take out a protractor and pencil. I remember Mr

Game Day back at Stevenson, who flashed a yellow 'You're My Hero' badge across the table at my IEP meeting, and who taught me how to use a protractor. I count to thirty, when the stage manager should give clearance to let the audience back in. Thirty passes, and then sixty, then ninety, one hundred and twenty. Mr Game Day didn't teach me enough about how to use protractors to occupy me for much longer.

When the doors finally open, the students file in, extremely silent for a group of teenagers. I don't look up to acknowledge their existence, but I notice that they don't sit down. They grab their bags and then walk back out of the theatre. An audience of nearly fifty is now an audience of five. Another minute or so passes, and the stage manager climbs down from her box. I look up at her briefly, and she has a look of confusion on her face, which matches precisely how I feel. She goes to the entrance of the auditorium and opens the door, walking out.

Now The Male Lead and I sit in our places, doing our stage business, with an audience of five watching us and no stage manager. This should never happen.

After a protracted delay, the stage manager comes back. She walks across the stage – where she does not belong.

'We will begin the performance in two minutes. This is clearance,' and she climbs her way up the ladder to her box.

Back in the green room after the show, I look down at my micro-waved dinner. I shake my head when The Dresser lifts the spoon full of hot goop towards my mouth. I have lost my appetite.

'The teacher said that her students were not prepared for your level of disability,' the new producer says to me. There is an element of disgust in his voice that does little to take the sting out of the statement.

And then Mr Bumbling decides to have an opinion: 'Well, a leopard doesn't change its spots, so what's the point in trying to change this teacher?'

The stage manager comes in and gives us the half-hour notice for the evening's production.

*

'Give us a call when you get into London,' The Wolf said, handing me his overly complex British phone number.

'I know how inaccessible the London Underground is, and I keep thinking, if I'm late, I'll be in trouble.'

'Don't be ridiculous – if you're late, you're late. Not like you're going to be the first person to ever audition for a drama school and be late.'

'I might be the first disabled person to audition for that drama school.'

'So? You have as much right to be constrained by London transport as anyone, if not more.'

At that moment, a deep tightness in my chest unwound. Why was The Wolf the first person to say this to me? Why did everyone else in my entire life just look at me, roll their eyes and go, 'You're late,' while making unknown notes in their records?

'Email me a schedule of what you have lined up in terms of auditions, and I'll clear what I can.'

The Wolf swung his duffel bag over his shoulder; his frayed black-and-white houndstooth coat matched his peppery hair. Everything about him was black and white, except for his eyes. His eyes were definitely blue; they reminded me of a husky that is equal parts high energy and safe place.

'All right then. I'll do that.'

I automatically began to collate the drama schools in my head. *This one is in London, it will be easy for him to get to. This one is in Scotland, it's not worth the ask. This one will be unlikely to go well, so maybe I shouldn't waste his goodwill on it.*

'Oh, I'm staying in Hounslow,' I blurted out as one more piece of information that might be useful.

'Hounslow? Who lives in Hounslow? That's like … not London. My brother used to live there and whenever I would visit him, I would say, "When do we get to go to London?"'

I smiled, remembering my own impression of Hounslow.

'It's just that my host mum and dad live there – I've always stayed with them.'

'Right. Hounslow. So, I will go from Surrey Quays to Hounslow to pick you up, to take you to drama auditions in central London and then back to Hounslow?'

For most people, this absurd transport journey would be justification for saying, 'Yeah right, not worth it, good luck, see you some other time.' But for The Wolf it was a genuine desire to clarify what I needed.

'I'm sure we can work out something easier.'

'No. Hounslow. It's fine. The Underground's easy, and I'll bring a good book. See you soon.'

And with that, I watched The Wolf get in the van that would drive him to the airport.

Weeks later, when I returned from my auditions in London, I ran into the head of the theatre department and her star student at the organic food shop. She asked me how my trip to London was.

'Good. Very good.'

'Did you get into any drama schools?'

'Yes, and I will be attending summer school at RADA in three months. How was your March?'

Graduation came along quicker than expected. Mr Varian had declared, back in that small high-school meeting room, that no matter where I went to college, he would be there for my graduation.

'Varian!' I screamed in disbelief when he appeared in the doorway of the theatre department. 'Varian! You're here!' With that, I moved away from the music stand with my script, and the male actor by my side. I ran my manual chair at full speed until I came into Mr Varian's arms, and he spun me around with the adoration of someone who once claimed to be my father during early-morning Forensics trips, 'just to see what it was like'.

'You made it! Sit! We're about to start the reading.'

'OK. All right. I will!' and he sat down next to my parents. My mother reached out and held his hand.

The story was something I had thought of two weeks before. I was on my way back from the communal pool and I had an idea for a play – a real play. A play that could win awards, I thought. I would write a play about a disabled student in love with a teacher who was a failed architect. Now, she wanted to be an architect, and he was using her disability and his control over her to stand in her way. The metaphors just came out again and again and again. Buildings, architecture, support system, a woman being placed on a pedestal only to be knocked off whenever she refused to kowtow to a man's expectations. That would be good. That could really put my mark on the theatre world. And I would love to play a role like that.

It was May 2006, and I was twenty-one at the time. I would call it *Schism*.

Chapter 15

My hands are shaking as I go to my contacts list and press the screen for The Twin. I can justify that I'm shaking because I have just done ten kilometres on the gym bike, or because the music in the gym was so loud that it was disorienting, or even because transferring from the bike back to my chair was more laborious than the workout itself, risking the effects of gravity as I put one leg in front of the other, walking through the tight spaces between the equipment. There was also a gym rat who felt the need to groan every time he landed a box jump at inconsistent intervals, but none of these are actually the problem.

'So, you know how we're going to meet in a bit for lunch over in the box park?' I search for the words and thoughts to string together in order to make what I am about to say have some sort of logic.

'Yeah, I'm about twenty minutes away,' The Twin responds.

'OK, so I need you to come to the gym rather than meeting me at the office because … um …' *This can't be happening*, I think to myself. *This is happening.* 'You know my chair?'

'Yeah, I know your wheelchair. I'm quite familiar with it actually.'

'So, it's decided to only drive backwards.'

'Backwards? Right ...' The Twin's slightest pause suggests she is having as much trouble computing the situation as I am.

'I need you to come and meet me at the gym so we can drive through the Elephant and Castle roundabout, back over to the office, and then we will hang out for dinner like normal people. Is that OK?'

I actually asked if that was OK. What is The Twin going to say? *No, you're stuck at the gym for the rest of time.* Or maybe I am trying to keep everyone else calm in a moment when my world is quite literally breaking down.

The iBOT, my twelve-year-old wheelchair, was the brainchild of engineer Dean Kamen, before he invented the Segway. It goes up and down stairs, navigates kerbs, has four-wheel drive and can balance on two wheels to raise the user to eye level.

Back in 2008, I received an email from the company informing me that they were no longer going to produce what my friends and I had dubbed the 'super-chair' ever again. Then in 2017 came another email: 'iBOT is back!' Or at least, it would be – in three years' time.

I had to hold out for three more years, but I could already feel the gears under my seat grinding with age, and every once in a while, the chair would cut out for no reason. Every time I came to a road crossing I found myself praying.

'Be aware that one of these days your chair is going to cut out and that will be it. With the way your iBOT is behaving now, it will be a miracle if it makes it to 2020,' the man from the Facebook iBOT group had told me. He had a side hustle of being a semi-professional cage fighter, but he worked for the company that originally made the chair and would make the chair again.

A cage fighter with an engineering degree was telling me that my mode of transportation was on life support. I believed him.

So, I turned my speed down, and drove with the care of a granny in an Oldsmobile. The few times the chair did die, my heart hit the pavement in a plea as I attempted to start it up again.

But now, in the gym, turning it off and turning it back on does not solve the problem of its current directional preference. I try a reboot seven or eight times next to the exercise bike. The erratic box jumper comes over and asks me if I need help. I insist I am fine, because it is easier than screaming, *Yes! My life is collapsing and on fire and the alarms are going off at full blast in my head because of a major wheelchair malfunction! Good God, man, this is an emergency!*

'Absolutely fine.'

A few minutes later I drive from the gym floor, into the atrium, down in the lift, to reception. Backwards.

Nobody looks at me. In fact, nobody gives us any strange looks as The Twin holds the back of my chair and guides me through the Elephant and Castle roundabout. Not a word is spoken, not a stare is stared, which says something about the state of Elephant and Castle, I feel.

In the office, over avocado on toast, we FaceTime The Cage Fighter, who walks us through the mechanical tasks needed to get the wheelchair headed in the right direction again.

'You do realise this is a sign of your chair wearing down?' he says in a voice that has the undertone of 'prognosis negative'.

'Yep, I don't want to talk about that, I'm in denial, thanks, goodbye!' I say as I slam my laptop screen down. Of course I am not in the denial stage about the death of my chair; I am bartering.

I know to be thankful every day it keeps going, and just maybe, if I am thankful enough, the chair can make it to 2020.

*

'And here is the instruction manual.' The physical-therapist-turned-iBOT-representative handed The Crew Gal and me a large spiral-bound notebook. 'You will have two days to read and study this, but at the end of our sessions, we are not able to give you the chair unless you can pass an oral test about its capabilities.'

The decision to buy my first $35,000 iBOT chair back in 2006 was in no way easy. It came about after having looked at the road-safety rules in the UK and clocking that every 'vehicle' used on the pavement, be it an electric wheelchair or scooter or myriad zippy electronic mechanisms that were to come, had to have some form of lights.

'Well, your old chair doesn't have lights, and this one does,' my mother helpfully put together. 'Case closed then, really.'

I did not for a second think that her shorthand logic made any sense at all. Surely the entire disabled, elderly and chronically ill population of the UK who needed some form of electric chair were not plunking down $35,000 in order to buy one? And, for that matter, I doubted the NHS was going to do so either.

But I wanted this chair. I envisioned myself walking with The Wolf, The Leading Lady and the other actors of the RSC on the South Bank at eye level, balanced on two wheels.

Having lived in London during that tumultuous period two years before, I knew that the pavements were crap. If I was lucky enough to get up onto them on one side, there was no guarantee of what would meet me at the end.

'I don't think I deserve it,' I said to my mother one night, when we were once again listing the pros and cons of buying the iBOT. My only con was its cost.

'Well, of course you don't *deserve* it; you're never going to deserve it – that's not how life works. You don't buy wheelchairs because you deserve them, you buy one because it's what you need to help you live the best life you can.'

I thought of those words as I sat in our LA hotel room with The Crew Gal and opened up the spiral user's guide. We decided to start at the beginning of the book, go page by page, and test each other just as we did back at Davidson for a Spanish quiz.

'Where should you not drive the iBOT?' The Crew Gal asked me.

'What the heck kind of question is that?! There are a million places where I shouldn't drive the iBOT.'

'There's a list of four of them right here.'

'Mars. Is Mars on there? I probably shouldn't drive the iBOT on Mars.'

'It says, don't drive it through water – that's one example.'

'Water. How deep?'

'Four inches.'

'Got it. What are the other three?' I said, shutting my eyes to put a recording of her voice into my brain so that I could play it back on command, listing the four specific places that I should not drive my new chair.

When I first stood up on two wheels, the feeling of inertia caused by the chair tipping back over its centre of gravity and then raising itself up was enough to make me squeal. Stranger still, the chair dithered back and forth, compensating for my shifts in weight. But equally, as the physical therapist pointed out, nobody, no person, stood completely still when they were upright. It was like being in a small rocking chair when you were a kid. Back and forth and back and forth when looking at the world around you, relaxed and calm, like the world ebbed and flowed and there was nothing I needed to do to control it.

*

'Andre, can I come to visit you and Fontaine? I have a new wheelchair I need to pick up in Boston.'

The bearded writer, who looks more badger-like than man, stares back at me. I can see him trying to compute what I have just asked him. During the previous year, I had received a grant from the UK Government, which allowed me to seek out a bespoke Master of Fine Arts, and I asked for his instruction/mentorship.

But now I am asking him to be more than a teacher; I am asking Andre to be a host for a reason that, I concede, makes no sense.

'You need to come here to pick up a wheelchair?' he repeats, as if the words, when coming out of his mouth, would make any more sense.

'Yep. You've got it. That's right. There is a very specialised wheelchair that I have been using for the past fourteen years, which is seriously on its dying legs and—'

At the term 'dying legs', I could see him start to double forward in laughter.

'OK, yes, no pun intended. I'm serious, though! This wheelchair is literally being held together by superglue, bad wiring and the grace of God. I've been waiting for Dean Kamen to reintroduce the chair to the market, and he finally has. But we have to go to a city just outside of Boston to train to use it.'

'Who has to train to know how to use a wheelchair?'

I start to explain the chair and its various features, making me sound more like a creature created by Gene Roddenberry than a human being.

'Next you're going to tell me it flies,' Andre says to me, and I don't have much of a retort, other than: 'Not yet.'

His wife walks into the room and he turns to her. 'Athena and her friend are going to come and visit us this autumn.'

Alarm bells of the patriarchy and bad etiquette start going off in my head.

'No, no, you're supposed to ask your wife first, before you announce that you're having guests! You're supposed to say: "Is it OK if …" She's the one who's going to have to do all the housework.'

'It's fine! This is how we do it. Of course you and your friend can stay, just let us know the dates and we'll make it work. Can't wait to see you!' And then he logs off. I am left with a number of questions: dates that would be OK with him, OK with her, not stepping on anyone's toes, house rules and expectations, his teaching schedule, and anything else I would need to do to minimise the burden on them.

Later that night, Andre emails me in response to my list of questions.

'Don't worry about anything, dear Athena. We have three kids who have grown and left home and a house my brother and I built ourselves in the middle of nowhere. We have plenty of room for you and anyone else you want to bring along. Come whenever you need to.'

And so, with a roof over my head, two bedrooms and meals for a week sorted, I begin to go through the motions, once again, of documenting the justifications for something it is obvious that I need: a wheelchair.

*

As The Crew Gal took the handle of the iBOT wheelchair and tilted its entire frame back, I heard the cluster of wheels rotate around themselves to go up the first step. Then she pushed the handle down further and it repeated the motion. We were climbing a mock staircase – or rather, a real staircase, but one that led nowhere.

I couldn't see what the chair was doing, but I could feel it. The new technology was not as smooth as you would expect a cutting-edge feat of engineering to be. I imagined that the cluster of wheels would bang into the riser of the next step as if it were unable to gauge where the step actually ended and the rise for the next step began. And I was right: it couldn't. It took human intervention to continue its climb. The cluster of wheels rotated and rotated, leaving the stair to stop its ascent before it could move to the next step. It was simply physics, and without much suspension at that. I again began to wonder if this machine was really worth the price tag.

'Good. Now, for this last step, I want you to get it wrong. I want you to act like there's another step above it. Don't pull it back at the top like I taught you – I want to show you both what will happen.'

The Crew Gal did as she was told, and I felt the cluster rotate once again, this time faltering because there was no step to catch the wheels and – BANG!

An alarm sounded – I found myself flat on the floor looking up at the ceiling, my legs in the air, my waist bent at a ninety-degree angle at the seat, but flat nonetheless. I was not harmed, and neither was The Crew Gal, but it was terrifying.

'Yeah, that's what I wanted to show you. If this happens, basically the chair is stuck in this position, and you're going to have to wait until one of us can come out to help you.'

'What do you mean, one of you to *come out*?' I said. Tilting my head back to try to make eye contact with the physical therapist, all I could see was his muddied trainers against the wood of the staircase-to-nowhere.

'That's the deal. We will come out and fix it ourselves. It's like a Rolls-Royce. There are some safety checks that we have to do ourselves. We can't give you the codes to override the alarms.'

'Wait, so if this happens in London, I'm just supposed to—'

'Someone from our European offices will come out to you.'

It's supposed to sound posh, but images start appearing in my head of presidents, mostly Gerald Ford and George W. Bush, not being able to walk down the stairs of *Air Force One* properly. But these are our leaders. What happens when it's twenty-two-year-old friends who might be mid-conversation and not paying attention?

This was the first memory I went back to when I opened my email in 2008 announcing that from 2011, the iBOT would cease to be serviced for the foreseeable future. Not only could my mobility be cut short by a single mistake, but that one mistake would now be irreparable.

*

I continue studying with Andre for my MFA.

'Tell me what it's like. Tell me what it's really like,' are the words that he repeats over and over again during our lessons together. Being primarily a playwright, I have the horrible habit of not thinking through the details that most prose writers find themselves swept up by. The things people wear, the way the light refracts into a room, the weather outside, the heat of the air.

'I don't know, that's what the costume and lighting designer are for,' I say.

'My father would have loved you,' he groans, signalling that I'm still on the right side of good and well behaved.

I also know that it's not exactly a compliment in the simplest sense of the word. Andre's father, Andre Dubus II, was a complicated man. He was also a writer and was known in literary circles by the varying titles of what he wrote, who he wrote like, who he was influenced by and what his relationships were.

I think on some level, even with all of his complexities and moral ambiguities, I would have liked Andre's father, too.

But the comment has a different meaning for both of us. In July of 1986, Andre Dubus II was driving home and stopped to assist two motorists whose vehicle had broken down on the side of the road. In the midst of him being a Good Samaritan, an oncoming car swerved and hit the rail, killing one of the motorists and crushing both of Mr Dubus's legs, ultimately resulting in a double amputation.

For a man who prided himself on his virility and his activity, often going for fifteen-kilometre runs well into his forties, the result was an uphill battle of both acceptance and, ultimately, letting go in a world that didn't have terms such as 'ableism' to explain common experiences for those of us with disabilities.

Whenever I prepare to spend an extended period of time with someone who is established in their career, I naturally do a deep-dive. Given the literary status of Andre III's father, I decided to read Andre Dubus II's book, *Meditations from a Movable Chair*.

It is interesting to me that he chose the term 'movable chair', and not 'wheelchair'. I understand why. 'Wheelchair' doesn't have the same poetic context. There is no real vocabulary that makes disability feel sensual, or beneficial. The words around disability often come out feeling clunky, jagged: a haphazard aesthetic that leaves no room for beauty.

I can see in Dubus II's work the hesitation to answer what his son asks of me all the time: 'What's it like? What's it really *like*?' How do you define trauma without any cultural context or a literary canon set behind it? How do you pin down the social problems of being othered when there is no language to use yet? So, Dubus II attempted to put the thing that resulted in the loss of his limbs into some sort of literary context.

I can hear the elder whisper out to me. Maybe it is a result of hearing his son's voice so often: 'What's it like? What's it really *like*?' But the words I also hear are, 'What's it like now? Has it changed at all? Or is it still just as difficult to find the words to explain our mundane trauma?'

I thought that these connections and reflections between my own work and Dubus II's were all in my head, until I read one of his essays. A friend tells him about a new wheelchair that could brilliantly balance on two wheels, go up and down stairs, and, in 1996, cost $25,000. It's created by a guy nobody knew the name of yet: Dean Kamen.

The essay ends with the reality that he very much wanted one, but the engineered negation of disability is only for those who can afford it, and that did not include him.

During my next lesson with Andre, I point out the essay. 'That's the chair! That's the chair I am coming to get!'

I want to put it down to some sort of miracle that the fates and the planets lined up in this amazing way – that the very chair his father wrote about was going to be sitting in my teacher's house. I want to feel like Dubus II is reaching out to me through time and space, seeing me as a writer because of our common love for this chair. But it is not a slim line-up of fate. After all, how many people can afford such a remarkable piece of equipment? The iBOT stopped being made because, over the course of ten years, fewer than 400 were sold. This is the chair that I have written plays about and sued British Airways over, the chair that has been mine for fourteen years. And a second one is coming.

What are the odds? Not wholly unremarkable when you break down the numbers.

*

'That's it. You're all set. Enjoy it,' the physical therapist said to me, as if he were handing me the keys to a convertible on my sixteenth birthday. We had passed the test. We could now take the iBOT back to Las Vegas to get used to the chair before flying out to London permanently. *Flying out to London permanently,* I reminded myself, *because that's where my adult life is going to be.*

I was still ill at ease with the world at eye level. The inconsistent dithering back and forth to remain balanced was something that I felt could too easily cause the chair to tip over into a body of water, or off a cliff, or simply injure the people surrounding me in a crowd. And yet, every time I went out in the chair, I was elated. This was a new world, despite having warning signs and potential dangers posted all over it.

There was an entire part of the world between the height of three and a half feet and five feet, which had gone unnoticed in my eyes. It was like the entire middle plane of existence opened up. Things like ATMs, valet windows, ticket sellers – anything just above seated level I saw and noticed in detail. How had I moved through the world for all these years, entirely missing this eighteen-inch sector of space?

Once arriving in London, we took a black cab to the digs on Charlotte Street that I was staying at for the summer RADA course. The next morning, I turned over and looked at the oversized black wheelchair with PVC plastic on its back and arms, made to look like leather.

When The Crew Gal came in, just as she had done during the days at Davidson, I looked at her as she shut the door to my room.

'Is it just me, or is the chair sitting at an angle?' I asked.

She looked at it, took a step back towards where I was lying on the bed, then took a step forward and put her hand on the headrest of the chair.

'No, I think you're right. That chair isn't straight at all.'

A quick call to the European iBOT hotline assured me, 'It's always going to be at a slight tilt; that's just the nature of the tyres.' *How could something cost so much but not even sit straight?*

The evening of my first full day in London, I called The Wolf to let him know that I was in town and rethinking every life decision that had got me to this point.

'I would think it very odd if you weren't rethinking everything,' he said to me in a voice that made my duality of thought seem normal. 'It is scary. You emigrated. You have literally nothing but a new wheelchair.'

'Two wheelchairs.' I had brought my manual as well. It was

sitting in a classroom at the Royal Academy of Dramatic Art, waiting for me to begin classes that Monday.

'Fine. Nothing but two new wheelchairs, a duffel bag and a suitcase. That, and the candy-bar phone you nearly dropped out the window when I called, is all you've got this side of the ocean. That's scary. You're allowed to feel a little off-centre at the moment.'

*

'Athena's here to get one of those chairs Dad always wanted – can you believe it?'

I am sitting at Andre's bar top in the kitchen; all my weight is pressed into my forearms for an added point of stability. Truth be told, I don't do very well on barstools. My feet swing back and forth, knocking me entirely off balance as they search to find the ground, or at least a platform beneath them. In this case, there is neither.

'What, one of those super-expensive chairs that go up and down stairs? I remember him talking about the article in the *Wall Street Journal* about them. Or maybe it was the *New York Times*,' Andre's brother says, putting a straw into the lime soda in front of me. 'That's incredible. I wish Dad was here to see it.'

'I wish Dad was here to joy-ride it, although I don't think he could've fitted into Athena's chair size.'

The brown-and-cream kitchen with wooden cabinetry sprawls into a great room. It is an American style of living space with few walls and multiple 'zones' in a single room because the room itself is so large. This is a house that Andre and his brother built by hand, laying every floorboard and every tile, fixing the plumbing, the lights and the wiring. It is beautiful.

It's also one of the least accessible homes I have ever seen. They have this house standing on stilts so that a mother-in-law suite can fit on the bottom floor. To enter through the actual front door of the house, I have to walk up about twenty-five wooden steps. I ask Andre when it was built, and he answers, 'Before Dad lost his other leg.'

The day before, I was in Manchester, New Hampshire, to train myself on a wheelchair I already knew how to use. There was a quadriplegic man receiving his first iBOT, and I could tell just by looking at him that he'd suffered a spinal-cord injury. Grinning from ear to ear, he looked at me with hope in his eyes, and I again remembered the privilege I'd had for the last fourteen years, one that he had not had access to until today. A world at a height he knew better than the waist-high one he had been sentenced to after his accident. Back when he, between the two of us, was the relatively privileged one.

'Here, watch this video and then we'll start the training.' In the fourteen years between receiving my first iBOT and now, the personal one-on-one training has been replaced by a video, detailing which buttons to push in which order to make the chair go to specific modes.

When they roll my new chair in, I lose my breath. She – and yes, she is 'she', like a boat – is elegant, with a curved space in her back that wraps around me as I sit down. Her sides hold my sides firmly, but with an implied grace. I insisted on ordering the side guards because I know that, otherwise, red-carpet gowns are prone to get caught in the wheels of any wheelchair.

She asks less of me. She responds to my commands more quickly once I have the button profile down. She doesn't shudder when she dithers.

This iBOT hides. When I am in it, you see more of me, and less of her.

'That's it then! You won't be going back to the old chair ever.' The physical therapist says this with such confidence that, at first, I resent him for it. That chair has been my friend. We have been through RADA together. We have marched against Trump, and I fought hard when British Airways damaged it. They are the wheels that have taken me inside Westminster for my political career thus far.

After seeing me sit in a new chair, to say that I won't go back stings. Does this man not realise the incredible bond my skin and soul have had with this piece of fourteen-year-old metal?

We're done. Thank you for getting me where I needed to be. Thank you for getting me here on your last bit of energy.

I reach out and touch my old chair, keeping my back enveloped and supported by the new backrest, finally made for a woman's figure. Without my kit or myself in it, the old chair seems stiff, cold, overly large. And maybe it is because the tyres are typically low, or because I am looking at it while supported by a new system, but I can swear its uneven lean is more exaggerated than when I discovered it all those years ago.

My new chair is a lady. This old one is like Hodor from *Game of Thrones*. It has got me where I needed to go. It has had a hard-working and unstoppable attitude, even after dying in the middle of the pavement numerous times. But it is time for me to leave Hodor behind, and become whatever this new phase of life asks of me.

Back at Andre's, I tell him about my last moments with the chair. Now, I suddenly find a knot in my throat, as my feet dangle and search for a point of stability.

'You should write an essay about that.'

I smile and roll my eyes, enjoying the connections I have found with a man who, when I approached him to teach me twelve months ago, seemed like a total stranger.

'I will,' I say, thinking about the chair his father wanted, now sitting, covered, in his car port downstairs. I love her, but the emotion of leaving the old one behind is still too raw.

So, I bend my head down to the lime soda on the table, put the straw in my mouth, and take a drink.

Chapter 16

The first time The Wolf and I went to audition for a drama school, he met my mother and me at Hounslow East station, true to his word.

We were on the way to Birmingham via Waterloo and my mother held our BritRail tickets, which were supposed to get us a good deal as American 'tourists' to travel throughout the UK for my auditions. He immediately took the back of my manual wheelchair from my mother and said, 'Birmingham's a factory town. I haven't been there in a while – it'll be good to go back.'

'All I know about it is that line from Noël Coward's *Blithe Spirit* when they talk about the piano cover and the husband says, "Lady Marshall got that for us from Burma," and the dead wife says, "Well, it looks like she got it from Birmingham."'

The Wolf laughed at this.

The bright daylight of Waterloo washed out the ugly greys of the Underground once we went up the escalator. The lift was out, and so The Wolf perched the front wheels of my manual chair on the one step rising out of the machine and the back wheels on the following step, slightly lower.

I was trying not to think about the audition I was facing in a few hours. It would just be another situation to say the speeches that I had done so many times. Maybe a workshop, if I was called back later that afternoon.

Before getting onto the train, we stepped outside with The Wolf for him to have a quick cigarette.

'Don't I look like the ultimate carer – wheelchair in one hand, cigarette in the other. Do people ever flick cigarette ash in your face without realising it? You're kind of at the perfect level to receive that.'

'Yes. That does happen from time to time.'

'Fuckers.' He lifted the tobacco wrapped with his own paper to his mouth and sucked again.

On board, we sat in the red fake-velour seats, beige hard plastic outlining them all, and my mother went through her handbag, taking out her tickets, mine, then removing my passport, and continuing to look.

'Where is my passport? I can't find it. I can't use the rail pass unless I have my passport. I'm going to have to go back to Hounslow to look for it.' Then she turned to The Wolf: 'You can take her to the auditions, right?'

'Yeah, sure. Absolutely. No problem.'

'All right – good luck, hon. I love you.' A quick peck on the cheek, and she was off.

'Do you think she really lost it?' The Wolf asked about a minute later.

'What, her mind?'

'I mean her passport.'

I had no idea. The train started up, and in my mind, I began to go through what the day would entail.

'I'll need to eat something at some point. Are you OK to feed me?'

'Of course.'

So, that wasn't a problem. He walked me to the train toilet, leaving my chair on its back so it wouldn't roll while I was on my feet in the inaccessible cubicle. He stood outside the door, waited as I washed my hands and came back out, then offered me a confident, firm arm automatically to stabilise myself as we made our way to the opposite end of the carriage where the accessible seats were.

How could this feel so … normal?

'You never had tuna mayonnaise with corn? What's wrong with you?!' The Wolf sat down next to me and casually unwrapped the top half of a baguette sandwich as if he had done this all before. He didn't even take the extra paper around the wrapping and put it over his hands. Then he held it up to my mouth and I took a bite.

He gave me a bite, then took a bite of his own baguette, and so forth until we were done.

The Wolf flagged down a black cab and helped me inside, ignoring the cabbie's offer to let down the fold-out ramp. 'This is just faster,' he said, and I agreed. Then he put my wheelchair in, wheels up, climbed inside himself, reached around my waist and snapped the seatbelt in place.

The audition required us to stay longer than we had anticipated. A callback for the same-day workshop was a favourable sign. I looked to read The Wolf's face at the news that we would be getting home later than expected; a lifetime of minimising myself and justifying my presence, and the effort it took for me to participate in anything, made this sense-check a reflex within me. There was nothing but a smile and a wink. 'I knew you could do it,' he said. 'Well done.'

In the workshop, The Wolf received a call on his phone. My mother had found her passport safe and sound, and the day was worry-free. He told me this after I exited the workshop.

'One down. Let's see what they have for you. It will probably be a few months before they get back to you with any sort of decision.'

'I don't know if that's the right place for me.' I was thinking about the black Marley floors and the wooden accents of the school. There was no sunlight – a trait common to drama schools in the mid-2000s. And this was only day one. I knew nothing except to question whether or not I could do 'better'.

Then I reminded myself of my college admissions experience – and that was with a good report card behind me.

In the unlikely event that I received a single invite, I would grab onto it, fully committed. I reminded myself again that I hadn't ended up with the numerous acceptance letters that I had been promised for college. I quickly shrank down my thinking and thanked him for the day.

'You don't have to thank me.' The Wolf said it with such ease, as if he meant that there was no expectation for me to see him as some overly generous person. 'I wonder what the next school will be like.'

Thus began our journeys up and down the United Kingdom: me auditioning for drama schools, him acting completely reasonably when the person running the audition would look at him with eyebrows raised.

'What's the problem? She's got an audition.'

'All right, our audition room is up a flight of stairs.'

'She can walk. I'll carry the chair up.'

After a few weeks of this, I couldn't help but interject: 'No, don't talk to him. He's a mute. I'm the one auditioning – talk to me.' The

Wolf was clearly not a mute, having just spoken ten seconds before, but it was so fun to watch the third-year drama student trying to figure out if they were being punked; almost as fun as watching The Wolf zip it on command.

We were never late. When the train dropped my mother, The Wolf and me off in Glasgow and it started to snow, he swung his black-and-white duffel bag over his shoulder, took my manual chair in both hands and started to climb up the hill out of the station. Despite me insisting that we could take a taxi, he seemed to think that the hotel was not far enough away, and that by the time we got in the car we would already be there.

'Oh, I don't know what we would do without you,' my mother began, pulling the drawstrings of her hood around her chin. Her feather-down coat, purchased to get through the Chicago winters, had been matted down over the years. While it was still warm enough for my parents' new life in Las Vegas, the loss of feathers meant that it was somewhat uninsulated against the March Glasgow snow.

'If I wasn't here, then you would take a taxi.'

*

Two years later, I sat on the floor in a champagne-coloured silk nightgown in front of the floor-length mirror of the Thistle Hotel in Glasgow. I had already dropped out of drama school, and the boy I had met at RADA had moved in with me. I thought that he was 'the one', and yet the flat had become so pervasive with cold turns and unspoken words, explosions avoided and precipices to fall off, that I needed a night's break. So, I stuffed some underwear and my one silk nightgown into a bag and checked into the same place that The Wolf, my mother and I stayed in during the audition for the Royal Scottish School of Music and Drama.

The hotel staff looked at me curiously as a disabled woman, alone, insisting that she just needed a room, but not an accessible bath, for the night.

My heart thumped as I put my debit card into the chip-and-pin machine. *This is so silly. I have a flat that I'm paying rent on just a hundred yards down the road, and yet* he's *staying there and I'm here. Surely it should be the other way around*, I thought as I typed my PIN.

I looked at the room-service menu, thought about ordering and remembered the cream of chicken soup the hotel had two years ago during the snowy March auditions. Then I remembered that it was served with a giant soup spoon, essentially the equivalent of a shovel in my mouth. I decided not to order anything. It was only for one night.

When a disabled woman who needs your help to eat leaves you, you can take that as a clear red flag against your character.

*

The first thing I had noticed about The Dancer was his posture, followed by his North Carolina drawl that made me feel like I was back at Davidson when it was at its best; before the institution had decided that I was too complex and difficult to be favoured.

To make ends meet, he taught ballroom dance, which made sense. A good-looking guy with big brown eyes and a dark complexion. Tall, slender, muscular. We were often put together side by side because our postures were 'too straight' according to the Alexander Technique teacher, and so, it was our job to 'soften' one another up a bit.

'You're blocking energies if you stay stiff. You won't be able to receive vibrations from each other if you're too focused on your own posture.' This seemed both like precious advice from one of the most well-respected movement teachers in the profession, and some sort of heavy-handed metaphor.

The words that are bestowed upon me very often are: Wonder Woman, strong, proud, stubborn, razor-sharp, scary – often delivered by people who believe these words to be compliments. They are not. They are words that can very quickly warp into something toxic. But I am all of these things. Part of our humanity is being too proud, too stiff, too challenging, not knowing when to let go and when to open our wounds because they don't need to be protected; they need to be healed.

We were both willing to soften our edges to become better artists and to see where we could take each other. For weeks that summer, we ran speeches from *Henry V* and *The Winter's Tale*, acting in a scene from *All's Well That Ends Well* in which I played The Dancer's daughter and he was the unreachable but overprotective king.

This was both the drama training I had always wanted and the relationship that I had always wanted.

One night, The Dancer and I were walking home along the South Bank with a few of our friends. In order to make me jealous, he half-jokingly grabbed the hand of Shakespeare's Blonde, then looked to see how I would react.

'Fine by me! You two would make a great pair!' I felt no need to turn possessive.

'Well, I don't want him!' Shakespeare's Blonde said. 'Don't I get a say in the matter?'

'You get the ultimate say in the matter. Let her go now.'

There was a flicker of darkness in his eyes when I noted that my friend had the power, and he dropped her hand just a little too hard.

Time blended that summer like watercolours.

The Dancer, myself and a few other students bought tickets to see *Gaslight* at the Old Vic. I was assured that the seats would be accessible, only to find out upon arrival that they were not, and the few accessible seats were already taken.

'Well, I guess we'll see you tomorrow in class then,' The Dancer said as he waved at me and then ducked with the other classmates into the auditorium.

I made my way home from the Old Vic to my flat just outside of Waterloo slowly that evening, knocking on the window so that Shakespeare's Blonde would let me in.

She was furious.

'No, calm down. He doesn't know any better,' I said.

'I don't care how ignorant he is! Even someone from the back-woods of North Carolina should have the decency not to just leave you and say, "Have a nice night," when you've been excluded like that. Throw him in the garbage!!'

I asked her to lower the red flag she was waving.

*

The Dancer was safely ensconced in the Tate Modern gift shop. When it comes to a store that will set fire to your imagination and make you feel like an elite artist, the Tate Modern gift shop is the best place to be. If you have cash to burn, that is.

I walked through the turbine hall with The Wolf. There was a crack that had been put into the floor of the massive exhibition space. It ran from the tiniest hairline fracture at the beginning of the entrance, all the way to a giant schism at the end of the room. The Wolf straddled the line and walked on both sides for as long as he could while talking to me.

I couldn't get past the bureaucracy of the crack. There would be a giant scar on the surface of the turbine hall for the rest of the building's existence. What kind of a museum coordinator would allow such a remarkable installation to occur? How much of it was planned out and how much of it was the artist simply saying, "We will wait and see how the crack manages itself"?

By the time we got to the opposite end of the turbine hall, The Wolf was on one side of the crack and I was on the other. I couldn't roll over to his side, even with super-chair.

If The Wolf wanted to, he could jump over. And he did. We looked at each other without saying a word. Because there was little choice to be made, we headed back to the gift shop, me two steps behind him.

'I know that I'm the problem. Just like I was the problem at the Conservatoire. I'll make this relationship work. I just need to figure out the code to unlock The Dancer.'

The Wolf, The Dancer and I then walked up and down the Tate Modern, battling its notoriously poorly managed lift, and saw nearly every room available without needing to pay admission tickets. The Dancer said nothing the entire time, and I enjoyed his silence for once. He walked from room to room with us and I told myself that this was healthy. The Dancer and The Wolf didn't need to interact, and I appreciated the freedom from the former.

It was The Wolf that I called the morning after The Dancer left me, forty-eight hours after he received rejection letters from both RADA and the Royal Scottish School of Music and Drama. I wanted to hear The Wolf's voice, but that morning I had also found five empty bottles of Jameson whiskey hidden around the house. Was that normal? The Dancer had moved in only eight weeks prior.

I explained this last detail to The Wolf, and he was silent for a moment. I didn't want to think about the reality that I seemed to have been a doll to be played with, to be shown off, to be used as a badge of honour and then set back on the shelf.

After a moment of silence, The Wolf spoke: 'Five bottles of Jameson is fine. I went through a phase like that – don't worry about it.'

Two hours later I called back. I asked him the same question, but this time about seven bottles of Jameson.

'Don't worry about it, honestly.'

A little while later, I sent The Wolf a text: 'Eleven?'

'Nope.'

I was aware that The Dancer was flying back to North Carolina. He must have still been in the air, the wheels not yet touched down stateside. I wondered what my moral obligation was if the guy I was living with actually turned out to be an alcoholic. He was in trouble and I wanted to help him; I wanted to put the pieces of us together again; back to the way it was.

'Stop worrying about him, Athena. Just stop.'

*

Seven months later, The Wolf helped me put together a desk for my computer work. Actually, to put it more appropriately, he put together the desk. I was just useful for the gags and to halve measurements in my head when needed.

'What's one hundred and fifty-four divided by two?'

'Seventy-seven.'

He held screws in his mouth while fixing together my own chipboard surface, covered by a sticker that looks like wood – a place where I could write my blog and pass judgements on the world.

'I think I ran over Yoko Ono's foot yesterday,' I dropped into the conversation.

'Well, that's OK. She has another one.'

The day before, I had been at the Frieze Art Fair with a friend, in awe of both its scale and its ability to divvy up spaces to individual artists. Yoko Ono was the headline speaker.

'She shattered a pot onstage, and she said that in fifty years' time, if we all took a piece, we should meet back where we were and put it all together again.'

'Well, that's not going to happen.'

I knew it wasn't going to happen. I knew that Yoko Ono was stretching the limits of both imagination and, more importantly, reality by this sentiment.

Still, I took a piece of Yoko Ono's terracotta jar because, for as long as I held that shard, I could keep my part of the bargain. If I didn't keep a piece, it would be lost.

'Well, I'm keeping it on my desk. I know it's futile, but I like the ideas this piece of pottery puts in my head.' I gave it to The Wolf after he finished plugging my iMac into the back of the chipboard unit, and he put the shard on the top shelf.

*

I had an ad-hoc consultancy job working for the London Underground. I had used my experience of the first time I had been to England, the inhospitality of the Tube system to bodies such as mine, as reasons for why I thought I was the right candidate for

233

the job. The work was once a month, and paid enough in a single day to cover bills as well as groceries for myself and the individual I was living with in a flat in Woolwich at the time.

This freelancer's paycheque wasn't all I had to my name, but it was all the money I felt was really mine.

The fact that the 2012 Olympics were coming to London in six years equally meant that the entire system was being looked at and critiqued. Every few months, I had an additional day's work to bill, which meant setting that money aside for the leaner months.

I was assaulted by a member of staff at Woolwich station numerous times while living there. He insisted that I didn't know where I was going and attempted to push my wheelchair without my permission.

Every time I went away from the Woolwich flat or returned home at the end of the day, I knew I was risking trauma. Trauma from the singular transport worker who still berated me and insisted I didn't know how the transport system worked; trauma from him touching me again; trauma at the broken promises of ramps and access that would meet me at either or both ends of my journey.

To go out in a body that is not built for this world is to risk daily trauma. To go out in a world that is not built for this body is an act of self-revolution, and one that is exhausting to muster daily.

'If he lays hands on you, that's assault by UK law,' The Wolf pointed out to me one afternoon as he was prising off tyres from my wheelchair.

'Yeah, it's assault, but that's OK.'

'Do you hear what is coming out of your mouth right now?'

'I mean, it's not like I can do anything about it other than move.'

'You are literally moving house because someone else didn't uphold their end of the bargain of accessibility. I'm not saying you have to start a whole lawsuit, but at least let that click into your brain for a minute.'

I moved to a flat about a hundred yards away from where The Wolf was living. I had my own personal Kwik Fit whenever the iBOT had a flat tyre.

On the days when I worked, I would walk from the Westminster Underground station to the Transport for London building in Victoria. I would go through Parliament Square, stopping to look at Churchill and Lincoln, and then cross over into the car park that is attached to Westminster Abbey.

'Is William Wilberforce here?' I asked the first time I entered the abbey on my own. I had just come from a meeting at the London Underground offices where I was sat in a room with five old white men, the epitome of 'male, pale and stale', playing with their trains. In the background was not the comforting tea and cookies of the typical meeting room. Instead, there were glass panels looking out into the monitoring room of the transport system. Digital tracks showed where each train was and how fast it was moving, and when it was due at the next station. It looked like a NASA space centre, not a place to make decisions on equality.

'He sure is,' the warm abbey worker replied to me. 'Would you like to see him?'

I visited him whenever I was frustrated about the glacial pace of change. Soon, the abbey workers knew my name.

As the 2012 summer Olympics approached, those 'male, pale, and stale' executives at the London Underground became increasingly agreeable, either because of the pressures of the delivery timeline or simply, though less likely, because their ideologies had changed.

And yet, as the days went by, my treatment at Woolwich station by South Eastern Railway was something I could not let go of. Here I was, the poster child for accessible transport, not taking legal action against what I knew to be discrimination simply because I figured 'it wasn't exactly assault'.

How could I say I worked for transport accessibility when I couldn't even call out an example of ableism, despite being one of the most privileged people with a disability on the planet?

'You don't have to fight anybody, Athena.' The Wolf, again, was fixing my tyres. It was yet another removal of rubber against steel and explaining to him the mess that was British law.

That night, I downloaded an application form for the small claims court.

Does anyone know the precise mathematical equation to compute if something is worth the fight or not?

When the brown envelope thudded onto my doormat, I learned that, were we to go to court, and I was to lose, I would be responsible for the other side's legal fees, as well as my own. This is common practice in the UK – a way of keeping frivolous lawsuits in check.

The insomnia and cold sweats that came with catastrophising only continued. For all I knew, South Eastern Railway could have hired Johnnie Cochran to be their legal representative! The legal representatives at South Eastern Railway argued that I accidentally misfiled my claim under the wrong name.

It was the overwhelming weight of being told time and again that I was privileged that made me want to do something. If privileged people hadn't helped me, I would still have been sitting in a beanbag chair in my own faeces.

In the end, it all came down to a meeting, an 'attempt to settle outside of court' as their lawyers put it. The Wolf attended with me, sitting on my left side, his legs crossed in this sort of man-spread that forms a triangle when one's ankle is balanced on the knee. He said little, and looked at the chipboard table in front of us.

'I'll only say something if you get yourself into a real mess. Other than that, I'm just here to be a witness.'

The legal representative from South Eastern gave me a number that they were willing to settle on and they in the end, they gave me everything I asked for. Later, The Wolf pointed out that they must have always had permission to give that amount and they probably simply expected me to get scared and settle.

The legal representative had silently left the meeting. What can you say when you know that there are many cogs in the wheel of injustice, and you are acting as one of them?

*

I heard The Wolf arrive in A&E before the curtain of my bed was pulled back. The sound of his slightly gruff 3.30 a.m. voice combined with my empty yellow manual wheelchair he pulled behind him probably made it very clear to whom he was referring when he asked, 'Where is she?'

When I was taken into the ambulance, it never occurred to me that I would need my own wheelchair at some point. Hospitals were full of wheelchairs, after all.

For three weeks, I had been either throwing up or in bed. The Wolf would often let himself into my flat during those afternoons to hold my hair back while I was bent over a toilet, or leave a cup of juice by my bedside with a straw if I happened to be asleep. He and I had gone back and forth about what was causing the illness, and the local GP offered no help. That night, after vomiting three times, I called my dad.

I was developing pain in my upper left chest.

'You need to go to the hospital right now,' Dad said. But I was so tired.

'If I still feel bad in the morning, I'll go then.'

'You could be having a heart attack. Go now.'

I was not having a heart attack, of course. Rather, as common sense will tell you, if you spend weeks on end uncontrollably retching, chances are that you will pull some muscles in your chest. Add some involuntary reactive muscle spasms to that pain and you have a nice, self-perpetuating response cycle.

The curtain around my bed was pushed aside without any pretence. The Wolf sat at the end of the mattress with his foot on the wheel of my empty yellow chair. It was hardly a cure-all, but I felt a little bit of the pain release from my chest as he looked at me.

'You're not going to like a word I'm about to say, but I don't care. This has happened because you're working too hard, you don't have enough help and you don't eat enough.'

'How do you know—'

'Because I have watched you go from Davidson, to not having structured time, to skipping lunch because it's easier than finding help. You don't eat enough and you "work" so much that you're not productive.'

Having never done well with unstructured time, any weeks when I wasn't acting were meant to be blocked off for writing. Writing was cheap; it was an activity that was independent of winning an audition or being noticed. Writing was something that you had to be self-driven to do every possible waking hour in order to be called 'a writer'. There was no time for so-called 'rest', because it was all supposed to be time writing.

'Let's be clear. I don't pity you and I'm not afraid for you. People go on for years as you are. Some of them even get a good bit of work done. You can exhaust yourself – I won't stop you. It's not even my business. But there's no reason to work past six at night when you've been writing that day—'

'Late at night is when magic happens for most writers—'

'And I think it would be really stupid if no one saw your best work because you never took enough care of yourself so that you could write it.'

*

I swiped my freedom pass across the yellow Oyster Card reader in the orange entryway to the Surrey Quays line. Primary block colours dominated the London transport system. Orange, red, blue, light blue, black, brown, yellow, green. I could see that there was a ticketing guard watching us.

'She's not allowed there. There's no lift.'

'I can walk,' I said. 'He'll help me down. It's fine.'

'I said, she isn't allowed downstairs.'

'She can walk, and I can carry the chair down. It's fine,' said The Wolf.

The guard stood directly in front of my chair, and The Wolf swerved me to the left in order to avoid him. He whispered in my ear, 'Keep going; we're just going to keep going and get you on the train.'

I interlaced my arm with The Wolf's, and he picked up my manual wheelchair.

'Stop! Don't take her down there!'

'Well, we're down. And the world's not exploding, mate,' The Wolf said.

The train started rolling up, roaring towards us, and The Wolf's voice was getting lost in a combination of the searing noise and the TfL employee shouting over them both repeatedly, to the point where the conversation had become absurd.

Another TfL employee was walking down the steps as the train slowed to a halt and The Wolf pushed the button for the door to open.

'Just get on!'

'Do not. Put her. On that. Train!'

The Wolf put his weight on the back of my chair and tipped the wheels up, then lifted the back wheels into the carriage. 'Are you OK?' he asked, putting one foot on the threshold between the train and the platform to keep the door from closing and cutting me off.

'Yes, I'm fine – go!'

He stepped his foot off the carriage and I heard the doors beeping to close shut. I turned around and saw him wait just long enough for the train to start rolling again. He looked at me and nodded. And then, before I was even five feet away, carried off by the train, I saw him turn to the two TfL employees and become the British equivalent of the Incredible Hulk. I heard him scream, 'What the fuck is wrong with you?' as he charged at the first man. The last thing I saw was his stance broadening, one foot well in front of the other as he pulled his fist back … and disappeared from my sight.

The Wolf did not get arrested, but things were never the same after that.

Chapter 17

It is a period of time where I am doing well in life. *Schism* has opened and closed. I've led the Women's March against Trump. It is a regular occurrence that my running commentary about society, feminism, inequity and inequality gets published in periodicals such as the *Independent* or the *Evening Standard*. I know how to create a Twitter brigade that makes corporations' lives uncomfortable when it is necessary.

It is during this time that a member of the alumni relations department contacts me from Davidson.

I'm doing so well! I'm so impressive! I'm a force for good! I am the epitome of what Davidson wants their alumni to be. Would I be interested in being interviewed for the alumni journal?

'Sure,' I say to the woman, momentarily choosing to set aside the pain the professors and administrators at Davidson caused me. I've always hoped that, with time, the attitudes and the people who broke my heart in college would have been replaced with people like my classmates who arranged a calendar on my dormitory door to figure out how I would get three square meals a day.

I agree to conduct the interview via email.

Her questions are … odd. They centre around my disability

– what I can and cannot do (mostly what I cannot), with only a passing enquiry about what my experiences were like at Davidson.

I am quite blunt in my responses, talking about the dean who said to my mother: 'But we already have a disabled student selected for the class of 2006.' I share honestly about my relationship with the theatre department, although I don't talk about the verbal battering from my advisor.

I reframe her questions, saying, 'The question you really should be asking is—' and then answering that question. I take the focus off my diagnosis and put it onto my mind, my methods and my work.

She follows up with a few additional questions about the nature of cerebral palsy.

*

It is a miracle that I arrive at the Arts Club. It is the hottest day of the year, and my battery is dying, both literally and metaphorically. I am exhausted, and my wheelchair is at 39 per cent.

I tried to take a taxi. 'My wheelchair ramp isn't working,' they said. To be clear, the ramps are foldable pieces of metal that are set inside the floor of each cab. It is illegal to pick up passengers if anything is wrong with their wheelchair ramps.

I am going to a programme run by two women I know. They've called it 'Words and Theatre', or something along those lines. The idea is to take great actors and match them up with great short stories – it is, in essence, an unending procession of stars who have been conned into giving a night to the arts.

I roll/steer/walk myself across town, spending 35 per cent of my remaining 39 per cent of battery just getting to the venue. When

I arrive at the Arts Club, which claims to be accessible, I see the two steps up to its entrance.

I ask if there is a ramp. There isn't one.

Usually, my very expensive piece of equipment, my iBOT, mitigates the realities of inaccessibility, even in buildings that claim to be accessible. But with a depleted battery, I am like anyone else with limited mobility. And the Arts Club is breaking the law by affecting my equality of opportunity to enter.

I point this out to the porters, who shrug their shoulders and apologise. I know it's not their fault, per se, but they are complicit by working in a building that does not have appropriate entrances.

I call a cab, which thankfully does have a working ramp.

When I get home, I write an email to the head of the organisation that bases itself in the building, explaining that this is illegal and that I was informed by their website that the building was compliant with the Disability Discrimination Act. Unfortunately, I could not attend the event.

*

My college friend refused to understand why I was suing the rail company over their unwillingness to put down a ramp whenever I came home to Woolwich, and their general treatment of me.

She said I was being angry. And I was angry, but this was not an action built out of anger.

She said I was acting entitled. She did not realise that assuming entitlement takes a whole range of revolutionary acts against society.

'They don't even *have* wheelchair access where I live,' she said over FaceTime, as if to justify why I should be thankful for breadcrumbs.

How could this woman and I have known each other for eight years, and yet somehow have misread each other so completely?

You live in a third-world country. Are we really going to judge human rights on the basis of what a third-world country provides in terms of equal access to its disabled citizens? was what I wanted to say.

Instead, what I said was: 'It might not be the law where you live, but it's the law where I live, and there are rules to protect me from the lack of access.'

We were both immigrants who moved far away from Davidson College as soon as we graduated, because we could not wait to see what was waiting for us in the big, wide world that was promised by our professors and our families.

'Why does it even matter? It's just a train. Take a cab if you need to get—' she began.

'Because I signed a lease based on the assumption that the rail company would enable me to exit at the local train station. I made my life choice based on a map that the rail company created to show accessibility.'

'Well, you shouldn't have lived where you needed a rail station to get into town.'

At this, my already damaged brain was about to explode with reasons why: I wanted cheaper rent, I wanted more space, I wanted to be able to live where I wanted to, I wanted South Eastern to keep the promise their map had provided.

I looked through the screen at one of my oldest friends. We had been through break-ups and mishaps and travelled all over the world together. Yet to her, having a ramp at an accessible station, or indeed having any accessibility at all, was something 'nice to have'. Not something that I was entitled to.

I didn't question how much she loved me, but I did wonder how much she had been paying attention during the past decade.

*

By the time the reporter from Davidson gets back to me, it's been almost a year since the original interview.

A cursory read of her article sets off every single alarm bell I have. My sense of self-preservation starts weaving mass-produced red flags with an automatic loom. It's hard not to cringe.

This is not only out of date, it's insulting: 'Cerebral palsy-ridden', 'disabled', 'inspirational', 'struggling despite everything'.

It says nothing about my work with the Women's Equality Party, or the Olivier I was just nominated for. It focuses instead on how I needed to depend on people in my hall to get ready and survive at Davidson. This is fine and true, I did. But by honing in on this, she has turned a story that was sold to me as being about my accomplishments into one about how Davidson rescued a pathetic little cripple from the gutter of obscurity.

I am not in control of my own story. The actions of the unnamed and faceless man who hindered my mother's labour and delivery has taken centre stage in my life and is the lens through which my accomplishments are judged, highlighted or ignored.

But maybe I'm wrong.

I show the draft of the Davidson article to one of the founders of the Women's Equality Party, Catherine Mayer, who is the former Europe Editor and Editor-at-Large of *TIME* magazine. I don't have to wait nine months for her to respond. Instead, her name pops up in my inbox within about ninety seconds.

'Good God, this is awful!'

She offers to write a letter to the interviewer at Davidson to set the story straight. To explain why this interpretation of what happened is way off and is insulting to me, and belittling of my accomplishments. I give her the green light. After all, if I'm not going to be able to change this woman's mind, a personal email from a former editor at *TIME* magazine will do so, surely?

When the reporter sends me the second draft of her article, it's even more revolting than the first. The inference made is that I couldn't even get into Davidson of my own volition, and I was selected because I was 'special'.

Catherine is in disbelief that it is possible to make the piece even more insulting, yet here we are.

I write back and inform the reporter that what she has written is an example of inspiration porn. 'I'm not going to explain to you what that is – you need to figure that out on your own. I suggest you see Stella Young's TED Talk for reference, but please learn to be a writer and not a pornographer.'

Call it brash or call it wisdom, but I post the interviewer's final draft of the article on my Facebook page. 'I think this is ableist,' I explain, and invite people to respond if they agree or disagree in the comments section.

Comments such as 'yuck', 'gross' or 'how can someone from Davidson even write this way?' begin to flood my page. The current Student Union President offers to write to someone at Davidson on my behalf: 'Please don't see Athena's accomplishments through the lens of what someone else has done to her. She deserves better than that. Her accomplishments alone are enough for Davidson to be proud of. Don't even mention her disability.'

But I write to the head of the college myself – Davidson's very first female president – and ask her if, due to the nature of this article, 'Perhaps disabled students at Davidson are feeling discouraged for some reason. Do they feel alone on campus?'

I'm trying to give everyone the benefit of the doubt.

A fellow alumnus tags the Disability Studies professor at Davidson on my post. This is about to explode. I take the article down; I want nothing to do with the Disability Studies professor, who is able-bodied. She gets very prickly if anyone suggests that there is ableism baked into the Davidson culture and that she is complicit in it.

I get a response from the suits at Davidson. They have decided to pull the article. The Disability Studies professor includes a quote about how she's 'disappointed' in me. I am again a disappointment to professors at Davidson College. Rather than try to get it right, it's easier for my college to not give my successes any publicity at all. I made a mistake, according to them, and now they are disappointed by my mistake.

*

'Why the fuck did you do that to us? We have worked so hard to get the support of this organisation and put on a good show, and you just trash us?'

I receive an uproarious phone call from the acquaintances who put on the event at the Arts Club that I couldn't attend.

'I didn't trash you. The building is non-compliant. You do have a knack for setting your shows in inaccessible buildings.'

'WE CAN'T AFFORD ANYTHING ELSE!'

'If you can't afford to do the event where there is equal access, maybe you shouldn't be doing the event. I am very sorry that I disappointed you both,' I say, feeling like I am the non-compliant one.

Clearly, I am the problem; I should have made sure my battery was charged. I could have mitigated this disaster before I left the house. I hang up the phone, wishing I hadn't said anything at all. Later, I learn that a fellow writer was sitting in the back of the car with the two women. Apparently, after we hung up the phone, he set them right by pointing out 'that these are civil rights issues, to be challenged just like racism was back in the Sixties'. His father-in-law was a civil rights lawyer, one who took cases that should have made history – and some of them did – but far too many were lost in a system that didn't recognise its own prejudices.

The next time I bump into them both, one of the women touches my shoulders even though I am too afraid to say anything. I am like a deer in headlights, saying as little as possible, expecting another explosion. But it doesn't come.

As they walk away, I can feel a tightness in my muscles begin to loosen. They don't hate me. We can move on with our relationship, and act like nothing horrible happened.

That's good, I think.

About a year after the Arts Club, all relationships smoothed over, my friend and I are staying with one of the women who yelled at me in her B&B as paying guests.

At dinner, another guest pulls out a chair to sit beside me.

'Oh, be careful if you sit next to Athena,' our hostess says. 'You say the wrong thing and she will bite your head off.'

I look at the woman I have paid to host me in my escape from the ableism of London for the weekend. I don't say anything in the moment, but later that evening I write to her, explaining how hurtful her comment was. Within twenty minutes, she barges into my room, which is, admittedly, in one of her cabins, on her estate.

'You know you can catch more flies with honey than you can with vinegar? You are aggressive and you do hurt people.' I know this is her way of punishing me for what happened at the Arts Club.

When I pack up the cabin to return to London a few days later, I don't say anything to my hostess other than thanking her for the 'pleasant' stay.

'I really do hope you come again. It's so great having you here.'

I don't say it, but I'm not coming again. I'm not paying to be treated like this again. After what she has said about me and said to me, I'm not ever seeing her again.

Her husband walks us to the train station. It is in the middle of nowhere, caught between two cities in the UK. There is a single train that goes back and forth every hour.

When the train conductor gets out, he asks if I need a ramp. And I say, 'Yes, I'm really sorry but I do ... Sorry!'

It's my fault that I need a ramp. It's my fault that I went on holiday. It's my fault that I ruined the relationship by bringing the inaccessibility of a venue to everyone's attention.

'Don't apologise for requesting the things that you are entitled to,' the husband says to me. He doesn't make eye contact, but I can hear him say it over the familiar clatter of the ramp being put down. And then he hands me my suitcase, turns and walks away.

*

The BFI building on the South Bank tried to look chic, but it had always struck me as cold and old. My friend, The Fellow American, had brought me here to introduce me to two film producers he knew. The men were interested in optioning my take on a contemporary romantic comedy version of Cyrano de Bergerac. Female-led, social-media-driven, good-natured catfishing that would ultimately show the audience the truth about their squeamishness towards dating people with disabilities, and how everyone lies in relationships.

I looked at the glass of fizzy lemonade that had been sitting on the table, bubbling away.

'That means she wants some,' my friend said. It was an old joke between us. Or perhaps there was a slight tinge of virtue signalling towards the movie producers about it. I couldn't tell. When we first met, I was so shy that I let glasses of lemonade just sit on the table undrunk, rather than asking for help. Eventually, he said, 'You're looking at the lemonade a lot. Does that mean you want it?'

'Yes,' I said.

'Well, you could just ask.' *Touché.*

The movie producers leaned into me and said, 'We're really excited about this film. You're so talented and, quite frankly, it ticks a lot of boxes. We're a new production company so we're optioning it for five years. I know that's longer than most, but it'll take that long to get our boots on.'

I knew it ticks a lot of boxes. I wrote it that way. But I wasn't going to tell them that. They'd think I was being cocky. A young woman who knew what she was doing and had a plan lying underneath her creative vision that was marketable, money-making and strategic? Impossible.

Five years was far too long to hold someone's idea, but I was eager, new, and I didn't want to say no to the producers.

'We've not worked with someone with a disability before, so you have to tell us when things aren't right.'

There was a still-small voice in my head that was saying, *They don't actually want you to call them out when they are ableist. They won't be good on their word. Walk away now and avoid the inevitable hurt that is coming at you.*

But instead, I said, 'I'm sure it won't come to that.'

After signing the contract, everything was all smiles for the first eighteen months. When I delivered my first script, it was returned with some notes but full of praise. The contract stipulated that payment is due 'on delivery of the first draft' but I was too nervous to say anything about it.

Three months after delivery, and I still hadn't been paid. The contract did not stipulate whether or not I should write an invoice. I wrote an email asking for payment.

Within a matter of hours, I received a six-page email from the producers, destroying my professionalism. They ripped into my work, saying that I was a 'very problematic writer' and I was lucky to be working with them at all. A surge of tension and adrenaline rushed through my body.

After going back and forth, The Fellow American sided with them. So now I am no longer comfortable having a relationship with the movie producers, or the man who introduced us.

*

'This is why you need me,' the writing agent says to me. 'It's my job to take on the producers who abuse you. Nobody with professionalism should be making you jump through endless hoops to get paid.' The agent has invited me into her office for a cup of tea and to ensure we jive. So far, so good. I am getting very weary of suffering people's slings and arrows of outrageous behaviour once I request any level of professionalism.

'People only behave this way because they assume they can get away with it towards a disabled person. After you sign with me, nobody will behave this poorly towards you again. You can trust me.'

Time passes. *What is my script-writing agent doing?* Or maybe a better way to frame the question is, *What exactly does she do?* I send her ideas, outlines, scripts, notes on television shows I'd like to write for each week, but I never receive an answer. Finally, after two years of supposedly working together without actually working together, she emails me. 'I don't think I can give you the level of attention you need from an agent. I think it's best if we part ways.'

Insta-guilt occurs. I write back to her to apologise. *I am the one in the wrong. I am the one asking for too much. I really like her as an agent, and I don't know where else I would go. Please keep me on the books.*

She never responds.

A year later, the agent emails me. *How exciting, a West End theatre has commissioned me to write a new play.* It's time for 'my agent' to take 'her' 12 per cent.

'I'm confused, because the last I heard from you, you sounded as though you didn't want to be my agent. But now, you very clearly do. Which is certainly fine,' I email back in the warmest possible tone. 'But please, because my brain injury finds it very confusing, don't go back and forth like this.'

Less than a minute passes before the agent emails me back.

'How dare you accuse me of having a brain injury. I am no longer representing you.'

I am stunned. I'm very clearly the one with the brain injury here, not her. The fact that she claims that brain injuries are something one can be 'accused' of screams ableism. But now I am left without an agent again.

*

He has been acting weird. I've never seen him act this way. Like I am a burden.

He has asked me to join him this evening but when we arrive, one of his students greets him. She is bouncy, overly chatty, with frizzy hair; the kind of hair that is charming to the outside viewer but that the girl looking in the mirror might place all of her insecurities on. She is flirtatious, and it is clear she does not want me there. She cuts off any chance I have to make conversation between the three of us, or even just with him. She stands in between him and me, leaning into him and casually bumping up against him.

The bar area is noisy and overstimulating – an environment where I know my speech won't be understood. She marches over to a high table, one that is above my head until I raise my iBOT up to standing. Then she turns her back towards me, and her face towards him.

*

A group of women sit in a circle around the perimeter of the overly large main room with their heads bowed, eyes closed, and they pray. No one is looking at me, so I glance around the room and my eyes land on the pile of presents.

I have bought my friend a diaper bag. All of the mummy blogs that I've read say this is 'the one', and the price tag agrees. Plus, it's hot pink, her favourite colour.

I suddenly feel very alone in this room as I listen to the women repeat, 'We thank you in advance for the health of this baby.' It seems a bit presumptuous. *Why can't we just thank God for the baby?*

I can't get the prayer circle in that oversized living room out of my head. So I pull my friend aside and point out that this has made me uncomfortable.

'But of course my baby is going to be healthy,' she tells me. 'Why wouldn't she be? All the scans are turning out great. She's growing as she should. Pregnancies end in happy endings: birth.'

I look at her, suddenly feeling like an underappreciated Cassandra.

'You know that's not always true,' I say pointedly to my friend. I am Maleficent visiting the royal baby shower. A cautionary warning, saying, *Hello! Labour is hard and it can go very badly …*

The next four days I spend with her are a marathon of passive aggression. I remind myself that this is her first pregnancy, and I need to give her grace. But it is difficult when I realise that I can't blame all of her actions on hormones.

I keep thinking of that line: 'We thank you in advance for the health of this baby.'

Did my mother pray for the same in the months leading up to my birth?

*

It is a really stupid idea to show off photos of a topless woman at a family dinner.

'I don't think you should show me those kinds of photos of your ex-girlfriend.'

It's a shock that I have to say this, and I wonder how exactly he was raised to make him so sure that this kind of behaviour is OK.

'Well, she doesn't care, so why should you?'

Reading between the lines of his words, he is really saying: 'She doesn't know, so why should you care?'

But I don't think that's true. I think she would care if she knew. Whether or not she would have the confidence to tell him off herself is another story.

And I care because I've met his ex-girlfriend; I like her. I remind him that *I* care. And that should be enough to make him stop.

It's not.

'Well, you just don't like me having sex with anyone else,' he claims.

That's not true. I just don't like seeing photos of topless women without knowing that they have given their consent.

*

I keep reminding myself that she's his student as she makes my friend buy her three drinks over the next hour. Downing them as quickly as possible, she laughs as she leans into him, and then backs away. It's textbook, and very irritating.

Every time I ask her a question, she looks at me blankly and says, 'Sorry, I can't understand you,' and then goes back to whatever she was talking about with him.

I wasn't expecting exclusivity; I knew that some of his students might be here. But this is different. I could fall into a crack in the floor and I don't think either of them would notice.

As much as I feel frustrated, I begin to feel equally unsafe, unheard and unseen. And it is this last triad that makes me excuse myself for the evening.

Yes, I am irritated. Yes, I am upset. But mostly I don't think it's appropriate for me to stay in an environment where I can't be understood and am not listened to. I have better things to do with my time, and I keep telling myself this. I walk to the Southwark

Tube station with her laughter and flirtatious vibes on loop in my mind.

*

I can't not say something. I text him and say I think we need to talk about what happened. I didn't feel comfortable with the way things were handled.

But he twists it into the excuse that I didn't have a good time because I wasn't drinking. Maybe if I had a bit more alcohol in me, I would've had a better time, but that's not his fault.

'I'm not saying it is your fault. I just want you to know that I wasn't comfortable with what happened.'

'Why don't you just stop talking about this before I lose all respect for you?'

This is the ultimate red flag pointing towards an abusive relationship. My factory-enabled red-flag maker is now loaded with cheap material and set to high speed, making as many items in the shortest amount of time.

Red flag! Red flag! Red flag!

*

The debate over topless photos and consent rises in temperature over the course of the coming months. I don't want to stop the friendship; I want him to get his pretty little blond head screwed on straight.

Using all the right words, gleaned from *Teen Vogue* and Vox documentaries, I try and fail to explain to him about image-based sexual abuse. Showing me those images without consent is legally considered sexual abuse; not just towards the woman in the photo, but towards me as a disabled woman. In the UK, eliciting any sort of unwanted sexual activity, including showing people images that they did not consent to see, is legally sexual abuse when it is done to a 'vulnerable adult'.

I think back on all the times I have gone out on his arm to public events: being shown off, smiled at, smiling back, laughing at his jokes. And then I remember the side glances he would direct towards everyone else, making sure there was an audience present.

Eventually he leaves a voicemail saying that he would show me topless pictures of his girlfriends because that's what he does with the women he loves – making it very clear that if I don't like it, it matters very little to him.

In saying he will do this again in his voicemail, I have on record that he has threatened me with sexual abuse.

My friend has sexually abused me, and he said he is willing to do it again.

*

I read my post once more and then hit send. News about Caroline Flack's suicide comes out of the speakers of my laptop on BBC Radio 3.

My flatmate is taking a once-in-a-lifetime opportunity to move to South Korea. I need to find someone willing to live with me and help me eat breakfast and dinner. It takes a total of about an hour a day to be my roommate in exchange for living in a large bedroom with an en-suite bathroom and a private balcony, for about £350 a month – enough to cover the shared bills on the house. The responsibilities are minimal at best, requiring no nursing degree. I dress myself, I toilet myself, I work with my company to keep my life moving and organised.

The forum I have posted the listing on is called 'BOSSY' – a Facebook forum for women in theatre who are looking for work, looking out for each other, looking to share tips and become assertive in an unfair world together. Two minutes after I hit send, a response comes in on Facebook. 'No, thank you. I don't have to work where I live.' I respond with: 'If it's not right for you, that's fine, but it might be right for someone else.'

Within an hour, a cybermob of hundreds has ganged up on me.

'You're an Associate Artist at the Globe Theatre! You're privileged! How dare you ask someone to pay for the privilege of working with you! What a presumptuous bitch you are!'

I go back online, explaining the reality of the situation from a disability rights perspective: I don't want to live in a care home. I don't need so much help to justify employing a carer. In the UK, there is a government dispensation for people with disabilities to hire at-home carers. As an immigrant, I'm not entitled to that, so if I wanted to hire any kind of aide in London, it would have to come from my own pocket.

Someone else goes online trying to explain the independent-living movement – how people like me have a right to decide what their own care looks like. The cybermob shifts and diverts to attack both of us. Apparently, there are 'homes for people like us'.

'You know, anyone can become disabled. And when that happens to you or you have the privilege of raising a disabled child, I really hope you remember your behaviour.'

That evening, a friend sends me a link to Reddit's 'Extremely Privileged and Arrogant Karens' thread. My post is on there. My name is blacked out, but I am recognisable because of who I am, what I've asked for and the location of my offer.

I email the moderators of BOSSY and explain what is happening. They are appalled to learn that my private information has been captured and the screenshot has been posted on Reddit.

'We're stopping the site. Those whose avatars we can track are being notified that this behaviour is unacceptable. I am so sorry this has happened. Please do go to the police. You never know when a record of this might help someone else,' they reassure me.

Another news story comes on the radio about Caroline Flack – suspicions about why she committed suicide, naming online forums as part of the cause of her depression.

It is 20 February 2020.

Chapter 18

'There is no right thing to do here. It's about what you want to do.'

I look at this man, made small by my iPad screen. Like many people from the past few years, I have no idea how he looks in three dimensions. All I know is that he's a damn good solicitor and seems to be on Planet Earth. He's also kind. There's the added bonus that he can keep up with my brain; four factors for which the overlapping area of the Venn diagram is painfully small.

This is the seventh solicitor I've collected in my menagerie since becoming an adult.

My life has been tangled up with lawyers from my Birth Day. I don't want them in my life, but they aren't foreign objects either. I call them in as a last resort, when alone I cannot hold the pieces shattered by inequality any more.

Judges are concerned with the weight and letter of the law, whereas lawyers sit next to a person as a fellow human who provides protection. They act as a brace to hold what has thus far been made irreparable, upright and balanced, shielding it from more harm.

I call in a lawyer when I need a rest.

Only not now. Now, this man on my eleven-inch iPad screen

has completely upended my cosmology and thrown me into a swirling chaos.

'There is no right thing to do here.'

What strange language is this Atticus Finch lookalike on my screen speaking?

'So, you're telling me, no matter what I do, I'm in hell. But at least I get to choose which hell I'm in.'

'Yes. You get to choose which hell you are in. What do you want, Athena?'

The concept of actually getting a choice, even at my age, ties me in a Gordian knot.

*

I basically had to pull my own teeth to sit down with the theatre's access director. I've had a lifetime of meeting people with such titles, promising to help, only to prove themselves obstructive – *This is a case of good, better, best, Mrs Stevens.* He asked me if I wanted a drink, then asked me if I needed a straw. *So, at least I get a peach lemonade out of the deal*, I tell myself. The Access Guy takes out his Moleskine notebook and a pen.

He has beautiful handwriting. Not the perfect Catholic-school 'nuns-slap-you-on-the-wrist-if-your-loop-de-loops-aren't-right' script, but actual 'wedding-invitation calligraphy'.

'You have the kind of writing that always makes me wish I could write by hand.'

'This is my chicken scratch, actually. I'm dyslexic and it's a coping mechanism. As a kid, I figured out that if I had good handwriting, teachers were less likely to point it out if a letter was backwards.'

Ah.

'Well, I'm here. What can I do for you today?'

I say this often. This phrase is the best I've found to cut to the chase and get to the meat of the conversation and away from the chit-chat of small talk. I frame it as an act of service.

'I was told I just had to meet you.' I see the sparkle in his eye, and I do not like it. It is the sparkle that says, 'We're gonna get along great, I'm on your team,' but actually means, 'You are going to make me look good.' There's excitement in that sparkle. Maybe it starts out as genuine, but far too often, I've seen it warp into something else.

'OK, let's get this out of the way. I'm in this building as a creative, not as an access consultant. I'm not willing to do the same work I do here as I do for the London Underground or Heathrow. I don't want to be measuring toilets or giving access advice.' Advice which able-bodied people then choose not to listen to.

'God, no. Toilets are my job. I spend half my time undoing the red assistance cords in all accessible loos that well-meaning people think shouldn't be touching the dirty floor. It's Sisyphean.' *Nice classical reference*, I think.

'Look, my job as the Access Guy is to take care of the loos, and the doorways, the gatekeepers, and anyone else who doesn't "get it", so that as an artist, you can do your best work. This conversation should have started with me asking how I could help you.'

I'm not going to buy it on the first offer. I would much rather be talking to a director or lighting designer at this point in my one wild and precious life.

'You don't like me, do you?' he says.

'I don't know you.'

At best, The Access Guy will see that as a joke. At worst, he will concede that I've got a point and back off a step. But even if he puts me down as 'aggressive at first point of contact', he'd have to give me some slack if he still wants to win me over.

'Why are you in this job?' I hold myself back from my usual enthusiastic performance of 'Like me, like me, you work for a theatre, please like me!' I look out the window at London streaming by, then take a gentle tug on my drink to avoid eye contact.

'I started out as a dancer. Got injured. Needed a second career.' I wait for the inevitable monologue about how it took him hobbling around London with a torn ligament for the scales to be lifted from his eyes, enabling him to see that his local Tube station had no lifts. My 'we are not amused' face was on standby.

'Plus, I saw that we have lots of people all ready to go in for a fight for LGBTQ+ rights. And I benefit from that. You shouldn't have to measure loo doors yourself.'

He's won.

'You need to know something upfront about this place, Athena. When we built the new theatre four years ago, several of our producers asked if it could be built to not include wheelchair seating.'

'Wait! What? Why?'

*

I could fall at mid-2000s Steve Jobs's feet and kiss them for inventing the Spotlight search engine. If it were possible, I would use the search bar in my email app until it's worn through. But the joy of digital rather than analogue indexing means that there are no warped gears grinding down each other's teeth. The switching between searching for keywords, first names, last names and phrases I remember in specific emails flows back and forth until I find the document I'm looking for.

Still, sometimes I panic when the email I thought would appear doesn't come from the first or second search. I have to think tangentially in my mind and dig through threads, trying to calm the tension of possibly tripping over myself. Then my breathing slows each time I land firm-footed on the information I knew was there. Each time the text in question strobes on the screen, I highlight the pertinent lines and hit the forward button. *Here are the receipts.* The millennial equivalent of a smoking gun.

It is 4.17 in the morning. I woke up at 2.37, sweating. I hate the mid-sleep ruminations and fears, but I am too well acquainted with them.

When it's clear the breathing exercises and the Hank and John Green podcast isn't going to send me back to sleep, a continuously painful parade of possible points of imperfection trample across my bed. The only way to stop it is to grab my phone and double-check my own sanity. Then, I might as well just pass it on.

Hopefully they have their notifications on Do Not Disturb.

Sometimes in looking for one specific email, a line or a text that has gone missing, I find details I've forgotten about, which prove to be helpful. Soon my heart rate goes back down. I am wise. I see the truth. Other people choose not to see it.

*

Four long chipboard tables were brought together to form a sort of rectangle with a gap in the middle. The tables came from various rehearsal rooms pulled together at the last minute in a sort of makeshift boardroom that only artists would be content with. There is no head, there is no bad seat.

I, of course, brought my own chair to the table.

'Southwark Council has a disproportionately high percentage of disabled people because of the number of care homes in the area.' The Access Guy says this in explanation to my queries, as well as to inform everyone else around the table who might not notice that having a 25 per cent disabled population in a single borough is not average. One in five people are disabled according to British statistics. If you account for age and remove elderly people, it goes down to about one in eight.

It's a meeting of the minds that the theatre has instituted to add an artistic voice alongside the board of directors. I'm not sure people realise that we around the table have no power. There's nothing in the charity's by-laws that stipulates our existence. We are a think tank, essentially, a nice thing to have, which can be easily pulled if proven to be a nuisance.

But the people around the table take themselves very seriously. It's an honour to be sitting around the table. You have made it in the theatre if you sit around this table. Unless you're The Access Guy. Then you haven't 'made it in theatre', you're just a nice thing to have around.

'I don't think we should be expecting our directors to hit quotas in their productions when it comes to disability,' says a well-known director. 'I think people might feel constrained or intimidated.'

The reality of having one in four people on stage with a disability would completely up-end the entire industry. For one thing, you would run out of experienced actors quickly if the West End had to have a cast with 25 per cent disabled people. Not to mention the fact that it would be a nightmare considering all theatre buildings that managed to survive the bombings of the Second World War are considered 'historically significant'.

The director would be standing on much firmer ground had we not decided ten minutes ago that all productions in the theatre would require a cast that fitted the proportions of racial and gender diversity in Southwark. Now, doing the same for disability is on the chipboard table.

I am the only one with a disability at the table. I have a fraction of the experience of everyone else in the room. I felt the weight of expectation that comes with eyes looking at me. Each of them could give me a job if they wanted.

'It's just not right to put such restrictions on creative people. You're going to curb everyone's creativity if you start policing every detail of a production. Does that make sense?' the director adds.

The Access Guy puts down his pen and his notebook covered with his perfectly beautiful handwriting with a sigh. He sits back in his chair, crossing his arms. I can see him looking at me from the corner of his eye.

After the meeting, The Access Guy and The Gal Pal hang back. I like The Gal Pal. After two years working off and on in a theatre, which assures me I belong but still has so much power over me, The Gal Pal has proven herself to be as much of an ally as The Access Guy. The Gal Pal has given me the low-down on which people in the building I need to steer clear of for my own sanity.

'Are you OK?' The Gal Pal says, grabbing my shoulder and kneeling in front of me.

I try to avoid eye contact as I zip up my bag.

'Yeah, that was awful,' The Access Guy backs up.

Only then do I notice that my leg is shaking, vibrating in tiny movements that I couldn't reproduce if I tried. With my elbows on my knees, I cover my head with my hands.

'I should have fought back harder. I should have argued more. Why didn't I say something? I'm privileged in this industry!'

'You're not privileged, Athena. These arses need to do the work, not you.' The Gal Pal puts her hands on the top of my head.

In this moment I hate her.

I hate her because she must be wrong.

Then The Access Guy speaks very quietly.

'They had their minds made up before the conversation ever began.'

*

My phone is a time machine. As is my saved email folder. I can't change anything going backwards in time, but I can relive what happened. And I have proof that my memories can be trusted, my brain can be trusted, and that when people around a chipboard table say, 'It's a shame she misunderstood our intentions,' or, 'Athena doesn't understand,' it's a form of gaslighting rather than truth.

A combination of hands that won't play ball on a good day, and the familiar, painful electrical surge of emotion charging through my body, means that it's nearly impossible to take screenshots. Instead, I end up turning on the lock screen when I can't flick the two buttons required at the same time, or push myself out of the app by mistake when brushing against the phone screen in the wrong direction.

I google 'Can text messages be used as evidence UK?' even though I already know the answer. My solicitor has asked for these screenshots, and now I am doubting my solicitor. But at least I'm doubting an able-bodied white man. It's probably evening out the universe somehow.

*

'This is a good start. But if we're going to have an anti-racism policy, where is our anti-ableism policy? Where's our gender-equality policy?' How many policies must a theatre have to make clear its anti-oppression stance? I've spent eighteen hours this week editing a document to try to give it some sort of cohesion. Our policy has been spliced and diced from a variety of other establishments' policies.

The document includes the wonderful musings of James Baldwin, Martin Luther King Jr, Pablo Picasso and Gandhi.

There is only one woman quoted. I did point out that Picasso's granddaughter had said that he flagrantly and purposely set out to ruin every woman he claimed to love, as well as the fact that he was a paedophile – as was Gandhi.

'We'll get to those,' the woman at the theatre's helm says to me from her *Brady Bunch* rectangle in the corner of my screen. 'This is … we'll get this one out first. I think it's important, given what's happened this summer, to establish this as policy in this theatre as soon as possible.'

The Access Guy is catty-corner to her. I watch his cheeks puff out as he exhales and then make as though his doorbell has rung, thus leaving the screen.

She thinks it's important to get the anti-racism policy out as soon as possible given the murder of George Floyd.

I think the policy is a complete mess and could do a lot of harm as is.

Whatever happened to not wanting to work in this building as anything other than an artist? Then again, with the industry shut down and my brain currently working at half-capacity thanks to brain fog, being an artist is not really an option for anyone. I should be thankful for the work and the opportunity to collaborate, even if it's on policy, rather than performance.

Working on policy during this time would lead to more opportunities for performance within this theatre, I tell myself.

'It's like … well, I was telling my husband this this morning, it just feels impossible to breathe right now,' she says.

'Well, it's a good thing you have someone who was literally born with a lack of oxygen and no pulse working for you,' I say in response. I say it because I can think of no other semi-intelligent response to the wording of her description. All the other responses that rattle through my brain either sound morally superior or snarky.

Covid has made me useful: a handy combination of knowing how to get things done without leaving the four walls of my flat and a parasympathetic nervous system that makes a state of emergency seem like everyday life means that the entire world shutting down weirdly plays to my advantages. I am the one now suggesting to the theatre how to stage classical plays for consumption on YouTube.

'Just think about doing *The Tempest*, but everyone onboard the boat has an iPhone and they're recording the island as they see it. The educational foundations would love us, and you could do all sorts of dramatic moments where people have low battery and need to make a solar charger or something environmentally sustainable.'

'Hopefully we will be back to normal before something like that can get made.'

By the time The Access Guy comes back on the screen, it's clear that any additional identity-based anti-oppression documents are going to be on the back burner.

*

'Tell me what happened.' The solicitor stares back at me, encased in the screen to my left. I'm poised over my laptop, ready to take notes as to what I need to do next to make this whole situation go away. But he wants to hear from me, in the words I choose. What do I tell him that I haven't already told the people involved?

The only words I can think to put together: *I thought I would be different. I thought I could change them.*

I was groomed to believe I was making a difference, and doing that was the sole function of my life, even if it harmed me in the process. How do I explain that I went along to get along, sitting around the chipboard tables thinking their decisions were wrong but they didn't apply to me? This rift happened because I fall down at the idol of other people's approval every time I am asked. Worse, I come on bended knee to this gilded figure not because I doubt my value, but as a strategy. The only way to get anything done as someone who this world isn't built for is to persuade other people to like me.

The directors who didn't want to feel 'required' to put disabled people in their productions didn't mean *me*. The producers and theatre administrators who didn't want to build wheelchair spaces in their new theatre couldn't have meant *me*.

The creative who thought she was exceptional in acting, writing, in the ability to analyse the resources and opportunities that are available, who pulls out the best in people, will surely dodge the discrimination simmering beneath the surface? Once I change them, then the wall would be down and such theatre-makers would never dream of building performance spaces that didn't have accessible seating.

This happened because I thought I could skip over discrimination.

Ableism, I thought, was about ability, and I had ability in overabundance by any establishment's measure.

Nobody ever told me that the nub which sits at the base of true discrimination is a desire to control. If they had, my teachers, mentors and therapists would have also had to tell me there was so much out of my control.

*

I jump body first onto my bed as the phone chimes with another voice note. The summer sun is streaming into the open window, and I have left a path between the porch and the inside of my room so that one can cool the other, but the temperature is such that I'm not sure which way it's working. A second voice note follows with a LOL emoji quickly behind.

'You cannot get yourself out of that hole you just dug! I'm never going to let you live that one down! I cannot believe you had a dream where Rishi Sunak was a camp counsellor. Where did your parents send you to camp?'

The few hours after the daily Covid briefings and before the sun sets is when The Gal Pal and I grow our friendship. The past few months have been wonderful in that way. I have given up texting since succumbing to Long Covid, but voice notes are great, particularly when both of you are working together in the same organisation but still under the urge to stay inside. Anyone who doesn't need to be in the theatre building gets to stay at home, which is great for a self-proclaimed introvert like The Gal Pal.

I can tell everyone is on high alert if I'm out and about; more so than before the pandemic. But for once I have an excuse to duck back inside for weeks at a time and not deal with the daily assault of mundane microtraumas that is living in London for anybody, much less any body.

I can feel my blood pressure dropping as the weeks go by.

'Yeah, yeah, you can hold that against me during the second lockdown,' I say.

Another LOL from her and then: 'Wait, what do you mean, the second lockdown?'

'You know, when we all have to do this again in winter.'

'What?'

'Because people will be indoors and we don't have a vacc—'

I realise mid-sentence that she hasn't thought of this, and as much as she is an introvert, for her, being single and alone in a one-bedroom apartment is an entirely different experience to what I am having. It feels as if I'm breaking apart the vulnerable foundations she's just laid down for herself in an attempt to return to normalcy. For weeks, we've been talking about green shoots appearing within the theatre world, and now I am taking my Dr. Martens and walking all over the ones she's found – with my very uneven gait.

'Nooooo! No! Fuck me, we're not going to have to do this … we're going to have to do this again, aren't we? Oh, Athena, I don't know if I can do this again.'

*

I run down a timeline in my own words for the solicitor.

I am proud of the words I've chosen, proud of the details I can condense into single lines and still make sense. I am proud that I can say this for the umpteenth time when someone asks me 'What happened?' in a way that might not convince anyone to help my cause, but will at least leave me with a shred of energy.

But brevity is not the soul of wit. Keeping it short has only come through months of not wanting to get off the couch; of keening; of rehashing why I didn't stop when I saw the warning signs screaming that I wasn't different, that these people I thought I could change were going to hurt me – all while watching K-dramas and looking at floorplans on Rightmove, also known as the millennial's form of dissociation.

When I disconnect from the Zoom call, I open a new email. Letter by letter, I type in Mr Solicitor's name and that of his assistant, thinking about how that word has such different connotations for the two of us. He has an assistant, and in the eyes of the world that is a symbol of his success. I have many assistants: The Dresser, The Movement Director, The Twin, The Lithuanian, The Roommate, and the list goes on. They assist me by feeding me meals, putting my bra on, taking my dictation, and somehow having them is not an emblem of success for me. My use of assistants is equated with me being deficient somehow, rather than a success.

And because I am assumed to be deficient, I know my words are not considered truth in situations like the one I have brought to my solicitor.

My character isn't enough.

It takes a paper trail, and an able-bodied man's law degree.

I will never have the latter, but I am an expert at keeping the former.

A quick line about how nice it was to meet him and here is the timeline of events I talked about in our conversation is all my brain can eke out.

I add this because I've been told that it's rude to simply send an attachment, and even more rude to send it just with the words 'hi' or 'as we discussed'.

A friend once told me that people remarking that someone is 'too blunt' can be a sign of neurodiversity. As is oversharing to gauge and conform to other people's expectations, and feeling the need to log every single interaction.

'What if you feel the need to do all of that, because experience has taught you that shit goes down if you don't balance on a knife edge? What if it's a logical cause and effect telling you that you can't make a mistake?'

'That's a trauma response,' was her deft and definitive reply.

*

'I'm going to tell you something, and I don't want you to be mad,' The Gal Pal begins. That's all her voice note consists of, but I could tell she took a deep breath before she said it.

'I'm not going to be mad. There is nothing you could possibly say in this moment that will make me mad.'

Why do people always assume I will be mad? The swing back and forth of being called a political revolutionary and then aggressive results in chronic whiplash, even when induced by a good friend. *Someday,* I tell myself, *I will figure out where the boundary is between hailed Wonder Woman and the harassed Angry Woman. Then I will do everything possible to make sure I never cross that line.*

The new message from The Gal Pal comes through.

'All right, here goes … Ummm … That actor you were friends with and then you basically broke it off with him – we're casting him for an upcoming production.'

The news didn't surprise me at all. He had worked for them before I did. I knew it was a matter of time before the theatre called his phone again.

'I'm not mad. But now you have a problem. I know this man sexually abuses women. He abused me.'

I hope, as I say these words, that I will stay safe. I hope the burden of the situation isn't about to fall on me. I want this to be a blip and then to move on.

For the next hour, I joke with The Gal Pal. I compare the actor to an angry cat meme, jokingly offering to play opposite him in the production. I tell her I am not mad. Theatre in London is such a tiny tribe; I had already figured this was going to happen someday.

'I promise you, I'm not letting him get through our door. I hate him for having life so easy in this industry.'

'Well, my dear Gal Pal, it might not be up to you. You can't kick him out just because I said he did something. There are procedures to follow, I'm sure.'

'Yeah, I guess there will be. Let me talk to The Access Guy. This will never happen, Athena. We won't let it.'

*

'Well, I'm really not happy.' I watch as the solicitor tosses the paper to the side of his desk. 'I mean, I wrote these guys a letter – what? – six weeks ago and I've not had any response. At all.'

I wonder if the solicitor can see my patronising smile from the camera of my iPad. So I look away. *Aw, Mr Solicitor, are you annoyed because they are ignoring you? Welcome to my reality.*

But I don't say that. I am paying him by the hour, after all.

'Oh, for the love of God, just hit send already,' I say, putting on a straight face.

'OK … I've sent it. We are now suing Shakespeare's Globe.'

Chapter 19

For every action there is an equal and opposite reaction.
Forces come in pairs.
An object at rest will stay at rest and an object in motion will
stay in motion unless acted upon by an external force.

Odysseus and Varian would lead our class in discussions around the theme of betrayal when we studied Benedict Arnold, Brutus, Judas and Cassius, as well as the summer they executed the Rosenbergs. Betrayal wasn't just a word whispered alongside 'infidelity' in the circles of church gossip.

'Betrayal is when the ground upon which you stand and thought was stable crumbles off the edge of a cliff. It's when the pillars you were leaning against suddenly give way.'

I have tested this surface, and it can be counted upon to steady me, you say. So, if it breaks, you blame yourself. You must not have tested it thoroughly enough. Something must have gone wrong in the preliminary calculations. Like so many avoidable disasters, you should have noticed where the support had worn thin over time.

The pain from the impact of the fall is your fault.

*

The Gal Pal and the Access guy are chosen to take down my disclosure about the abuse. That's a formal, institutional attempt at pleasantries for the term 'to take a witness statement'. Witness statements are tied up with a legal system. 'Disclosures' are about giving information to people and institutions, not legal processes.

It takes over an hour to explain the abuse. I talk about the fact that I am not alone in being abused by this person, and that I feel the position Shakespeare's Globe is hiring him for is how he could find his next victim. I speak freely, having been through the emotional and creative work needed to sit with the pain of a friend lost and the perception of love shattered in my heart. That pain, like the brain injury and the so many other human failings in life, won't go away. But at least I have done good work on it. My brain's inability to rest when things are left unfinished means that I have been able to create paid, award-winning work out of what has happened. It also means I'm very good at telling the story.

There is silence when I am done with my monologue.

'The first thing that needs to be said – and, Athena, I know you probably don't like the term, but legally, you are considered to be what is called a "vulnerable adult".'

I don't mind the term. I tell The Access Guy I love that word – vulnerable. Any person who calls me 'vulnerable', not to deny me power, but as a way to give me the privilege of rest, is a person I need for support.

I'll need all the support I can get as I work in that building. The alternative is that this person gets the job and I'm not in the building. So, while this person works, I lose work because I am 'vulnerable'.

After the years of #MeToo pulling abuses into the light, as well as my own work to protect artists – paid for by the Globe, ironically enough – I'm not supposed to be the one losing work when someone else is dangerous.

I am thanked for my disclosure and told that I won't need to repeat any of it again. I can take care of myself now. The Access Guy and The Gal Pal will take it further. They tell me I am safe at the Globe and they will take care of me. I don't need to worry.

Before I go to bed that night, I sit in front of my television screen and pull up a YouTube video of a ball bouncing back and forth across the screen. This will help my brain's hemispheres talk to each other and increase the chances of extinguishing any rumination that might keep my brain up that night. Little Grey Cat sits next to me and watches the digital ball bounce back and forth, too. That night I sleep for a full eight hours.

*

The Gal Pal calls me forty-eight hours later. 'The Access Guy is not letting him in the building.'

'Why?'

'Because he believes women, Athena.'

I burst into tears. The iPhone sits on my lap, blurred in my vision. Someone just believed me. My character was enough.

But I also know what The Access Guy is doing isn't enough.

'He can't do that. You can't simply not hire someone because of what I say. There have to be processes, procedures.' I think of my high-school history classes, how our civilisation is claimed to be built on the presumption of innocence.

I hear all the stories about women telling lies with regards to their abuse, and how people fall back on the phrase 'Athena doesn't understand' when I say something they don't like.

'No, Athena. We believe you. You said it. You were brave and you said it, and that's all it takes. You're done. You did well. Rest.'

I believe her.

There is nothing else to do for the next six weeks.

My mind is made up not to worry if my artistic home hires the person who abused me or not. Outside of disclosing my lived experiences, I don't know what else I can do, and what action the theatre should take. I have zero control over the situation, nor do I have any legal qualifications.

For the first time maybe in my life, I decide not to take up the weight of outcomes. And it feels good.

*

It has been six weeks since that meeting. I check my email before going to bed when a new one appears.

Executive Nobody Special has emailed me an invitation to meet on Friday evening for an 'informal chat' about my 'conversation' with The Access Guy and The Gal Pal. They 'don't want to rely on second-hand information'.

I am alone and I start convulsing, sweating, and my muscles go into spasm and seize. This has never happened to me before. Doctors have often told me that, because of my brain injury, if a panic response is activated, my body can go into more extreme shock than those without brain damage. But I have never experienced any response that could be considered out of the range of 'normal' before. After all the overcoming I have accomplished in my life, it takes one email from Nobody Special to literally knock me off my seat and onto the floor.

Shaking, reaching blindly on top of my desk, I pull my phone down with a clatter and a thud. I need to communicate what is happening, and I am a writer; writing is how I put into words what is happening; to tell someone. *I can't breathe.* Words from my high-school psychology class like 're-traumatisation' become audible in my head. I can hear my teacher talking about how people are more likely to change their story if they're asked to repeat it over and over; not because the victim is being deceitful, but because layer upon layer of emotions on the brain frustrate clarity.

I finally control my fingers enough to send a voice note to The Gal Pal and The Access Guy. It is late, so I don't expect a response, but I get two.

'They're not talking about your disclosure with us. I have no idea why Nobody Special would want to talk with you. Do you want me to tell them to stop?' The Access Guy offers.

The Gal Pal's voice note raises my alarms more: 'They have locked The Access Guy and me out of all conversations. We're not allowed in meetings where they talk about you. Any effort I make is shut down.'

'But I need The Access Guy,' I send back to Gal Pal. 'He's a reasonable adjustment because communication is hard. The Globe can't take away my reasonable adjustment when they've already given it.'

The voice messages flying back and forth cause my heart rate to return to baseline when I hear confirmation about what I am experiencing. And then it shoots back up again when the next details are unveiled, so much so that my Apple Watch sends me a warning about overexerting myself.

'I don't think Executive Nobody Special has dealt with any abuse victims in their life,' says The Gal Pal.

'Have they had any disability-rights training? The Access Guy said I was a vulnerable person; do they know that? I thought I was done with having to do this again.'

'Honestly, I don't think they know what a vulnerable person is. I don't think the Globe even has a safeguarding policy.'

My head spins as I try to figure out which way is up in this world; where what I had is suddenly taken away. Where discussing my sexual abuse can be framed as an 'informal chat' on a Friday evening.

What do I have left to use as a point of stability? To hold me upright? I have the worst of any possibility for someone with cerebral palsy: no way to know which direction was up, and no stability.

Everything I have attempted to hold on to is crumbling. This isn't the theatre that I have worked for years to help create.

I know these people. I trust these people. I have done nothing but outstanding work as a performer and director on their stage, as a strategist during the pandemic, even representing them while making speeches to Westminster.

And then The Gal Pal says something that makes everything go from emergency to sudden death: 'The Higher-Ups have known about your disclosure for six weeks. The project starts in a few days and the director has no idea this has been disclosed to us.'

My life has been shaped by inaction and complicity.

One of the most common things I hear is: 'Be patient with me, be gracious, I'm still learning, and I don't know how to handle people like you.'

It is a privilege afforded to very few to be allowed an authentic reaction in this world, even in times of great distress. Women bite their tongue for fear of being labelled as 'aggressive'. People of colour slowly inhale and exhale against the risk of the word 'angry' being placed in neon lights above their head. People like me should be thankful for what they have been given because it can all be taken away at someone's whim.

How long do you give someone patience, allowing them to learn and hide behind ignorance before they trample on that grace; until you finally realise they are not actually interested in 'still learning'?

But that wasn't where I was with the Globe, right? Far from it, I thought. I have earned the right to an authentic reaction with them, particularly in the middle of poor procedure and strife. It would be dishonest not to show them my reaction, which is tied up in my neurological condition. They, with their anti-oppression policy, can afford me my own grace and genuineness.

I have been good enough to earn that. And so, while I respond to their emails, I set boundaries to protect my mental health when none of the procedures legally required from them are in place.

I am also clear over these emails that I am having a heightened reaction due to both my disability and my past abuse, and it may take days to undo what has happened tonight.

No constructive help is offered. Instead, there is silence for another week.

Inaction.

*

The project start date gets closer.

I record my statement on video and hand my phone to the Globe, outlining evidence on it: abusive messages and threats directly from the person they wanted to hire.

At the very least, they can't ask me for my statement again and I can't be proved inconsistent. All they have to do if Executive Nobody Special and the Higher-Ups have any questions is pull up the recordings that contain all the information.

Within a week, the Globe returns my phone. They say it is a police concern, not theirs. They will hire the abuser, and the role I have been doing for the last few years will be put on pause for the time being. I have effectively lost my first full-time job.

I tell myself that the Higher-Ups at the Globe will see sense and logic, and the law will prevail. I am not going to lose my job. How could I lose my job when I was harmed by their lack of procedure? It's like being locked in a car that is heading towards a cliff with no one at the wheel, and then complaining about taking a wrong turn in a useless attempt to avoid disaster.

The Access Guy spotted right away that I was a vulnerable adult. Have people somehow forgotten all the meals they've fed me? Literally put food on a fork and fed me. The cups with straws they held?

'I don't think of you as having a brain injury,' must be the new progressive answer to disability.

Three days later, I receive an email from someone at the Globe I have never met. Apparently, he works in HR. I had no idea that the Globe had an HR guy. *Where has he been for the last eight weeks?* He says that The Gal Pal and The Access Guy will not be allowed to contact me for the foreseeable future.

A while later, I visit the Globe for the first time in months. I don't expect to see The Gal Pal, or The Access Guy, or any of the Higher-Ups there. And I don't.

Instead, I see an eight-foot-tall picture of myself performing in my wheelchair hanging above the box office.

I laugh. *See, they still like me! They still want me as part of their establishment! How could someone who has caused a loss in their 'trust and confidence' also be their poster child?*

If I think about the photo too much, I feel objectified. But I just have to trust and use the same optimism that everyone else cleaves to in times of crisis. Even if it means not looking at reality.

*

It is now April, six months since the email putting my position at the Globe on hold. With my picture still hanging larger than life above the box office, I am told I won't be getting my job back.

Three separate solicitors tell me that I am too late to file a discrimination complaint; I should have done it when I was 'fired' in October.

'But I didn't know I was fired in October! I was waiting while giving them the opportunity to fix their mistakes.'

'Employment tribunals give you three months to file for discrimination. Judges don't take any excuses for falling outside that timeline.'

'But it took longer than three months to do the investigation. It took six.'

'They probably knew that, and drew out the investigation on purpose. Sorry.'

*

I ask the Globe for updates about their safeguarding procedures being put into place. I get no response. I have someone else start correspondence for me in hopes that an able-bodied person will be respected where I am not.

285

There is still no answer.

From April until August, I remember nothing except staring at the wall and obsessively waking up in the morning to write and rewrite, edit and rewrite, edit and rewrite a letter giving up my place as Associate Artist.

I don't want to send this letter. The idea of giving up this position that I earned finally rattles me out of mental paralysis and into some sort of action.

I look at every other London theatre's website and, with the exception of the Old Vic, none of them has their safeguarding policy for vulnerable adults posted. Many of them have anti-racism documents, pronouns are discussed, and rainforests will be saved, all while still on a theatre's homepage. *Trees before cripples, apparently.*

There are tiny theatres that have a fraction of the budget that these West End theatres are privileged to have, and yet their safeguarding policies are up to date and online. What happened to me could happen at almost any of the highest-profile theatres in the UK. An industry-wide problem, and I am the only one who seemed to be aware of it.

My friend has kindly taken it upon herself to communicate with the Globe on my behalf. I tell her to send them my resignation letter if she thinks it would be safe for me to do so. She doesn't send it; instead, we go to *The Stage*.

After all, to stay silent; to not take any action; to wait and see what happens, is to remain complicit, and that would be a mistake.

The editors of *The Stage* ask for timelines and emails, documents to prove what I am saying is true. I have it all on hand, everything they ask for. I hand over contracts and text messages, answer every question with supporting evidence like the well-trained, good little disabled girl I've always been. A lifetime of being told you misunderstand things results in the keeping of an encyclopaedic paper trail.

The Stage decides that, rather than publishing my letter, they want to write up my being fired from one position and stepping down as Associate Artist as a news story, citing that they don't want me to accidentally libel anyone.

Fine by me. The fewer of my words used, the better. But I am concerned that a news story means The Highest Up would be asked to respond.

'They will need to respond, that's only fair. But we will keep an eye on what they say and edit the story to tell both sides.'

The Highest Up doesn't just get a quote in the article, they get a full statement. My solicitor counts nearly fifteen inaccuracies in their 500-word statement. 'Fifteen new counts of post-employment victimisation,' is what Mr Solicitor says, including that the Higher-Ups suggested that we all meet up so I could fill everyone in on what happened to me.

Sorry, when did that happen? Was that before, during or after ignoring us and our requests to be updated on the new safeguarding policy?

There was also no sense of how having a neurological condition as well as being a victim of abuse would put me at a massive disadvantage in a face-to-face meeting.

The Globe and their legal team will go on to say that, although I do have cerebral palsy, which is caused by a lack of oxygen to the brain, I do not have a *neurological* disorder. Suddenly, even the conditions and ramifications around my Birth Day are something they suggest I 'misunderstand'.

'You saw copies of my contract. You know what they said in their statement doesn't reflect my true hours of work. Why did you print the wrong thing?' I respond to *The Stage*, after the release of their article.

'There were so many documents flying around, it was hard to keep track of them all, and we didn't want to get into a back-and-forth between you and them.'

'OK, here, I am sending you my contract again. Correct the error in the article. Or at least address the error.'

'That's what The Highest Up said. We're not going to correct it.'

So, one man says something is true, and it wipes out the disabled woman's mountain of evidence: this is what abuses of power and privilege look like.

I try to contact the Higher Up myself, without success. So, I finally write to their boss, The Highest on High. I enclose my contract, the timeline and a copy of the evidence.

All I know is that my contract hours are misquoted publicly, so I ask to get this changed. The Highest on High is able to do this and, finally, they do, before they, too, cut off all communication.

*

It's the run-up to Christmas and I am again huddled up in the daybed under the staircase of my friend The Movement Director's house as I wait for her to get home from work. I pull on another top because I can't figure out how to work the heating of the 100-year-old Welsh terraced house, short of setting it on fire.

Head stuck in the knitted torso of a sweater, I hear the double ding of my iPhone, which means a text coming through. Then another double ding. I don't even have my head through the neck of my top yet. A third double ding, too quickly to be the repeat of the first. *Who is it that has so much to say to me?*

It's The Gal Pal.

My gut goes through my groin and solidifies at my knees with a weight that causes them to buckle. The muscles in my hands fire off in a way that is well outside my control. The spasms cause the phone to fly out of my grip and fall onto the floor with the screen flat. The object's sound against the wood worries me that it has cracked.

Scuttling on my hands and knees, I reach for the phone under the table. Being picked up causes the screen to turn back on. The display, which thankfully hasn't cracked, says 'The Gal Pal: 3 messages'.

Heart rate high, I do an inventory. I remind myself that no matter how my hatred for inaction spurs me, I don't have to answer The Gal Pal now.

I don't even have to look at it.

I don't have to answer her when I do look at it.

I don't have to answer it when I look at it, even if she can see the two blue tick marks showing that I have read her messages.

These are new and uncomfortable thoughts. Even after repeating them, they make me feel unsettled because I want this whole situation to be all right again. I miss The Gal Pal and The Access Guy. But they are going to say I hurt them, I know it. That's one of the first things people reach for when I don't respond the way they think I should.

So, I take stock: do I have sleeping meds with me? Yes, I do. I check my Apple Watch to make sure I've had enough sleep the past few nights. I have three meals a day lined up until I go home after Christmas. I've been happy this season, no sign of the Christmas grief that has so often snuck in during my adult years. There is no need to take public transport, or expose myself to the risk of unexpected trauma from strangers while I am at The Movement Director's house. I am safe.

I can have whatever reaction I need to have in this moment without an audience. And when my friend gets home, if it feels like there is still a flurry of electrical activity in my brain, or a gaping hole in my heart, she will accompany me in the pain by holding me and allowing me to cry. Even if it takes all night, somebody will bear witness and I will not be alone.

The hope that everything can still work out, that I can say the right words to make it so, is what drives me to pick up the phone again and unlock it.

The Gal Pal wants to wish me a happy Christmas so badly, but she is afraid it will make me mad. So, she is doing it now instead of on the day. She wants to still be friends if I do, but she doesn't want to talk about what happened at work. Indeed, it's probably better if we don't talk about it and just move on. Can we simply be friends again and act as if this whole debacle never happened?

I know her intentions are good, but what she is suggesting is not healthy. It's societally correct, sure, and there is an army of Miss Manners types out there who would insist that this is the way forward. But I'm not sure how our relationship can work if we gloss over something like this. What would the two of us have 'in relation' if reality is just deleted, and the debris of my heart is brushed under the rug like she is suggesting?

That's not the kind of relationship I want. And I don't need it.

I tuck myself underneath my friend's high-gloss stairs-of-death and fold my knees into my jumper. 'Ghosting' or 'leaving her on read' isn't the right thing to do; The Gal Pal is a genuinely brilliant friend and deserves better. If I don't text her back, she's going to assume that I've turned hostile and written her off, and nothing about that is true. I love The Gal Pal, and I miss her terribly.

We both deserve the opportunity to grow. Here. Now. In this moment.

> Merry Christmas to you, too. Thank you for reaching out. It means a ton. But I didn't make this problem, The Globe did. I'm not willing to act like this has gone away, because for me, it hasn't. The parties who made this mess need to address it and clean it up. It's not my job to fix the problem. It's not my job to minimise the problem. I don't have to. The Globe does.

After I hit send, I never question my response.

Chapter 20

The shipping container in Elephant and Castle that I've turned into my office is a place of cheer and warmth. We've kitted it out with a desk and narrow bookshelves that wouldn't take up much of the container's eight-foot width, and painted it green, with some gold-painted beading lining the otherwise fake hardwood floor we laid down. It won't be until later in the year, when the weather turns, that I realise my mistake: that a floor needs insulation under it, particularly when you're in a shipping container and there is nothing between you, the floor and the concrete slab exposed to the elements underneath.

I find the gears of my brain smoking from friction during the weekdays of 2016. Brexit has been passed. The inevitability of Trump being elected is already set in my sights. I try to balance the realities of relationships that I thought held me stable falling apart.

On weekdays, there is a barrage of putting out fires, trying to straighten out people and their attitudes, sudden appearances on the BBC during a feminist crisis. The outside world is impossible to block out unless I reach back to my childhood habit of waking up early before dawn. Back then it was for physio, now it is replaced by writing when the hours are quiet and the world is still asleep.

The weekends are for creative writing only – plays, essays, commentaries to be posted on online – anything to keep my voice going in a world determined to shut it out. I recently hired a new support worker funded by a government grant. *Enter The Dresser.* She and I sit at neighbouring desks and write for a few hours, stopping for lunch – other shipping containers sell Mauritian food or Jamaican jerk chicken, or French duck burgers – and then starting work again. When she leaves at three, she sets out a nourishment shake for me so that I can keep working a few more hours.

I bend over to take a last tug of my shake while I log on to Facebook. Then comes the disappointment of taking one last swig of a milkshake before realising it is gone – my afternoon snack is complete, and I can no longer use that as an excuse to evade writing.

The excuse that does present itself, however, is wildly unexpected. My friend from college – The Fireman's Son – has started a Facebook Live session. The city of Charlotte has been under riots the last several nights. Last night, the police decided to release tear gas on protestors.

'There was a man in a wheelchair that couldn't run away because there are no kerb cuts on the streets. They kettled us all in.' The Fireman's Son texted me earlier. Now he is outside the Charlotte Panthers stadium with a gas mask in his backpack. The police have outlawed all masks as a form of 'aggressive behaviour'.

The police have killed people who look like The Fireman's Son. And so, when I see him recording himself with a selfie-stick as a police officer stops him, I can't help but stop scrolling my feed, clicking the video into full screen mode and hitting unmute.

The incident is already well underway. The Fireman's Son opens his bag and pulls out the gas mask when requested.

'And you're sure you're not out here to protest, son?'

The Fireman's Son responds that you can't be sure what you're going to run into on the streets of Charlotte right now. After all, he has a wife and two baby girls at home.

I push my nutrition shake away from my laptop, accidentally knocking it to the floor so that a small sliver of fortified chocolate milk falls on the cold ground with a clang as the tin succumbs to gravity.

I start typing slowly, with the one finger I am able to communicate with.

'Stay calm, bro. You are doing great.'

In between the two sentences, I briefly debate whether or not I should send them separately, just so he knows as soon as possible that I am watching – all the way from my shipping container in London – and I will spring into action if needed.

Ultimately, I figure that if he sees one message, then seeing the full thing would be better than only seeing half of it. I hit send, not before accidentally hitting the button next to it, causing a slash at the end of my statement. That is how much my hand is shaking as I try to communicate. As much as my hands are unsteady, his must be worse.

*

'How's The Tuesday Morning Girl?' my dad asked, looking at the pixelated photo of her on my desktop.

'She's really sick, Dad.' I said it with a finality in my voice that I'd never used when referring to any of my friends.

The Tuesday Morning Girl had been sick to the point of being bedridden off and on, ever increasingly, for three and a half years. She wore an anti-nausea patch to go to a friend's wedding, and I was the one who held her hair back as she threw up from the vertigo in the ladies' room accessible stall. She never drank alcohol in college.

Every morning, she woke up and the world was spinning. Listening to podcasts and the radio made it worse. Television and reading were completely out of the question. Her husband had become a full-time carer, as well as balancing a job in a DIY store.

It took years of guesswork and internet searching to figure out what was wrong, until we found an umbrella term that seemed to capture all of the symptoms: postural tachycardia syndrome, or PoTS.

I looked at Tuesday Morning Girl's photo on my desktop, taken well before she got sick. She had a cowboy hat on and a green shirt against a sky-blue wall, holding a sign that says 'Do Not Fear' – a biblical reference that feels pathetic on multiple levels.

Throughout our days at university, if I felt bad about taking up too much of one person's energy, she was there to pinch it with her unending bounciness, full of giggles and cheers that bordered on manic, but also good advice.

On a particularly hard day, I looked at her and said, 'I thought I was doing the right thing when I did what I did.' She wrapped her arms around me and said, 'One of the hardest things about this life is realising that even though you do the right thing, the ending still might not be what you want.'

How could someone who folded T-shirts at Walmart to make money over the summers in college get asked if she needed a wheelchair every time she walked into the same store as an adult? How could her options be so limited? How could someone my age suddenly fall under that category? A category that I was meant to eradicate: disabled.

*

The Fireman's Son uses the word 'sir' every chance he gets when responding to the police officer. More officers approach, standing with their hands on their waists. We only see their legs, man-spread apart.

'Yes, sir … No, sir … I have no plans on creating any sort of disruption, sir.'

At my desk, I think of all the times in college The Fireman's Son would say to me, 'You don't have to be perfect, baby girl. Just be you.'

No, we do have to be perfect. Here is why: his 'sir' is used to stop any misunderstanding that may turn into misinterpreted words, which may turn into a collapse of justice.

The number of viewers going up in the top corner of the screen says that something is brewing. People want to have eyes on what is going on behind the Charlotte stadium right now.

'If you end up in court, we all are here as witnesses,' someone puts in the chat. We are holding him like the precious human he is.

The officer asks dispatch to confirm that gas masks are prohibited on the streets of Charlotte at the moment.

The dispatch does.

My feet don't reach the floor when I sit in my desk chair, so I have to press my arms into my desk's surface to stay upright. Still, I feel like the floor is coming up to hit me, even though I know I'm upright.

The reports and tweets with hashtags, #SayHerName and #SayHisName, all start to run together so that I can't remember Breonna Taylor's name, or the young man who was killed just outside of Saint Louis, or that other man who was holding a book.

It feels like there are too many people to name. The moment

I need to remember names, the sheer number of them overwhelm me and there is just one name I can think of right now: the name of a friend whose father was a firefighter on 9/11, who I am watching as he gets arrested five time zones away.

Braxton Winston.

*

I fell from my chair onto the floor of my rented flat as I heard the news. Tears splattered as I felt the reverberation of my knee hit the ground.

'Yeah … I know. It was really hard.' The Photographer repeated these sentences whenever my grief started to slow down, causing my sobs to start up again.

It had started with a joke when The Photographer and I were talking about The Crew Gal.

'Did you know about her first pregnancy?' the voice on Skype asked.

'What's that supposed to mean? Don't tell me that she had a baby without me knowing it!'

'Well, sort of.'

The Crew Gal had a baby without me knowing it because she had gone into labour at five and a half months. Had the boy remained in her womb just two days longer, the doctors could have done something.

The Photographer drove from Atlanta, Georgia, to North Carolina to witness the labour and delivery of our friend's first child. She arrived in time to see him, tiny and breathing for only a handful of minutes.

'The thing that struck us the most was how much of his

personality you could see even in those few hours. He was a human being.'

I wasn't there. I had no idea. The Crew Gal had gone into labour so early that I didn't even know she was pregnant. She hadn't told me yet.

How could she have had to go through a labour that would end with sadness, while I was halfway across the world, partying it up at press nights and plays in London.

The Crew Gal was not supposed to go through that.

My mother went through it.

*

When the police officer wants Braxton to turn off his video camera, an explosion erupts in the chat. He clocks all of our protestations of 'absolutely not' and 'we'll never see you again', and 'if you turn off that camera, I am calling a lawyer'.

'I don't think that's a good idea, sir. I think things will escalate if I do that and I don't want that to happen.'

Will that be interpreted as a threat? I can't tell. Everyone who has to fight for their existence knows that the only way you can win is if you're a blameless victim.

The police officers take one look at the phone. We see a glimpse of their faces through the selfie lens. It's the first time their faces are on the screen.

Waves of 'good, now we have a face' and 'I can describe that ugly mug' come across the screen, and I hope Braxton doesn't have to take the fall for our commentary. Because that's another way that this could go so terribly wrong.

The primary officer says something into his walkie-talkie and there's a beep and click as he waits for a response. I feel all of us pushing the volume key on our laptops in order to hear better. We are literally listening to a voice from a police station coming through a walkie-talkie on the streets of Charlotte, through my friend's phone microphone and coming out of our respective devices.

'Got it, thanks for that.' The click beep of the police officer's walkie-talkie goes off again. 'Right, son. I'm afraid we're going to have to take you in. Sorry about this.'

And the way the police officer says it, I believe him. Not everyone in the chat agrees. The kaleidoscope of lifetime experience has rightly led us all to interpret tone of voice and word choice differently.

The screen goes black, and we are left within a text chat trying to figure out where our friend has been taken, who can post bail, who has a lawyer, what any of us can do next.

Someone suggests putting up an Amazon wish list for things Braxton is going to need in the immediate future. And then a new screen name appears in the chat.

'This is Braxton's mum. Will someone please tell me where my son is and what is going on?'

*

It's another sleepless night. I'm worried. I am ruminating. *How can I read people's minds to navigate away from potential problems? How do I phrase things differently so that people don't immediately jump on the panic and defence button when I point out something has been knocked off centre?*

I grab my phone. There is a text waiting for me from Belle.

'I just want you to know that I think about all you went through fighting Stevenson so often now with my own daughter. I came out of her IEP meeting last week in tears. What do we need to do to get equality in education?'

I had seen pictures of her daughter on Facebook, smiling, awkward as any tween is. Why is Belle sitting through IEP meetings for her daughter the same way my mother did for me? Because Belle has a daughter with complex learning disabilities, and this is news to me.

I know that Belle and her family are in Stevenson's district. Belle herself is a teacher there. Those are the two things she wanted to be: a schoolteacher and a mum. Now she's getting a master's degree in education, trying to figure out what her daughter needs alongside everyone else in her classroom.

It may be 3 a.m., but this conversation seems like the most important one in the world.

'I think of you so often and how you navigated this so well. I am trying to remember what you did.'

I see Belle and myself sitting at our lunch table, me taking out my SlimFast and she her Caesar salad. Prototypes for the character of Wednesday Addams, repeating 'I just want to die!' because, as teenagers, that was the only way we knew how to express the fatigue that no one told us was legitimate.

I roll back over into bed, smiling at myself, thinking of me and Belle going through the halls of Stevenson. At first, upon reading her message, I was elated. Not because Belle is struggling, but because I know that we didn't waste our early years together as teenagers. We used them to learn what was ahead and what challenges had to be faced.

But as I stare up at the dark ceiling for longer, I think to myself,

'Why is Belle going through this at our school *now*?' If Belle and her daughter were going through the same thing in a different state or even the next town over, it would make some sense. But Belle is literally teaching in the building where we fought these same battles; where I had to become an icon of perfection in order to get the education everyone else was guaranteed.

I don't sleep for the rest of the night, bouncing between memories of Belle acting as my assistant when I was given an unqualified adult, and of us passing notes, making plans for our Sims' next house. In high school, my friend and I had to organise ourselves, to cover for the adults. Now, as an adult, my friend is stuck on lather, rinse and repeat.

This isn't how it is meant to be. I was told by my teachers, by my parents, by physiotherapists that I was breaking down boundaries so other people wouldn't have to.

Why had this not been sorted in the past two decades?

While still in my bed, I am cross-examining my eighteen-, seventeen-, sixteen-, fifteen-, fourteen-year-old self like a lawyer during a hearing, rather than like someone who is set to care for a teenager who doesn't know any better.

Inevitably, my mind slips back to the teachings in Mr Game Day's class on how to give geometric proofs, and the subtle liberal theology given to me by Mr Varian in his Miata with a Queer America sticker on the back bumper, and Ms Up/Down teaching us about the gravitational forces that hold our world together. And that rainy August day with the words 'All men are created equal' written on the whiteboard.

*

How do you tell a mother that you've just watched her son be arrested on Facebook?

The chat against the blackness of the now-ended Facebook Live session is at full tilt, explaining what we have witnessed, along with the gathering of ideas and suggestions. Within three seconds of each other, two people say that they are heading to Amazon to create a wish list for what Braxton needs. Reading each other's statements, they then agree to collaborate on the list together. Someone else has called the Southern Law Office to start getting him representation; maybe even before he steps out of the police car, that matter will be sorted.

'I'm here, too! In London.'

Someone adds a heart reaction to my statement, but it is clear that Braxton is taken care of, at least for now. I pick up the Nourishment can from the floor, and walk the forty feet to the end of the shipping container as if it is just another Saturday afternoon. The can makes more of a clang in the empty bin than I expect.

Later that evening, the Amazon list has been posted, as well as news that Braxton has a representative and is expected to be released on bail any moment now. His camera equipment and microphone have been lost, and it is unclear whether 'lost' is a euphemism for 'destroyed' or 'confiscated', or if he dropped it somewhere. I buy him three RØDE Lavalier microphones, the kind I use for my own YouTube interviews.

I write on my planner in ten days' time to message Braxton, imagining his phone currently blowing up in some dark, shut locker somewhere in the Charlotte police station. The outpouring of support once he gets his phone back in his hands will be overwhelming.

Better to wait a few days, because that's how long it takes for complications to begin to rear their ugly heads. That's when you need a friend the most. I know the timeline because I've been through it on repeat. Then I kick myself for assuming that Braxton is new to this game, because of course he isn't.

It's been three days since Braxton's arrest. The Woman Who Taught Me How to Walk at the therapy centre in Chicago visits me with her son in the shipping container. He is starting a degree in English literature at Oxford, and they have this weekend in London to see the sights before settling him into his university digs.

As soon as I see her coming through the eight-feet-by-eight-feet window, I recognise her as the other woman, next to my mother, who was there for the majority of my childhood milestones: milestones like graduating kindergarten; milestones such as being able to sit upright without any support; milestones like my first period; milestones like learning to get up from the floor without holding on to anything; milestones such as liking a boy for the first time; milestones like learning how to hold my head straight long after all of the former occurred.

We hug and we laugh about the time I face-planted my teeth into her skull, or the time she was filming me walking down the hall and I was unable to stop myself once I started putting one foot in front of the other, unless I ran into a wall or fell backwards, hitting my head on the thinly carpeted but otherwise concrete floor. When she left the clinic I was seventeen, and my parents and I saw little reason for me to start with another therapist when I was about to go off to college.

The Woman Who Taught Me How to Walk has the date of 23 May ingrained in her mind because I would start to get excited about my birthday as soon as Christmas passed.

'I will be ninety years old and not know my own name but repeating the day 23 May until I die!'

Knowing how overly exuberant I was regarding my birthdays as a child, she's not wrong.

'I caught up with another boy from the clinic not that long ago.' She tells me his name. 'Do you remember him?' I don't, but I say I do.

'He writes to those of us from the clinic that still meet for dinner every month. He went through a phase where he was really depressed. He didn't know how impossible it would be to get a job, despite having a PhD. Oh, man, that was so hard for me to read. It feels like we told him lies growing up. Did we lie to you? I remember when I had to tell you that you were always going to have cerebral palsy. That it didn't matter how much work we did – your brain injury would always affect how your body moves. You turned to me and asked, "So what's the point of doing any of this?" And I didn't know what to say, but I told you that you could stop if you wanted to. No one was going to make you keep doing therapy if you didn't want it. You could stop any time.'

I look down to the floor. There is still a spot of chocolate from where my can fell from a few days before.

At this moment, I don't want to look at The Woman Who Taught Me How to Walk. I don't want to face the reality that there was a point in my life when I wasn't my cheery self, completely supported by an assumed but fictional equality.

Belle's child's brain isn't the right brain for this world. The Fireman's Son's skin colour isn't the right colour for this world.

Or so much of this world isn't right for them.

The Woman Who Taught Me How to Walk, who was present

the countless times my skull hit the floor and I had to pick myself up, now has to pick herself up to fight back tears as she tries to continue to tell me about her other clients. Now grown, they are trying to sort out their place in a world that they always assumed had a place for them. Because that's what we were taught to believe.

I took it to mean that I was going through torture so that nobody else would have to fight as hard in the future.

That was the failure of my logic.

'You came back the next week,' she tells me, as if it is a matter of fact.

Of course I came back – there was no way on God's green Earth my mother and this woman were going to let me just stop going to therapy.

I don't remember that week. I probably still woke up at 5 a.m. to turn on *M*A*S*H* and do my daily exercises. When the calendar passed seven days and it was time to go to the clinic again, I returned.

'I asked if you were willing to keep working, and you said yes.'

Chapter 21

'This was always going to be a horrible idea.'

I say this as I lie naked on the tiled bathroom floor, looking up at the vaulting skylight three metres above my head. The grout in between each of the tiles rubs into my back, a sensation that would probably be more acute had I not just heard the sound of my skull rattling against the floor.

It is my birthday, the day that defined every movement I would ever make in the world. The day when I can say beyond a shadow of a doubt that harm was done to me. None of it was my fault. Four decades after 23 May 1984, I will be expected by both society and my own expectations to minimise and mitigate the reality of my brain injury – to make other people more comfortable; to pass in this world; to receive the education and resources most people in the developed world get to claim as a birthright. Whenever I feel as if my body is bringing nothing but chaos into this world, when a body affected by cerebral palsy yearns more than anything for a point of stability, I go back to my genesis.

Even the way I hold my toothbrush is affected by the actions of a man I have never met other than on my Birth Day. I have looked for decades to find one small corner of my life that he has not made an indelible thumbprint on.

All I wanted was a shower.

People slip all the time getting into showers and bathtubs. Statically it's one of those normal, 'everyday' dangerous things we do. So, maybe I would be on the floor, naked in front of my shower on my birthday, even without being deprived of oxygen four decades ago.

You never know. Brain injury or not, gravity is always at work. Maybe it was 'meant to be' this way.

My watch vibrates on my wrist. At first, I think it must be the fall-detection sensors doing their job. But when I raise my wrist, my assumptions are corrected. It doesn't think I've fallen. Instead, my Apple Watch wants to make sure I know that a college friend five time zones away is messaging me.

It is The Student Union President, who has now turned his adult life to entrepreneurship. Specifically, he is creating an app for those at risk of violence – originally for people at risk from the police, then for victims of domestic violence, and now for people with disabilities who may be encountering anything from discrimination to full-on hate crime. The Student Union President's thinking is simple: an app that can, hands free, start recording incidents and upload footage to the cloud as it's recording. It will provide an eyewitness account of what has happened, at least until the phone is destroyed by the perpetrator.

Because of his race and my brain injury, there are some people in this world who are less likely to believe our words to be reliable, and even with a recording of what happened, justice might not win the day.

I tap my watch over my head to read the message, still lying on the ground after bouncing my skull off the tile.

'Hey, can you think of an easy verbal cue for people with severe disabilities to activate the Legal Equalizer app?'

My mind attempts to bend itself around the irony of being asked, 'What would you say if you needed help?' immediately after I have fallen and am unsure if I have the capacity or the will to get back up.

I dictate to Siri.

'What about something like, "Help, help, help"?'

In this very meta moment, I decide that, no matter what the odds are of people slipping and falling when getting into the shower, there is no other world in which I would be here, on this or any other floor, giving software programming advice to a friend five time zones away after rattling my skull on the tile.

It's hard to find anything in my life that is not affected by what happened on Day One. That doctor's action is always an external force in every relationship and interaction I have. Sometimes the effect of that force is mitigated for years until a withdrawal of support makes it clear the negative momentum was always present.

I activate my core, folding my elbows back and pressing them into the ground to raise myself up. I do a quick scan of my body, finishing it by saying all forty-five US presidents in my head, my usual final check to make sure I am of sound mind and body.

Yeah, I'm fine.

I stand up.

I can feel a purple bruise starting to form on my right leg in that liminal region between my upper thigh and my arse-proper. That will hurt for a few days, then turn green as the blood vessels knit themselves together. No lasting damage, though.

Beats the heck out of my first birthday.

I step over the threshold of the shower and bat the shower head so that it will spray against the wall when I turn it on. Before I do, though, I sit on the floor. This is the position I bathe myself in, to avoid falling. Clearly, it's worked well so far. As soon as I am assaulted by cold water, I regret wanting a shower. The cold water bounces off the wall tiles and hits me, causing a spike in my heart rate; every muscle tenses and my breath grows shallow.

My mind grasps for all those YouTube superstars, mostly male, who swear that taking cold showers will cure all sorts of man-made ailments. *Yeah. If only it were that simple.*

I can feel the water running against the wall getting warmer. My breath slows and I study my watch as my heart rate comes down. Then, in a move that took me months to perfect, I use the hose of the showerhead to twist the outpouring of water directly onto me.

I raise an arm up against the wall over my head, trying to release the near-constant and familiar pain that goes from my upper back and shoulders, wrapping around to just above my eye socket. I count to twenty before switching to my other arm.

I get to twelve when I feel the warmth of tears well up in my eyes.

No one will know that I started my birthday on the floor. It's not something that really works itself casually into conversation:

'*Happy Birthday, darlin'! How's your day going?*' The Wolf will ask me at dinner tonight.

I will resist the urge to respond, '*Oh, you know. I started the day a victim of gravity brought on as a direct result of the malpractice done to me on this day decades ago. Are those lavender and rose French macarons for me? My favourite! Thank you so much!*'

I am so tired. And so frustrated. And not even my closest friends, who feed me my birthday dinner, know it.

It feels like my mind has separated from my body. The corporeal is on some sort of biological boomerang, repeating heaves and sobs that reverberate against the tiles around me. The sound cycles around the cubicle until I'm pretty sure the noise perpetuates itself.

My mind, however, stays on a straight track. It runs in logical order, like writing a geometric proof based on a set of given circumstances in Mr Game Day's class:

Given the laws of physics that govern the universe we live in ...

Given the biological realities of what happens to a brain deprived of oxygen for longer than four minutes at birth ...

Given the human condition and cultural realities that people are averse to change ...

Given the pressure that has been and always will be on the person who was harmed to minimise the impact of that harm ...

I don't want to.

I don't want to live in a world where we have to invest in venture capitalism so that The Student Union President can spend his life building technology in the hopes of holding people responsible for their acts of violence.

I don't want to have a birthday that starts with me falling naked on the bathroom floor.

I don't want to have a birthday that starts in tears, without anyone knowing.

But that is what today will be.

Either out of habit, perseverance, or simply because I have yet to come up with any sort of alternative, I will smile and say thank you for the birthday wishes. I will invite everyone around the table to help me blow out the candles of my cake, covering the fact that I cannot blow any of them out on my own.

I don't want to live in a world where everybody is fighting undetected battles, trying to stay upright despite their unique pain.

As always happens, the heaves of emotion stop, and then eventually so do the tears. I go back to raising my arms and leaning against the shower wall, trying to stop the muscles in my back from their chronic ache – an inevitability from a life in a body whose shoulders don't move the way evolution intended.

Reaching behind me, I pull the pump bottles of shampoo and body wash forward, squirt some of each out, one after the other, wash, and then sit in the steaming cubicle for a little bit longer.

I am waiting for the puffy redness to ease out of my eyes. I am waiting for the energy to face whatever absurd and harmful obstacles this world has in store for me today, my birthday, though at this particular moment I'm not sure I even want to leave the shower.

By the time I am towelled off and dressed, The Student Union President has messaged me back asking if I have any ideas about how someone with disarticulate speech could activate the app.

The question makes me circle back to what a gift my friend, The Student Union President, is trying to give to a world that is so broken it assumes that just because someone can't say the word 'no', they wouldn't. Or, at the very least, such a person wouldn't have the time, or money, or energy, or resources, or gall to contest what really happened in court.

I give him the name of a woman who babysat me as a child. She is now a professor of speech and language pathology at one of the best universities in the US. She specialises in augmented assistive communication, or how people communicate when their mouths cannot form the words. I like the idea of the two of them working together.

A certain percentage of my income is invested in The Student Union President's company. It's OK if there are days when I can't come out from under the duvet, or emerge from the steamy enclosed shower, because he is taking up the torch to fight inequality on the days that I cannot.

When his world becomes too much, I am at my desk writing, or onstage, breathing life into a story that will give someone else the language to shape words around their own unspoken truths.

I also remind myself that Braxton, The Fireman's Son, was elected to City Council weeks after his arrest. Right now, he is listening to police officers and community members, ensuring that the city never again throws people in jail just for trying to protect themselves.

And I remember that, as The Wolf says, I don't have to do any of it. If I want to stay in bed and cry and not be productive, not try to make the world right, that's OK too. My value is not dependent on anything I do. It is innate, as Varian and Mr Odysseus taught me.

At this early hour in the American Midwest, Belle is packing her daughter's bags for school, after meeting with teachers for IEPs around the same chipboard table as my own IEPs. She will take her daughter to our school, get out of her car, put on her lanyard and enter the building as a teacher herself. She walks the halls she once pulled me down, and goes to the IEP meetings of her students, advocating for their rights as much as her own daughter's. As much as my mum had to for me.

Another friend video-calls me from Hawaii. She is the first to wish me a happy birthday. Once that's out of the way, she opens the script of my latest play, which debuts in three days. Running lines with nothing but her face on the screen in front of me is the last great hurdle I always put before myself to ensure I know my lines. Her youngest son has a mind that is proving to both dazzle and baffle in equal parts. Multiple playschools have asked for him to be removed from their classrooms, citing that they don't have the facilities to give him 'the attention that he needs'. Each time this happens, it is hard for my friend to recover from the blow.

'But I am beginning to see myself in how he feels within the world,' she tells me after we are done with my lines. This is how she phrases that her brain may be different, too, and that she is now starting to question how our education failed her own brilliant and baffling mind.

A member from the ensemble stayed with us for several months last year. He writes on Messenger, 'Happy Birthday x.' I think about the morning I came into the kitchen and found him close to tears.

'I'm worried about my boy,' he said to me. 'It's been months since he's made any progress in his developmental milestones. What if he never learns to walk?'

The Ensemble Member's son had just turned two years old. He was born with a rare chromosomal mutation, making the boy quite nearly one in a million. The statement of 'that never happens' seemed so capable of bearing the weight of the unknown in our younger days. But after the unthinkable, they seem like pithy words of comfort.

'Oh, my friend,' I quietly said to The Ensemble Member. I placed my fingers on the surface of our glossy grey kitchen table lightly. I allowed him to take in my fingers as they moved to their own jerky, halting rhythm, to listen to the staccato breath support of my voice, without having to look at me.

'I don't know if what I am about to say will help or not, but when I was your son's age, I did a whole lot of nothing. Couldn't roll over. Didn't lift my head. I just stared up at the ceiling while my parents thought: *Is this it? Is this all our kid is going to be able to do?*'

The Ensemble Member lifted his head and took in all of me.

*

When the doctor, whose name and face I do not know, brought me into the world, the choices he made broke me.

More specifically, his choices caused oxygen deprivation over seconds and minutes that permanently killed nerves and dendrites in my brain. And the two factors together – an affected brain and an affected body – affect how I move throughout this world; how I receive the sensations that come at me from outside myself; how I file away necessary information so that no one can suggest I am somehow less than, and the prejudices people bring into a relationship with me.

> *Every action has an equal and opposite reaction.*
> *Forces come in pairs.*
> *An object at rest will stay at rest. And an object in motion will stay in motion.*

I want to believe that, if the above is true, there is an equal and opposite force acting upon this mysterious doctor. As a result of the impact of what he did to me, not only was my body harmed, but his soul was as well. But maybe that is not true. Maybe the laws of physics don't apply here.

There are days when I try to account for all the forces acting

315

upon me as a result of one man's choice. Sometimes I draw them out on the whiteboard in my head, the same way that I was taught in vector physics.

The force of air that is meant to expand my lungs is in equal and opposite measure to the muscles in my torso, tongue and throat constricting my breath in my core's constant search for stability.

The forces unfurling out of me to be understood, to help, to know and to create are pushed back, equal to the impediments of resistance found in bus drivers, false allies and people who swear that I misunderstand their oppositions.

There are poorly calibrated counterbalances in my body as it tries to remain upright. It wants to keep up with the constantly straight bodies it witnesses; aligned, and effortlessly defying gravity. But the second this body feels itself fighting to remain on its axis, I end up falling down a flight of concrete stairs, or onto the tiled floor.

'Rest,' The Movement Director tells me. 'Don't worry about any of it. Instead of feeling the fall, try to feel the force of the floor acting to hold you up.'

She doesn't say 'Just rest' as many people would. The word 'just' suggests that it must be the easiest thing in the world for anyone to do, an entitlement. But in my world, there is no simple stopping of effort or motion. My brain sending a message to 'stop' means a host of neurons firing out the message in all directions. A generalised command being barked across the board, leading to any number of my muscles responding with a startle.

It is other people's choices that have added more turbulence to my attempts to remain upright than anything I have ever tried to 'make happen'. A doctor's decision not to act; a friend's determination to show me topless photos even after I say 'no'; an institution's decision to give me 'good' while everyone else gets 'better' or 'best'. If forces come in equal and opposite pairs, how can I be asked to stop, do nothing and 'just rest'?

'Wait for the overly corrective spasms to pass,' The Movement Director says to me. 'Wait until your body doesn't fight so much against your desires. Wait until the right people are here to accompany these forces and hold you while moving through them.'

It would be easy for me to equate waiting with doing nothing, but I don't think it is the same thing at all. Waiting is a radical act of both defiance and hope. I am being defiant because I refuse to minimise the disruption that my body causes to a world that is built for you.

But I am hopeful that, somehow, the function of my life is found in the forces that it impacts. In taking up the act of supporting me as I move through this world, I lean against people and support them with the equal and opposite force they allow me. It is here that stability is found in the world, both in terms of physics and in terms of souls bumping into each other. When we talk about 'leaning in', we do so not hoping to fall, but with the expectation that what we lean into is strong enough to support us as we push against it.

To live in this unaligned body, with a brain that fires signals at an unsteady and erratic rate, means I am constantly looking for a point of stability, which can only come from outside of myself.

We are not meant to lean on people to become dependent upon them. But we all need multiple forces that hold us upright, either in body or spirit, in order to avoid collapse. We can only survive in a broken and unstable world if we hold each other steady in our hopes and bind each other together in our griefs. Without that, any of us would struggle to stand.

*

'Mama says it's time to eat,' The Little Girl says. Over the past three years, she has somehow changed from a toddler shrieking after The Little Grey Cat, baffled as to why no one in this house 'talks normal' like they do in Lithuania, to a very small person, switching fluently back and forth between languages. The Little Girl is still little enough that she managed to slip into the doorway of my room without so much as a sound. My startle reflex is activated with her words and yanks me away from my book.

'OK,' I say, with the finality of a human determined to take everything this child says very seriously. Closing the book, I shuffle myself upright, away from the headrest of the bed. First one leg then the other swings off the mattress and onto the floor, landing near my slippers, which I'm supposed to wear whenever possible to avoid falls.

The Little Girl shifts her balance onto a single foot, the other one at an angle in midair. With her arm taking her shifted weight onto the doorframe, she looks like a five-pointed, smiling star. When I came home from rehearsals today, I watched as she spun around on a kitchen stool, knees folded and legs underneath her, licking the batter off the whisk as her mother poured yellow cake mix from a silver mixing bowl.

A child in motion seems to be always in motion. A child in motion should always be in motion. There should be no opposing force acting against her.

'Do you need help walking?' she asks, still sparkling like a star in my doorway.

'Sometimes I do, yes.' I slide the front half of my foot into the grey felt slipper, and carefully lift them both to cross that leg over the other and use my index finger to run the heel of the shoe around my foot, effectively sliding the rest of it on. 'But that's all right. I can manage it,' I tell her as I do the same on the other side.

The Little Girl has never asked me questions like this before. To her, I have always been myself. I wonder what connections have formed in her remarkable brain today to ask this. I worry that my relationship with her will change now that she has begun asking about my disability, and I don't want that to happen. Not yet.

'Do you need help now?'

'No. I'm home. I'm fine when I'm home, for the most part.' Tacking on the last four words, I think of looking up at the skylight this morning from the tiled floor. This morning was an exception.

'You know what?'

'What?'

'If Mama's not around and you need help, I can help you.'

This child has knocked the wind out of me. My brain runs back the record of what I have just heard, selectively filtering out the elements of 'five-year-old' and 'bilingual' to make sure I've understood properly.

The Little Girl stands on two feet again, hand on her chest and head bowed slightly. She's obviously seen in the pictures from her books that this is the pose you strike when you solemnly offer to help someone.

'Maybe I do need some help, thank you.'

She skips over, and with a jump in the air, holds out her hand. After I stand up, she takes my arm firmly, confidently, so it lends me her stability.

'You know, Little Girl, it goes both ways. If you ever need help and your mama's not around, I can help you.'

'Yes, there are two adults in this house.'

At this point in time, I am very much feeling as if there are two adults in this conversation.

We walk together, her step matching my uneven gait, out of my bedroom and towards the kitchen for dinner.

We are already seeing differences in The Little Girl's brain than other little people her age. Some mornings, while she is still sleeping, I speak with her mama about it: what it means when she gets into school, how we can make sure she always gets what she needs. The Lithuanians know that I am particularly ruthless when it comes to knowing the games institutions play. I will sit at any chipboard table where her future is being discussed to ensure she isn't harmed. The other people around that table might say I don't belong there. They won't like me. But they don't need to like me.

The responsibility of changing the world and making justice happen should never have been placed upon my shoulders, but I will do everything I can to keep her away from the terrifying instability that comes from other people's complicity.

I can do this for one little girl.

Will she be hurt the same ways I was?

Probably.

Right now, holding The Little Girl's hand and staying upright with the stability she is giving me, all I can do is wait and see what she must face. When harm inevitably comes to her, for whatever reason, I want to make sure she knows that it's not her job to set this world back on its axis. It's not her job to keep everyone happy. I want her to refuse to minimise herself when something is wrong. I want to tell her it is never her job to go without what she needs to flourish. I want to drill into that wonderfully complex mind of hers never to hide any part of herself as a way of winning applause. In this unsteady world, it must never land on a child to be perfect or to keep those with power over her happy. I want her to know the innate value of her soul. Her worth has nothing to do with 'overcoming'. Because there shouldn't be anything to overcome in the first place. I want to tell her to flee from anyone who claims she somehow needs to become 'good enough' to earn equality. She knows she is more than 'good enough' already, just as she is. I want to tell The Little Girl these things, because I need to hear myself saying these words out loud.

The Very Bad Thing done to me on the Very First Day is something I cannot fix. And the weight of bearing it shouldn't be mine.

Acknowledgements

It is a very odd thing to be asked to write acknowledgements for a book. It is an even odder thing to write acknowledgements for a book about your own life. Are you acknowledging the book or the overcoming of the odds? Or are you acknowledging what it takes to write the book, or perhaps simply your own existence? I'm still untangling all of this, but I have been told I need to write acknowledgements. And apparently, I need to write them now. So, here goes:

This book would have remained a series of disconnected voice notes on WhatsApp were it not for the efforts of Sally Wippman, who ensured those voice notes became a cohesive first and very tight draft. Parts of this book would have stayed lodged in my head and I would have stayed under my duvet during some of my darkest days had it not been for the faithful help of Olivia Wakeford. And of course, this book would have remained an unwieldy, rambling mess – with a word count longer than *Spare* – were it not for the watchful and sometimes carrot-and-stick approach of Haley Catherine Selmon. Without these three remarkable women, good ideas would have stayed trapped in the labyrinth of my mind, weighed down and slowed down by the friction of my thoughts and the belief that this story was for 'someday,' but surely not for now.

I am deeply grateful to Lisa Milton, who tracked me down at the Primadonna Literary Festival with a book contract, despite the fact that I had no agent. Though we both initially agreed that writing a memoir was a terrible idea, it became clear I needed to write a memoir rather than a book of feminist history. It's to her credit that we pivoted to create something that is indeed done – and can never be undone.

My heartfelt thanks to André Dubus III, with whom I had the honour of working thanks to an Arts Council England grant to develop my creative practice. He encouraged me to learn to write via dictation, producing more words than I ever could by typing one-fingered across a yellow keyboard. Thank you for asking all the irritating questions and reminding me that prose writing, unlike scripts, doesn't come with a production team – it's up to the writer to deliver the costumes, lighting, and sound on the page.

To Marleigh Price, whose sharp sense of humour and complex worldview allowed me to be unapologetically myself: thank you. You protected me from the worst parts of writing about what has been done, brought Haribo gummies when I was stuck in my flat with a broken lift (yes, it still happens…), and made sure this book didn't veer into the realm of the "inspirational porn" and trauma-mining so often expected from writers like me.

To Hannah Boursnell: your keen editorial eye ensured every joke landed perfectly while avoiding any major grammatical sins – though, given we are from opposite sides of the Atlantic, we may still disagree on what the rules actually are!

To Sasha Billingham: your early feedback and encouragement

gave this book the push it needed. For years you knew what I was capable of and how many people stood in my way. I hope this book gives you the satisfaction of showing the obstacles we faced together in full.

To Mbye Njie, aka "The Student Union President" and founder of the Legal Equalizer app: thank you for reminding me that the most terrifying stories are the ones that never get told. Thank you for making sure my story will be told.

To Bill, Jason, and Merryn, who have loved me like older brothers and supported me in becoming the writer I am today. I hope you get a glimpse in this book of how I see you.

Sue Buckley and her colleagues at Pathways Center for Children: thank you for teaching me to stand up straight with my shoulders back and my head held high – literally. Thank you also for teaching me how to get up from the floor when I fell. These small details are the difference between a life lived well and a life seen as a victim. There are countless other things to be grateful for from my time at Pathways, but I can think of no better way to express what you gave me as a small child, when no one – other than you and my parents – expected me to be more. In no way do you mislead us by expecting children like us to be more. Rather, you expect the world to change in the face of our remarkable existence. That is exactly how it ought to be.

To my beloved parents, who gave me placemats with George Washington and FDR and read to me every night up until the night before I left for university: our little family was so unique and so remarkable that it is only as an adult that I recognize – or am at least beginning to recognize – how much love you bathed me in, even as we moved against such heavy forces.

And finally, to those who stood as obstacles in my way: perhaps you recognize yourself in these pages, or perhaps you don't. Either way, you were a force in my life. While some vectors should never have been set in motion, and no silver lining can cancel out the harm caused by their direction, it looks like the trajectory worked out just fine. I'm here. And I've made sure nobody knows your name. Except me, of course.

ONE PLACE. MANY STORIES

Bold, innovative and
empowering publishing.

FOLLOW US ON:

@HQStories